MULTICULTURAL
LITERATURE FOR CHILDREN
AND YOUNG ADULTS

Recent Titles in
Contributions to the Study of World Literature

Essays on the Fiction of A.S. Byatt: Imagining the Real
Alexa Alfer and Michael J. Noble, editors

Victorian Writers and the Image of Empire: The Rose-Colored Vision
Laurence Kitzan

Immigrant Narratives in Contemporary France
Susan Ireland and Patrice J. Proulx, editors

Aristocracies of Fiction: The Idea of Aristocracy in Late Nineteenth-Century and Early
Twentieth-Century Literary Culture
Len Platt

Salman Rushdie's Postcolonial Metaphors: Migration, Translation, Hybridity, Blasphemy,
and Globalization
Jaina C. Sanga

Imagining Africa: Landscape in H. Rider Haggard's African Romances
Lindy Stiebel

Seduction and Death in Muriel Spark's Fiction
Fotini E. Apostolou

Unorthodox Views: Reflections on Reality, Truth, and Meaning in Current Social,
Cultural, and Critical Discourse
James L. Battersby

Judgment and Justification in the Nineteenth-Century Novel of Adultery
Maria R. Rippon

The Late Modernism of Cormac McCarthy
David Holloway

The Colonial Conan Doyle: British Imperialism, Irish Nationalism, and the Gothic
Catherine Wynne

In My Own Shire: Region and Belonging in British Writing, 1840–1970
Stephen Wade

MULTICULTURAL LITERATURE FOR CHILDREN AND YOUNG ADULTS

Reflections on Critical Issues

Mingshui Cai

Contributions to the Study of World Literature,
Number 116

GREENWOOD PRESS
Westport, Connecticut • London

Library of Congress Cataloging-in-Publication Data

Cai, Mingshui.
    Multicultural literature for children and young adults : reflections on critical issues /
Mingshui Cai.
       p.   cm.—(Contributions to the study of world literature, ISSN 0738–9345 ; no. 116)
    Includes bibliographical references and index.
    ISBN 0–313–31244–3 (alk. paper)
    1. Children's literature—History and criticism.   2. Young adult literature—History and
criticism.   3. Pluralism (Social sciences) in literature.   4. Multiculturalism.   I. Title.
II. Series.
PN1009.A1C29   2002
809′.89282—dc21   2002017139

British Library Cataloguing in Publication Data is available.

Library of Congress Catalog Card Number: 2002017139
ISBN: 0–313–31244–3
ISSN: 0738–9345

First published in 2002

Greenwood Press, 88 Post Road West, Westport, CT 06881
An imprint of Greenwood Publishing Group, Inc.
www.greenwood.com

Printed in the United States of America

The paper used in this book complies with the
Permanent Paper Standard issued by the National
Information Standards Organization (Z39.48–1984).

10 9 8 7 6 5 4 3 2

#48857619

Copyright Acknowledgments

The author and publisher gratefully acknowledge permission for use of the following:

Excerpts from Cai, Mingshui, "Can We Fly Across Cultural Gaps on the Wings of Imagination?" (1995). *The New Advocate, 8* (1): 1–16.

Excerpts from Cai, Mingshui, "Multiple Definitions of Multicultural Literature: Is the Debate Really Just 'Ivory Tower'?" *The New Advocate 11* (4): 311–324.

Excerpts reprinted by permission of the publisher from Rogers, T., & Soter, A.O. (Eds.). *Reading Across Cultures: Teaching Literature in a Diverse Society*, (New York: Teachers College Press. © 1997 by Teachers College, Columbia University. All rights reserved.), pp. 199–212.

Excerpts from Cai, Mingshui, & Sims Bishop, Rudine. (1994). "Multicultural Literature for Children: Towards a Clarification of the Concept." In Anne Haas Dyson & Celia Genishi (Eds.), *The Need for Story: Cultural Diversity in Classroom and Community* (pp. 57–71). Urbana, IL: National Council of Teachers of English. Copyright 1994 by the National Council of Teachers of English, Reprinted with permission.

To my wife, Jianrong, and son, Shuofeng

Contents

Contents

Acknowledgments

This book is the result of my learning, teaching, and research. However, others have contributed their thoughts and ideas as well. I have drawn on the works of such scholars as Rudine Sims Bishop, Violet Harris, and Joel Taxel. I am indebted to them for their insights, which have informed and inspired my writing. My deepest appreciation goes to my mentor, Rudine Sims Bishop, for her constant encouragement, support, and guidance. I also want to thank Charline Barnes, Penny Beed, Bonnie Johnson, Dale Johnson, David Landis, and Rick Traw, whose comments and suggestions were most helpful when I composed and revised the manuscript. Another thank-you goes to Matthew Kollasch, who provided technical support for the preparation of it for publication. Finally, I am most grateful to my wife, Jianrong, and son, Shuofeng, whose love, care, and support have sustained me throughout the whole process of writing this book.

Introduction

Do we need a category of books called multicultural literature? If yes, how do we define it? And who can create true multicultural literature? Can "outsiders" create culturally authentic works about a culture? How do we evaluate and select multicultural literature for use with children? What functions do we expect it to serve for educational purposes? How do we incorporate multicultural literature into the curriculum? These are some of the critical issues that have been discussed and debated for the past two or three decades. Writers, critics, educators, and librarians are divided in their opinions regarding these issues. Ever since I was a graduate student at Ohio State University, about ten years ago, I have been thinking and writing about them. This book collects my reflections on some of the major issues in multicultural literature for children and young adults and presents them in a systematic way.

Many of the issues I address in this book are controversial. To clarify the controversies, we need to know how they arise. One of the major factors that causes the controversies is largely political. As Joel Taxel (1997) points out, the debates surrounding multicultural literature for children and young adults "are best understood in the context of historical trends and development in the American society" (p. 417). The rise of multicultural literature is a political, rather than a literary, movement. It is a movement to claim space in literature and in education for the historically marginalized social groups, rather than one to renovate the craft of literature itself. It has grown out of the civil rights movement and feminist movement in the 1960s and 1970s (Cai and Sims Bishop, 1994; Taxel, 1997). Since the day it came into existence, multicultural literature has been closely bound with the cause of multiculturalism and confronted with resistance from political conservatives. Recently there has been a "backlash against the multicultural movement" (Taxel, 1997, p. 417) in general literature and in multicultural literature in particular. Political conservatives view multiculturalism as an evil force "bent on undermining Western culture" (Cope and Kalantzis, cited in Taxel, 1997, p. 427) and "multicultural literature as a threat to the very fabric of Western civilization" (Taxel, 1997, p. 417). In the terminology of political conservatism, the concepts of Western civilization and culture do not cover those of the historically disenfranchised social groups. Any attempt to further their cultural and political interests in education and literature is regarded as a challenge to the dominant position of Western civilization and culture. McCarthy (1993) argues that in the past few years, "conservative educators and commentators have responded vigorously to the multicultural challenge" and made "a virulent reaffirmation of Eurocentrism and Western culture in debates over school curriculum and educational reform" (p. 290). A tactic they employ is to "give the dog a bad name and hang it." They label proponents of multiculturalism as advocates of political correctness, who politicize education, literature, and art; censor thought and speech deemed unfavorable to women and minority groups; and seek to reduce intellectual disciplines to "therapies whose function is to raise minority esteem" (Schlesinger, 1992, p. 171). Outright misrepresentation of the multicultural movement aside, to take the issue of racial and cultural equity out of historical context and "redefine it in terms of 'political correctness'" is "an easy put-down for anyone who questions the authority of people used to unquestioned privileges" (Sims Bishop, 1996, p. viii).

The political nature of the controversy is also clearly visible in the power struggle over the creation, production, distribution, and consumption of multicultural literature. Most nonwhite writers and illustrators were denied access to the publishing industry until the 1960s and still do not have equal access as their white counterparts (Harris, 1996; Taxel, 1997). Keeping this big picture of the power struggle in mind will enable us to put the controversies in perspective. Take the question of "Who can create true multicultural literature?" It should first be viewed as a political issue of equity and then as an issue of literary creation. It can be argued that any writer can write about anything he or she chooses. But whose work gets published and praised? Why are books by Europe American authors that grossly misrepresent parallel cultures[1] still highly acclaimed and widely circulated? When multicultural literature is taken over by the political and economic establishment of the dominant culture as a means to perpetuate the misrepresentation and suppression of parallel cultures, anyone who truly supports the movement of multiculturalism has to think soberly about which forces pose real threats to the existence of multicultural literature (Harris, 1996; Taxel, 1997). The imbalance of power is still very much to the disadvantage of the historically disenfranchised. Faced with this reality, do we stress the author's freedom of artistic creation and the power of imagination to cross cultural boundaries or do we emphasize the author's social responsibility and the social effects of this imaginary creation? The choice will be determined by where we position ourselves in the power struggle. There is nothing wrong with the claim that authors have freedom of artistic creation and that imagination can help outsider authors to write about cultures other than their own, but whose interest do we serve to raise a hue and cry about it when the integrity of parallel cultures is being destroyed and their hard-won space in literature eroded by many mainstream culture authors who jump on the multicultural bandwagon? To emphasize authors' social responsibility and the social effects of their works, it should be noted, does not mean that we will not seriously deal with the literary aspects of their work. But political concern should be our first priority for anyone who cares about the future of multicultural literature. Controversial issues should, first and foremost, be examined in the context of political power relations and struggles.

Another factor that causes controversies is ideological differences among professionals who believe in multiculturalism as an embodiment of democratic ideals and accept it into the classroom. They have different notions of multiculturalism and different agendas for advocating multicultural literature. Kincheloe and Steinberg (1997) classify five types of multiculturalism: conservative, liberal, pluralist, left-essentialist, and critical multiculturalism. They argue that critical multiculturalism is preferable to other forms of multiculturalist, for it is "dedicated to the notion of eqalitarianism and the elimination of human suffering" (p. 24) and advocates fundamental changes in the power structure. It is, in essence, an emancipatory theory. If a person subscribes to any of the other varieties, his or her multicultural position will differ from that of a person who espouses critical multiculturalism. For example, one who believes in pluralist multiculturalism will engage in celebrating cultural diversity but not in challenging and changing the status quo of the power relations between the dominant and dominated social groups. In contrast, one who believes in critical multiculturalism will not only value diversity but also deal with issues of equality and equity in society and in education. Take the issue of defining multicultural literature, for example. The pluralist multiculturalist is likely to indiscriminatingly include any culture in it, whereas the critical multiculturalist will include only the dominated cultures. Unless people accept the same form of multiculturalism, controversy is unavoidable.

A third factor that gives rise to controversies lies in the fact that parties involved in these disputes focus on different aspects of multicultural literature and talk past each other in emotional debates. Multicultural literature has a tripartite configuration: it is an aesthetic form of literary creation just like any other kind of literature, a political weapon in the cultural war, and an educational tool to change people's attitudes toward cultural diversity. These three major aspects of multicultural literature—literary, sociopolitical, and educational—are interrelated, yet each has a particular domain, with different objectives and criteria for evaluation. In the debate over issues in multicultural literature, one party may be primarily concerned with the political or educational aspect while another is concerned with the literary one. Because they aim at different goals and use different criteria, they probably cannot come to an agreement, just as two persons' paths will never cross if they run parallel to each other. Take the evaluation of multicultural literature, for example. Those who are primarily concerned with the sociopolitical and educational functions will value books with positive portrayals of parallel cultures and present strong ethnic characters as role models for young people. On the other hand, those who intend to defend multicultural literature as a form of art will object that to present only—the positive aspects and images of parallel cultures violates the very principle of literary creation and reduces litera- ture to documents for social study, or even worse, to propaganda. In my opinion, criteria for selecting books to use with children are different from criteria for evaluating books in terms of literary criticism. When each side has a different agenda and criteria, dispute is inevitable.

As long as we differ in terms of political positions, concepts of multicultural- ism, and concerns and criteria, the debate over issues in multicultural literature for children and young adults will continue. I doubt that we will ever see eye to eye with each other over these issues, but through discussion and debate we can at least see where each party stands. It is my hope that my reflections in this book may help clarify, if not resolve, some of the major issues.

The issues I discuss in this book are divided into three categories: issues re- lated to the conceptualization of multicultural literature, issues related to the creation and critique of multicultural literature, and issues related to the use of multicultural literature in education. The book is organized accordingly into three parts, each of which addresses one category of issues. The following is an overview of the book.

PART I: ISSUES RELATED TO THE CONCEPT OF MULTICUL- TURAL LITERATURE

Chapter 1, "Defining Multicultural Literature," examines the multiple defini- tions of multicultural literature. They are divided into two types: literary and pedagogical (Cai and Sims Bishop, 1994). The former defines multicultural lit- erature in terms of its intrinsic literary nature, whereas the latter defines it in terms of the pedagogical purposes it is supposed to serve. The pedagogical defi- nition is the most widely used, and controversial, one. The focal point of the controversy is how many cultures the concept of multicultural literature should cover. Defining multicultural literature actually becomes a matter of determining the parameters of the prefix multi. At one end of the wide range of definitions, multicultural literature is limited to books by and about people of color; at the other pole, all literature is seen as multicultural. There is a trend toward embrac- ing all cultures in the concept, and thus making no distinction between dominant and dominated cultures. The debate over the definition of multicultural literature is not just "ivory tower" bickering, however. The trend of all-inclusiveness en- dangers the very existence of multicultural literature.

Chapter 2, "Classifying Multicultural Literature," discusses three methods of classification: by content and intended audience, by cultural specificity, and by geographical and cultural boundaries. The first classification consists of social conscience, melting pot, and culturally conscious books (Sims, 1982); the second one includes culturally specific, generically American, and culturally neutral books (Sims Bishop, 1992); and the third one comprises world literature, cross- cultural literature, and parallel cultural literature (Cai and Sims Bishop, 1994). Classifying multicultural literature may help us better understand its nature and functions. In its own way each kind of classification sorts out multicultural books for different critical and pedagogical purposes. All three classifications have great implications for publishing, selecting, and using multicultural literature in the classroom.

PART II: ISSUES RELATED TO THE CREATION AND CRITIQUE OF MULTICULTURAL LITERATURE

Chapter 3, "Imagination, Ethnicity, and Cultural Authenticity," tries to answer the question, "Can outsiders rely on imagination to create culturally authentic books about cultures other than their own?" Many authors and critics maintain that there is no deterministic one-to-one relationship between authors' cultural backgrounds and their abilities to write about another culture, but they often underestimate the difficulty of writing authentically across cultures. There is no denying that imagination is a powerful creative faculty, but it is not the master of reality. "Brute facts" impose constraints and limitations on the author's imagination. It is impossible to imagine the specific customs, beliefs, attitudes, perspectives of cultures other than the author's own. First-hand experience and research are needed for an authentic representation of other cultures. In terms of literary creation, the crux of the "insider versus outsider" issue is not the relationship between authors' cultural background and literary creation, but rather that between imagination and experience.

Chapter 4, "Reader Response Theory and the Author's Role in Multicultural Literature," argues that concern with the effect of the author's cultural identity and perspective on the creation of multicultural literature is justifiable in terms of reader response theory. To some critics, emphasis on the author's influence on the text of multicultural literature seems to run counter to the assumptions of reader response theory, which has shifted the focus of literary criticism from the author and the text to the reader. As a matter of fact, the principles of mainstream reader response theories acknowledge the author's role in the meaning-making process. The concept of implied author specifically defines the author's presence in the text. It explains a possible discrepancy between the real author and his or her "second self," the implied author in the text, between the author's intention and the actual effects of his or her literary creation. Well-intended authors may create literary works about an ethnic culture that are unacceptable to the people of that culture. Their cultural identity and perspective may adversely influence their literary choices without their knowledge.

Chapter 5, "Stereotyping and the Politics of Representation," examines the issue of stereotyping. In multicultural literature, stereotyping people of marginalized cultures is not merely an issue of literary creation, but also one of a social-political nature. Historically, the dominant culture has been able to enforce blatantly racist stereotypes in literature and the mass media in order to distort the image and destroy the dignity of the dominated cultures. Stereotypes, old and new, have detrimental effects on all children. Sometimes it is hard to determine whether an image is a demeaning stereotype or a realistic portrait. To detect and dissect stereotypes, we would do better to examine them in the big picture of the social-historical context and the whole literary text rather than stress how stereotypes may be partially true, as do some critics. Special caution should be taken to ensure that realistic portraits of the dominated cultural groups, especially in historical fiction, are not mistaken as stereotypes.

Chapter 6, "Cultural Correctness and the Evaluation of Multicultural Literature," addresses issues of evaluating multicultural literature. A basic criterion for evaluating a multicultural literary work is that it should be culturally correct. To be culturally correct does not mean that it should present only positive aspects and images of a culture. A distinction should be made between critiquing a multicultural book as a literary piece and selecting it for classroom use. A culturally correct book may not be developmentally or emotionally appropriate for children of certain age groups or immature readers. To achieve more accurate evaluation of multicultural literature, some sorts of pseudo-objective content analysis and so-called overburdening criticism should be avoided and cultural criticism should be imbedded in closer literary analysis. Readers should be educated to understand and appreciate the total artistic effects of a multicultural book.

PART III: ISSUES RELATED TO THE USE OF MULTICULTURAL LITERATURE IN EDUCATION

Chapter 7, "Crossing Cultural Borders," discusses different views on how to use multicultural literature to facilitate crossing cultural borders. There are three kinds of cultural borders: physical borders, borders of differences, and inner borders. Reading multicultural literature helps us to vicariously experience crossing these borders. While all agree that we should cross cultural borders, some argue that we should find, and focus, on universals in multicultural literature, which define every individual as a human being and help to form a human bond among different cultures. From their perspective, to emphasize cultural specificities is exclusionary and segregational. However, although it is important to find human commonalities, to cross cultural borders, paradoxically, we need to recognize and define them first. Without accepting and respecting cultural differences, no truly equal rapport can be established among different cultural groups.

Chapter 8, "From Informing to Empowering," deals with the issue of incorporating multicultural literature into the curriculum. Multicultural literature should be made an essential part of a pluralistic curriculum rather than an add-on. When using multicultural literature in the curriculum, it is imperative to move from informing to empowering students. To empower students is to help them develop the ability to identify, critically analyze, and even take action to solve problems related to cultural differences. Informing and empowering are interrelated processes, and both important. But empowering is the ultimate goal and should be emphasized at all levels, starting with children in the primary grades. In this chapter, ways by which to move from informing to empowering is explained with examples of successful classroom practices. When general literature rather than multicultural literature is read, reading multiculturally can be a means to empower students. In order for multicultural literature to perform its functions of informing and empowering students, teachers need to inform and empower themselves.

Chapter 9, "Investigating Reader Responses to Multicultural Literature," proposes a multidimensional model for studying how readers respond to multicultural literature. Studies of reader responses to multicultural literature have great implications for multicultural education. They provide insights into what happens when readers read multicultural literature, which in turn informs its instruction. The proposed model has three dimensions: cognitive-developmental, affective-attitudinal, and social-communal. For researchers, this model will provide guidance for reviewing previous studies and conducting further investigations. For teachers, it will engender a deeper understanding of the scope of students' responses to multicultural literature. A survey of studies in reader responses to multicultural literature and analysis of their findings is furnished to show how the model works.

A selected bibliography and an appendix of websites related to multicultural literature are provided at the end of the book. They are designed to help the reader access resources on multicultural literature for children and young adults, which will provide further information on the issues discussed here.

This book is intended for people who are involved in the creation, production, critiquing, and consumption of multicultural literature for children and young adults. I hope I have covered issues that deserve their attention and have argued my points convincingly. However, I will be pleased if they find something in the book that makes them pause and think again about those issues, even if they disagree with me. The future of multicultural literature hinges on the results of the discussion and debate of the critical, theoretical, and practical issues. We will be better off if, when debating the issues, each side can be more attentive and sensitive to the other's arguments. Otherwise the debate will be "reduced to a case of good guys versus bad buys, of racists and sexists versus those committed to justice and equity" (Taxel, 1997, p. 433), and it is unlikely that we will achieve a certain degree of consensus, not even among true advocates of multicultural literature.

NOTE

1. The term "parallel culture" was first used by Virginia Hamilton in her acceptance speech when she received the Boston Glove-Horn Book Award in 1988. "Although the term may not be perfectly suited as a substitute for the uncomfortable term 'minority,' it has the advantage of according equal status to the cultures designated as parallel" (Cai and Sims Bishop, 1994, p. 70).

REFERENCES

Cai, M., and Sims Bishop, R. (1994). Multicultural literature for children: Towards a clarification of the concept. In A. H. Dyson and C. Genishi (Eds.), *The need for story: Cultural diversity in classroom and community* (pp. 57-71). Urbana, IL: National Council of Teachers of English.

Harris, V. (1996). Continuing dilemmas, debates, and delights in multicultural literature. *The New Advocate, 9* (2), 107-122.

Kincheloe, J. L., and Steinberg, S. R. (1997). *Changing multiculturalism.* Buckingham: Open University Press.

McCarthy, C. (1993). After the canon: Knowledge and ideological representation in multicultural discourse on curriculum reform. In C. McCarthy and W. Crichlow (Eds.), *Race and representation in education* (pp. 289-305). New York: Routledge.

Schlesinger, A. M. (1992). *The disuniting of America.* New York: W. W. Norton.

Sims, R. (1982). *Shadow and substance: Afro-American experience in contemporary children's fiction.* Urbana, IL: National Council of Teachers of English.

Sims Bishop, R. (1992). Multicultural literature for children: Making informed choices. In V. Harris (Ed.), *Teaching multicultural literature in grades K–8* (pp. 37-54). Norwood, MA: Christopher-Gordon.

Sims Bishop, R. (1996). Letter to the editor. *The New Advocate, 9* (2), vii-viii.

Taxel, J. (1997). Multicultural literature and the politics of reaction. *Teachers College Record, 98* (3), 415-448.

Part I

Issues Related to the Concept of

Multicultural Literature

1

Defining Multicultural Literature

There has been an inordinate amount of discussion about the meaning of multicultural literature, but no consensus has been achieved. "Like the term 'postmodern,'" Marilyn Levy (1995) observes, "'multicultural literature' seems to have taken on a life of its own, meaning different things to different people. To some, it's all inclusive, to others, it's all exclusive. To still others, it's simply confusing" (p. 11). The debate over the definition is not just a bickering over terminology in the ivory tower of the academia, but rather is concerned with fundamental issues of a sociopolitical nature. We should not underestimate the power of naming, "for the notion of giving something a name is the vastest generative idea that ever was conceived" (Langer, 1957, p. 140). Like a signpost, the definition of multicultural literature points to a direction for the choice and use of multicultural literature. Each definition reflects a different stance behind a different course of action. Although it is unlikely to achieve consensus on a single definition, clarifying the concepts may help us get a better understanding of the different perspectives and positions on multicultural issues. In this chapter, I first point out that there are two types of definitions of multicultural literature, literary and pedagogical. Then I argue that the controversy over the pedagogical definition is focused on how many cultures multicultural literature should cover. Finally, I discuss three different views on the definition of multicultural literature and their implications for educators.

LITERARY AND PEDAGOGICAL DEFINITIONS

Multicultural literature can be defined in terms of its intrinsic literary nature or the pedagogical purposes it is supposed to serve in education. The first is termed a "literary definition" and the second, a "pedagogical definition" (Cai and Sims Bishop, 1994, pp. 59-60).

Dasenbrock (1987) offers a literary definition: multicultural literature consists of literary works "that are explicitly about multicultural societies" or "are implicitly multicultural in the sense of inscribing readers from other cultures inside their own cultural dynamics" (p. 10). According to this definition, there are two types of multicultural literature: the explicitly multicultural and implicitly multicultural. The first type is easy to understand. A book that explicitly depicts the reality of a multicultural society like the United States is explicitly multicultural. For example, Gary Soto's (1991) *Taking Sides,* tells how a Mexican American boy tries to maintain his cultural identity after he and his mother move from an urban barrio to a predominantly white suburb. Because this story depicts the interaction between cultures in a multicultural society, it is therefore explicitly multicultural literature. The second type is more complicated. The intended audience and linguistic medium are used as the defining factors in the definition. Dasenbrock (1987) explains: "Literature in English has become increasingly cross- or multicultural, as writing about a given culture is destined—because of its language, English, and its place of publication, usually London or New York—to have readers of many other cultures" (p. 10). For example, Maxim Hong Kingston's (1989) *The Woman Warrior,* which portrays the author's experiences of growing up Chinese American in Stockton, California, is not just for a "local" audience of Chinese Americans but also for readers from other cultures. In varying degrees authors like Kingston make their text intelligible or difficult for those readers in order to "inscribe" them in the work's cultural dynamics. They may have to explain to outside readers what is plain to the readers of their own culture, or they may deliberately make the text difficult in order to challenge outside readers to understand a different mode of expression in a culture other than their own.

By the pedagogical definition, the term multicultural does not designate the multicultural nature of a single work, but that of a group of works used to break the monopoly of the mainstream culture and make the curriculum pluralistic. For example, *Lon Po Po* (Young, 1989), the Chinese equivalent of "Little Red Riding Hood," portrays only one culture, the Chinese culture. The book is classified as multicultural literature because it is one of those books that depict the underrepresented cultures and can be used to promote multicultural education. Similar works are *The Boy Who Lived with the Bears and Other Iroquois Stories* (Bruchac, 1995) and *The Piñata Maker* (Ancona, 1994). Each features only one culture, the first, American Indian; the second, Mexican American. They qualify as multicultural literature because they serve the purpose of expanding the curriculum to include literature about nonwhite cultures. Thus, instead of designating unifying literary characteristics of multicultural literature, the pedagogical definition of multicultural literature is predicated on the goal that this category of literature is supposed to achieve: creating a multicultural curriculum and implementing multicultural education. We are less concerned with the nature of literature itself than with the role it plays in education. "In this sense, multicultural literature is a pedagogical term, rather than a literary one" (Cai and Sims Bishop, 1994, p. 59).

No one seems to take issue with the literary definition. The controversy centers around the pedagogical definition. Many pedagogical definitions of multicultural literature have been offered, which vary in their extent of inclusion:

Works that focus on "people of color"(Kruse and Horning, 1990, p. vii)

Literature about racial or ethnic minority groups that are culturally and socially different from the white Anglo-Saxon majority in the United States, whose largely middle-class values and customs are most represented in American literature (Norton, 1999, p. 580)

Books that feature people of color, the elderly, gays and lesbians, religious minorities, language minorities, people with disabilities, gender issues, and concerns about class (Harris, 1994b, p. 117)

Literature by and about people who are members of groups considered to be outside the sociopolitical mainstream of the United States (Sims Bishop, 1992, p. 39)

Books other than those of the dominant culture (Austin and Jenkins, 1973, p. 50)

Of all the definitions, the last is the most inclusive, compassing all cultures other the dominant one in the whole world. The first is the narrowest, covering only racial groups. According to this definition, a book about the Amish such as *Growing up Amish* (Ammon, 1989), or about the Appalachian region, such as *Appalachia: The Voices of Sleeping Birds* (Rylant, 1991), will be excluded from the list of multicultural literature.

Despite varying degrees of inclusion, these pedagogical definitions of multicultural literature have something in common: they are contingent on the distinction between dominant and dominated culture; they all agree that multicultural literature is about groups of people that are distinguished racially, culturally, linguistically and in other ways from the dominant white, Anglo-Saxon, Protestant, patriarchal culture (Cai and Sims Bishop, 1994). The distinction between dominant and dominated cultures, however, is not acceptable to all educators. Some would argue against it and hold that even the most inclusive of these definitions is not inclusive enough.

THE FOCAL POINT OF THE CONTROVERSY

It is obvious that the controversy surrounding the definition of multicultural literature focuses on the prefix "multi" rather than the root of the term multicultural. Although culture is defined in various ways (Banks, 2001), when people try to define and redefine multicultural literature, there is little dispute over its definition. Many would not object to a dictionary definition of culture like this one: "the totality of socially transmitted behavior patterns, arts, beliefs, institutions, and all other products of human work and thought" (*The American Heritage Dictionary of the English Language*, 1992). The difference lies in how many social groups—whether they are racial/ethnic groups, classes, social sectors, communities or populations—should be included in the definition of multicultural literature. In an article entitled "Sorting through the Multicultural Rhetoric," Sara Bullard (1991) comments on the difficulty of defining the parameters of the prefix "multi." "Educators disagree, first, over which groups should be included in multicultural plans—racial and ethnic groups, certainly, but what about regional, social class, gender, disability, religious, language, and sexual orientation groupings?" (p. 5).

A brief look at the evolution of the term "multicultural" may provide a historical perspective on the controversy. In a recent article on the connections between multiculturalism and literature for children and young adults, Karen Smith (1993) traces its origin to the 1940s. In one of its earliest appearances, in a 1941 *Herald Tribune* book review, according to William Safire (cited in Smith, 1993), "a multicultural way of life" was held out as an antidote to "nationalism, national prejudice and behavior" (p. 341). Used in this sense, the term involved a broad representation of diverse cultures. Just as the term minority was not used to designate America's ethnic groups until the 1930s, in the 1940s, the reference of the term "multicultural" was not limited to ethnic cultures. However, in the 1980s, when the dominant status of Western civilization was more widely challenged, the term became more exclusive, "a college curriculum code word for 'not dominated by whites'" (p. 341). It encompassed the major ethnic groups in the United States that were politically and socially disenfranchised: African Americans, Hispanic Americans, Asian Americans, and Native Americans. Later, as American society continued to recognize the needs of various cultures, "multicultural" has assumed a broader representation, including people with disabilities, gays and lesbians, and "in short, any persons whose lifestyle . . . distinguishes them as identifiable members of a group other than the 'mainstream'" (Smith, 1993, p. 341).

Historically the prefix "multi" varied in its inclusiveness, the extent of which was determined by the sociopolitical concerns of the time. At present, the controversy continues to focus on how inclusive it should be. Defining multicultural literature is still a matter of determining the parameters of the prefix "multi." At one end of the wide range of definitions, multicultural literature is "books by and about people of color"; at the other extreme, it is all-inclusive—"all literature is multicultural" (Fishman, 1995, p. 79). The trend is toward all-inclusiveness. In the following section I examine three views that reflect this tendency.

THREE VIEWS ON THE DEFINITION OF MULTICULTURAL LITERATURE

The first view holds that multiple + cultures = multiculturalism. Therefore, multicultural literature should include as many cultures as possible, with no distinction between the dominant and dominated. The second view objects to a focus on racial and ethnic issues in multicultural literature. The third view maintains that every human being is multicultural (e.g., an Asian American who is female, middle-class, Buddhist, and has a disability) and all literature is multicultural (Fishman, 1995).

Multiple + Culture = Multiculturalism

How many cultures should multicultural literature cover? Some people argue that multiculturalism means the inclusion of multiple cultures and therefore multicultural literature is the literature of multiple cultures. They believe that the more cultures are covered, the more diverse the literature is. Both underrepresented cultures and mainstream cultures should be included; for example, not only Mexican but also Spanish, not only American Indian but also British, not only Vietnamese but also French. Thus, virtually any culture in the world should be encompassed by the prefix "multi." According to this view, a folktale from Russia is as multicultural as one from West Africa. However, this kind of undiscriminating inclusion is inconsistent with the fundamental assumptions of multiculturalism.

Multiculturalism involves diversity and inclusion, but, more importantly, it also involves power structure and struggle. Its goal is not just to understand, accept, and appreciate cultural differences, but also to ultimately transform the existing social order in order to ensure greater voice and authority to the marginalized cultures and to achieve social equality and justice among all cultures so that people of different cultural backgrounds can live happily together in a truly democratic world. This is an ideal embodied in the founding documents of the United States. However, before the ideal can be realized—and it may never be fully attained (Banks and Banks, 1997)—it is, paradoxically, imperative to empower marginalized cultures. If the issues of inequality, discrimination, oppression, and exploitation are excluded from consideration when we try to define multicultural literature, there is a danger of diluting, or even deconstructing, the social-political concept for which the term stands. When, in the definition of multicultural literature, culture is used as a broad concept and not in the strict anthropological sense of the term, it incorporates nationality, ethnicity, class, gender, religion, disability, age, sexual orientation, family status, geographic difference, linguistic variation, and any other possible differences from the mainstream culture. In each of these categories there are subcategories of differences. In religion, for example, how many different faiths are there in the world? Buddhism, Hinduism, Shintoism, Islam, Christianity, Judaism, to name just the major faiths. In each of these faiths, there are various denominations. A multitude of cultures exit in the world. Are we to include them all in our multicultural list?

A few years ago I circulated a proposal for a new course in the study of multicultural children's literature in my department in order to get faculty feedback. In the course description, I wrote, "The main focus of the course will be on Native American, African American, Hispanic American, and Asian American cultures. Other ethnic groups, such as Jewish and Appalachian cultures, will also be discussed." A colleague questioned this focus: "If it is a multicultural literature course, why doesn't it include Caucasian cultures?" The comment implies that multicultural literature must encompass all cultures. Caucasian cultures are no exception. If they are not included, it could mean reverse racism. Multicultural-ism does not mean the sum of multiple diverse cultures. Rather, the thrust of its conception is to decentralize the power of the mainstream culture. "Diversity must be framed within a politics of cultural criticism and a commitment to social justice" (Estrada and McLaren, 1993, p. 31). Instead of embracing the literature of all cultures, a definition of multicultural literature should therefore draw a demarcation line between the literature of the dominant mainstream culture and that of marginalized cultures. If multicultural literature includes all cultures, the term loses its meaning. In other words, the concept is deconstructed by dissolv-ing its opposition to the literature of mainstream culture. Without the binary op-position, what is the point of using a different name? All-inclusiveness reduces multicultural literature to simply literature (Sims Bishop, 1994).

The view that multiple plus cultures equals multiculturalism amounts to a "tourist's conception of multiculturalism" (Hade, 1997, p. 236). It assumes that the mainstream culture in which we live is essentially fair and suggests that we "travel" to as many cultures as possible to learn from them. We will overcome ignorance and bigotry when, on our return, we become more aware of cultural differences and more respectful of other cultural groups. From this perspective, a hierarchy of cultures is nonexistent and issues of social justice and social change are not primary concerns. This tourist's view of multiculturalism is idealistic at best and deceptive at worst, as it glosses over the grim reality of conflicts be-tween races, classes, genders, and other social groups. This equal treatment of different cultures recalls the insightful remarks of former U.S. Supreme Court Chief Justice Oliver Wendell Holmes when he said, "There is nothing as unequal as the equal treatment of unequals" (cited in Cortes, 1994, p. 30). If the playing field is to be made level for everyone, Banks and Banks (1995) suggest, histori-cally underrepresented groups need to be given unequal focus in the classroom.

"Multiculturalism Should Not Focus on People of Color"

Whether multicultural literature should focus on people of color has been dis-cussed and debated intermittently for some time, and recently there was a heated exchange between Patrick Shannon, Rudine Sims Bishop, and Violet Harris over this issue in the *Journal of Children's Literature* (spring 1994). While acknowl-edging the multiple dimensions of cultural difference, some educators contend that we should focus on racial issues. Harris (1992) believes that we should "concentrate on those who are most excluded and marginalized, people of color" (p. xvi). Sims Bishop (1994) also argues for a focus on people of color when selecting multicultural literature: "This is not an attempt to exclude other groups from the body of multicultural literature. It is an attempt to call attention to the voices that have been traditionally omitted from the canon . . . the part of the picture that needs most to be filled in" (p. 7). Others (e.g., Kruse and Horning, 1990), simply define multicultural literature as books about people of color. They believe the issues of race are so critical that they should be the focus of

multicultural literature. Their view harks back to the conception of multiculturalism in the 1980s.

In actual circulation, the term of multicultural literature is also treated as
equivalent to multiethnic literature. Books dealing with class, gender, and other
differences are usually not classified as multicultural literature by teachers or
librarians. For example, if we give a schoolteacher or librarian Anthony Brown's
(1986) *Piggybook,* which addresses the issue of gender roles in the family, it is
most likely that they would not classify it as a multicultural book.

Concentration on people of color has been criticized for reducing multiculturalism to racial essentialism that excludes many cultures from the concept of multiculturalism. "Such treatment," Shannon (1994) comments, "allows most teachers and students to stand apart from multiculturalism, as if it were only about The
Other and not about themselves" (p. 2). Because the majority of teachers and
students in his institution are white, Shannon goes on to say, they find multiculturalism irrelevant or even an imposition when it is limited to issues of race.
Rochman (1993) also argues vehemently against emphasizing racial issues:
"Multiculturalism means across cultures, against borders, and multiculturalism
doesn't mean only people of color" (p. 9).

No party in the debate seems to disagree with the noble goal for multiculturalism as stated by Shannon (1994), namely, "changing the definition and reality of
America until they stand for equality, freedom, and justice" (p. 5). To achieve
the goal of multiculturalism, in Shannon's view, all teachers and students should
be involved in talking about multiculturalism and should acknowledge cultural
biases by "making issues of culture problematic" (p. 2) in *all* the books we read.
Shannon argues that instead of focusing on literature about people of color, we
should discover and discuss the cultural aspects of any children's literature,
which itself will "[demonstrate] the complexity of multiculturalism" (p. 3). One
of the examples he uses to illustrate his point is *Farmer Duck* (Waddell, 1992), a
fantasy story about some farm animals revolting against a farmer who does nothing but make the duck toil for him. The "multi-racial," "multi-lingual" animals
form a united front against the common class enemy. This book normally would
not be classified as multicultural literature, but Shannon touts it as "a multicultural book at its best"(p. 3) because it has the *potential* for serious discussion of
economic class and the injustices of capitalism" (p. 3; my italics) as well as the
issues of gender, race, and language difference.

In his argument, I believe, Shannon sets up a false dichotomy between reading
all books multiculturally (Hade, 1997) and reading books about the Other. To
read literature multiculturally, as Hade defines it, is to read and interpret the
signs of race, class, gender, and other issues in literature. Willis (1997) also advocates "adopting a multicultural perspective towards literature" (p. 137). By
reading from a multicultural perspective, the reader will be able to analyze and
understand the ideological positions that have supported and sustained race,
class, and gender oppression. This critical approach to literature does not exclude reading multicultural literature. Actually, it is complementary to reading it.
To read books by and about people of color does not exclude whites from the

discussion of multiculturalism. Books about people of color may not directly reflect the lives of white teachers and students, but they definitely expose them to racial issues in their country, which at some point of their lives they will inevitably confront. Exposure to these books may help them become aware of racial discrimination and the oppression to which people of color have been, and still are, subjected in a white-dominated society. Whites are involved, rather than excluded, when they read books about people of color.

Take Mildred Taylor's (1976) *Roll of Thunder, Hear My Cry*, for example. It depicts the sufferings of an African American family, the Logans, under racist oppression during the Depression years, and so is definitely a book about the Other. How could white readers rightfully say that it has nothing to do with them? If they recognize the fact that whites have contributed to the oppression of people of color, how could they feel that reading the book is irrelevant to their lives or an imposition? A book like *Roll of Thunder, Hear My Cry* concerns everyone in the United States, regardless of ethnic background. Although its text is mainly about the African American experience, the book presents an opportunity for every reader to ponder the racial issues that have plagued this country. In this sense this book is about all of us.

When Katherine Paterson (1991) heard some teachers and librarians say that they do not buy books by Mildred Taylor and other African American authors for their libraries because they have no African American children in their schools, she made the following comments:

That's about the worst reason I can think of for not buying these books. Every child deserves the chance to hear those authors' stories. In a school review of *Coming Sing, Jimmy Jo*, the librarian said that the children in her upper-class suburban school would not be interested in the story of a country singer from Appalachia. With this kind of reasoning, a whole generation of children will grow up to sneer at persons who are different from themselves. (p. 36)

Contrary to the belief that emphasizing issues of race and ethnicity exclude whites from the discussion of multiculturalism, in fact such an emphasis calls attention to a critical aspect of multiculturalism, which concerns everyone. We live in a racialized society (Morrison, 1992; West, 1993). People of color have been discriminated against, oppressed, and exploited throughout our history. They still experience varying degree of inequality and injustice today. W.E.B. Du Bois said at the turn of this century: "The problem of the twentieth century is the problem of color-line—the relation of the darker to the lighter races of men in Asian and Africa, in America and the islands of the sea" (cited in Sims Bishop, 1994, p. 7). Although progress has been made, American society is, unfortunately, still torn apart along racial lines at the end of the twentieth century. And there are indications that race will continue to matter in the next century. Anyone who recognizes the urgency of the racial issues will not "fear, demonize, and dismiss an ideology that attempts to redress historic and on-going inequalities and institutionalized racism" (Harris, 1994a, p. 9).

"All Literature Is Multicultural Literature"

Shannon (1994) makes a valid point about implementing multiculturalism through the exploration of all children's books. From the premise that every book demonstrates the complexity of multiculturalism, however, he comes to the faulty conclusion that we should not have a separate category of literature called multicultural literature because the separation would make general literature appear as the norm and multicultural literature as alien. Shannon's argument about the multicultural nature of literature is shared by Andrea R. Fishman (1995), who explicitly states that "all literature is multicultural" (p. 79). Different from the first view, that multicultural literature is multiple plus literature, this view denies the necessity of creating a type of literature about various specific cultures, whether dominant or dominated.

The view that all literature is multicultural has the merit of expanding our understanding of literature from a multicultural perspective. We should try to read any piece of literature multiculturally in order to discover, and deal with, the cultural issues it contains. However, to make a concentrated study of underrepresented cultures, we need books directly dealing with them. Multicultural literature is still a much-needed, separate category of literature. Its existence also poses a challenge to the domination of all-white literature. Eventually, multicultural literature will cease to exist and the world of children's books becomes one of democratic pluralism. But we still have a long way to go before we realize that goal.

Whether multicultural literature is alien or exotic is not inherent in itself, but rather lies in the perception of the reader. From the perspective of marginalized ethnic groups, this new category of literature is not alien or exotic at all. Instead, it represents their world, reflecting their images and voices. When it is incorporated into the curriculum, children from these groups find characters with whom to identify in the books they read in school. Think of the all-white world of children's literature that Nancy Larrick described in 1965, with less than 7 percent of children's books published between 1962 and 1964 including African Americans in the text or illustrations. For African American children, the all-white world represented by this huge majority of texts was the exotic one.

If we argue that multicultural literature should be integrated into the content areas of the curriculum instead of being excluded from them and treated as an appendix, that is another matter. In some standard children's literature textbooks, such as those by Huck et al. (1997) and (1999), there is a chapter or a section that deals exclusively with multicultural literature. This treatment of multicultural literature does not necessarily make it appear as alien if it also permeates the discussion of children's literature in general. In the beginning of the chapter on multicultural literature, Norton (1999) notes:

This chapter is not intended to isolate the literature and contributions of racial and ethnic minorities from other literature discussed in this book. Instead, it tries to place multicultural literature in a context helpful to librarians, teachers, and parents who wish to select and share such materials with children or develop multicultural literature programs. (p. 580)

To make multicultural literature permeate the curriculum does not, and should not, entail the oblivion of multicultural literature as a category of literature deserving special attention. To emphasize that all literature is multicultural to the exclusion of multicultural literature as an intimidating force that sets up barriers between "them" and us, may as with making the term multicultural all-inclusive to the point of deconstructing its sociopolitical concept, contribute to its possible demise. In the present publication of children's literature, historically marginalized cultures are still underrepresented. Numbers of books by and about people of color, for example, are still disproportionate to the population. As Sims Bishop (1997) points out, despite the fact that the number of multicultural books has "increased significantly in the past years, the proportion of such books remains quite small" (p. 7). Recently, some professionals expressed concerns about the future of multicultural literature. When predicting the future for the publication of children's books portraying the Puerto Rican experience, Nieto (1997) was apprehensive that the conservative political agenda of the 1990s might bring it to a sudden stop. Horning, Kruse, and Schliesman (1997) worried that "the collective span of Americans is beginning to move away from multicultural literature," and stressed that "it is critical that multicultural literature be viewed as a substantial component of children's book publishing, rather than a passing fad" (p. 10). What is especially at stake is literature about parallel cultures, not multicultural literature broadly defined. As Sims Bishop (1994) points out:

White students and their teachers will find *Farmer Duck* . . . But will they find Jacob Lawrence or Lulu Delacre or Shonto Begay or Yoshiko Uchida on their own? And if they do, will they turn away because they think it represents something and someone alien to them? (p. 7)

Historically, protest against the virtually all-white world of children's literature played an important role in bringing about multicultural literature. To keep this fledgling literature alive, educators, librarians, parents, and students need to raise their voices to demand its continuing publication, which will not happen if they are confused by the controversy over the definition of multicultural literature. In the interest of multicultural education, I believe we need a narrow, not an all-inclusive, definition of multicultural literature. In this book and elsewhere I adhere to the definition generally accepted, and widely circulated, by teachers, librarians, and publishers, according which, multicultural literature is "[l]iterature about racial or ethnic minority groups that are culturally and socially different from the white Anglo-Saxon majority in the United States, whose largely middle-class values and customs are most represented in American literature" (Norton, 1999, p. 580). It also includes literature about these groups' root cultures outside the United States.

IMPLICATIONS FOR TEACHERS AND TEACHER EDUCATORS

The debate over the definition of multicultural literature has great implications for teachers and teacher educators. It has raised general questions about upholding and pursuing the goals of multicultural education and specific questions about incorporating multicultural literature into the curriculum. In the foregoing section I have already touched upon some of these questions. In the following section I will highlight two key issues: the relationship between diversity and equity and that between reading multiculturally and reading multicultural literature.

Diversity and Equity

Multicultural literature is an important component of the multicultural education movement and a tool to achieve its goal: diversity and equity in education. The view that multiple + culture = multiculturalism emphasizes diversity without distinguishing between dominated and dominant cultures. Educators who accept this view will aim at teaching about diverse cultures more than addressing issues of equity. When considering adding multiculturalism to the curriculum, they will expect the curriculum to represent all the diverse cultures that constitute the vast demographic web of the United States.

In view of the fact that dominated cultures have been, and are still, underrepresented in the curriculum, we should focus on the disenfranchised cultures rather than all cultures. To include every culture, the curriculum would not only be unmanageably big but would also miss the ultimate goal of multiculturalism. For example, in an instructional unit on the Revolutionary War, we cannot, and should not, try to cover every cultural group. Rather, we should focus on the underrepresented groups, such as African Americans and women, because their perspectives are not included in the textbook interpretation of the historical event and their contributions to the war are neglected. Instead of books about every cultural group, we should include books such as *Jump Ship to Freedom* (Collier and Collier, 1981) and *When the World's on Fire* (Edward, 1972), both of which reflect the Black experience in that historical period, or *The Boston Coffee Party* (Doreen, 1988), which depicts women fighting on the home front.

It is not my contention that in all cases we should exclude books about the mainstream cultures. In instructional activities that compare and contrast different cultures in order to show human commonalities, books about the dominated groups are usually used along with books about European cultures. Consider, for example, thematic units on food, housing, or the family. Books about various cultures will certainly be included. But if the historically underrepresented groups are not included in the unit, the attempt to affirm diversity is not successful because it does not address the issue of equity. Sometimes it might even be counterproductive to let an Eurocentric perspective be used or implied. Consider an activity comparing different versions of the same traditional tale (e.g., Cinderella story), which is popular in school. The Chinese tale *Yeh-Shen* (Louie,

1982), an equivalent to the Cinderella story, is a likely choice for the activity. Even though its origin is traced back to more than five years before the earliest of the so-called Cinderella tales, as Yamate (1997) observes, it is likely that the comparison will be, not between the variations of the Yeh-Shen tale, but between variations of the Cinderella tale. Although this activity does expose students to different cultures, Yamate (1997) warns, subconsciously it may also instill in them the notion of European American cultural superiority. To affirm diversity is to ultimately achieve equity. Diversity without equity is not the goal of multiculturalism.

A multicultural activity aimed at diversity may backfire if we do not teach equity at the same time. It may generate, instead of eliminate, prejudice. Glenn-Paul (1997) finds that at some "multicultural days" at her school, "some children were cruel to others" (p. 269) because their contributions did not measure up to expectation. If diversity is presented with little respect for the less known culture, a multicultural activity may build, instead of break, cultural barriers. Mildred Lee (1995) reports that on a field trip to a cemetery to celebrate the Chinese Clear Brightness Festival, a teacher ignorantly encouraged her students to tour the cemetery and make rubbings of the tombstones. The Chinese families who were cleaning the graves and making offerings to their ancestors were offended by the intruders. For the Chinese, this festival is a solemn occasion to pay respect to their ancestors and ask for blessings from them. The ceremonial meal they eat at graveside is not a family picnic as the teacher thought. The teacher might be well intended in organizing the activity but, due to her lack of knowledge, her efforts to foster diversity proved counterproductive.

Reading Multiculturally and Reading Multicultural Literature

The view that all literature is multicultural and should be read multiculturally opens new channels for multicultural education. Reading multiculturally enhances our multicultural awareness and helps us see multicultural issues which were not previously apparent. When explicating the idea of reading multiculturally, Hade (1997) uses the children's classic *The Secret Garden* (Burnett, 1987) as an example. According to Hade, it can be interpreted as a subversive story in that children triumph over adults. A multicultural reading, however, reveals a different meaning:

The poor and women, though apparently each with more sense than rich males, have been put on earth to serve rich males. The working-class people in *The Secret Garden* exist for the upper class. . . . A romantic view of class pervades the book. The poor are noble savages. They don't need modern medicine or money, just fresh air and starchy food. They are uncorrupted by wealth; innocently happy in their destitution. (p. 245)

A reader who reads *The Secret Garden* in this way brings to bear on it a multicultural stance—one that seeks out the meanings of race, class, and gender in a story (Hade, 1997)—and interpret its cultural implications. The multicultural stance provides the reader with an instrument, a magnifier if you will, to expose the assumptions about race, class, and gender hidden in a story. We can adopt this stance to many other classics such as *The Adventures of Huckleberry Finn*, *The Merchant of Venice*, and traditional folktales such as *Cinderella* and *Little Red Riding Hood* and find similar problems of race, class, gender, and other differences. College courses in children's and young adult literature should help students develop this stance and learn to analyze cultural issues involved in the books they read. I return to this point in Chapter 8, which discusses multicultural literature in the curriculum.

Although we should read any literary work multiculturally, we also need to read multicultural literature that concentrates on oppressed groups, especially ethnic groups. In *Farmer Duck* or *The Secret Garden,* race is not a central issue. If a reader wants to learn about the history and reality of racial issues in the United States, which can provide the information and perspectives, *Farmer Duck* (Waddell, 1992) or books about people of color such as *Tar Beach* (Ringgold, 1991) and *Roll of Thunder, Hear My Cry* (Taylor, 1976)? Obviously the answer is the latter (Sims Bishop, 1994). Teachers and librarians need to help children find these books and engage with them.

Some students of the mainstream culture may find it hard to engage in multicultural literature because it reflects experiences different from their own. Educators are obliged to help them find ways to begin the engagement. Shannon (1994) and Fishman (1995) both believe that a reader's "multiple cultural identities" may provide "ways in" to literature that seems owned by Others. They have a valid point. Shannon demonstrates how this might work with the example of *Tar Beach* (Ringgold, 1991), which depicts an African American girl's imaginary flight over New York city. In her imagination, she and her family are free from the bondage of discrimination and poverty. "Clearly this book is about race and racism in America," (p. 2), as Shannon points out, but the racial issues are situated "within a complex social context which cuts across other social groups" (p. 3). There are other cultural markers such as class and gender in the book with which white readers can identify. They may not belong to the same ethnic group as the characters in the story, but may be in the same social economic status or have other connections with the characters. These connections enable them to engage in the story and empathize with the characters. Some teachers who listened to Shannon read the book, for example, wrote in their response about devastating experiences of their spouse or parents being laid off and about their desires to move from the working to the middle class—experiences similar to those of the black girl's family.

However, if the response and discussion stop at seeking out the common experiences with the characters and fail to examine closely the social inequality and injustice caused by racism, as reflected in *Tar Beach*, it misses the point of reading about the Other. To see the commonalities among cultures is important, but to study the differences is equally, or even more, important. Through a discussion of differences conducted while reading *Tar Beach*, white students may become aware of their privilege and power over African Americans, and also of their bias against them. Some of Shannon's students reveal their bias when they snicker at the fried chicken, watermelon, and beer the black family has at a picnic. How these students formed the negative image of African Americans should be given serious attention (Sims Bishop, 1994). If the issue is not addressed in their discussion of the books, then, even if they can relate to the story, the activity will be largely counterproductive because instead of removing the negative stereotype, the literary encounter perpetuates it. For white readers, reading various cultural messages in a book about people of color should not end with narcissistic self-reflection but should eventually lead to a change in their perspective on the Other.

Multicultural literature embodies a dream of equity for the oppressed groups. We should hold fast to that dream (Reimer, 1992). Since its inception, multicultural literature has gained some ground in the curriculum but is still far from permeating it. To place pluralism at the core of education, we need more, not less, multicultural literature.

NOTE

An earlier version of this chapter was published in the fall 1998 issue of *The New Advocate, 11* (4), 311-324. Reprinted by permission of *The New Advocate*.

REFERENCES

American heritage dictionary of the English language (3rd ed.) (1992). Boston, MA: Houghton Mifflin.

Austin, M. C., and Jenkins, E. (1973). *Promoting world understanding through literature, K–8*. Littleton, CO: Libraries Unlimited.

Banks, C. A. M. and Banks, J. A. (1995). Equity pedagogy: An essential component of multicultural education. *Theory into Practice, 34* (2), 152-158.

Banks, J. A. (2001). *Cultural diversity and education: Foundations, curriculum, and teaching* (4th ed.). Boston, MA: Allyn and Bacon.

Banks, J. A., and Banks, C. A. M. (1997). (Eds.). *Multicultural education: Issues and perspectives*. Boston: Allyn and Bacon.

Bullard, S. (1991). Sorting through the multicultural rhetoric. *Educational Leadership, 49* (4), 32-36.

Cai, M., and Sims Bishop, R. (1994). Multicultural literature for children: Towards a clarification of the concept. In A. H. Dyson and C. Genishi (Eds.), *The need for story: Cultural diversity in classroom and community* (pp. 57-71). Urbana, IL: National Council of Teachers of English Press.

Cortes, C. E. (1994). Multiculturation: An educational model for a culturally and linguistically diverse society. In K. Spangenberg-Urbschat and R. Pritchard (Eds.), *Kids come in all languages: Reading instruction for ESL students* (pp. 22-35). Newark, DE: International Reading Association.

Dasenbrock. R. W. (1987). Intelligibility and meaningfulness in multicultural literature. *PMLA, 102* (1), 10-19.

Estrada, K., and McLaren, P. (1993). A dialogue on multiculturalism and democratic culture. *Educational Research, 22* (3), 27-33.

Fishman, A. R. (1995). Finding ways in: Redefining multicultural literature. *English Journal, 84* (6), 73-79.

Glenn-Paul, D. (1997). Toward developing a multicultural perspective. In V. Harris (Ed.), *Using multiethnic literature in the K-8 classroom* (pp. 257-276). Norwood, MA: Christopher-Gordon.

Hade, D. D. (1997). Reading multiculturally. In V. Harris (Ed.), *Using multiethnic literature in the K–8 classroom* (pp. 233-256). Norwood, MA: Christopher-Gordon.

Harris, V. (Ed.). (1992). *Teaching multicultural literature in grades K-8.* Norwood, MA: Christopher-Gordon.

Harris, V. (1994a). No invitation required to share multicultural literature. *Journal of Children's Literature, 20* (1), 9-13.

Harris, V. (1994b). Review of *Against borders: Promoting books for a multicultural world. Journal of Reading Behavior, 26* (1), 117-120.

Horning, K. T., Kruse, G. M., and Schliesman, M. (1997). *CCBC Choices 1996.* Madison: University of Wisconsin Press.

Huck, C. S., Hepler, S., Hickman, J., and Kiefer. B. Z. (1997). *Children's literature in the elementary school* (6th ed.). Madison, WI: Brown & Benchmark.

Kruse, G. M., and Horning, K. T. (1990). Looking into the mirror: Considerations behind the reflections. In M. V. Lindgren (Ed.), *The multicolored mirror: Cultural substance in literature for children and young adults.* Fort Atkinson, WI: Highsmith.

Langer, S. K. (1957). *Philosophy in a new key: A study in the symbolism of reason, rite, and art.* Cambridge, MA: Harvard University Press.

Larrick, N. (1965). The all-white world of children's books. *Saturday Review, 48,* 63-65.

Lee, M. (1995). Building bridges or barriers? *The Horn Book Magazine, 71* (2), 233-236.

Levy, M. (1995). Reflections on multiculturalism and the tower of PsychoBable. *The ALAN Review, 22* (3), 11-15.

Morrison, T. (1992). *Playing in the dark.* Cambridge, MA: Harvard University Press.

Nieto, S. (1997). We have stories to tell: Puerto Ricans in children's books. In V. Harris (Ed.), *Using multiethnic literature in the K-8 classroom* (pp. 59-94). Norwood, MA: Christopher-Gordon.

Norton, D. E. (1999). *Through the eyes of a child: An introduction to children's literature.* Columbus, OH: Merrill.

Paterson, K. (1991). Living in a peaceful world. *Horn Book Magazine, 69* (1), 32-38.

Reimer, K. M. (1992). Multiethnic literature: Holding fast to dreams. *Language Arts, 69,* 14-21.

Rochman, H. (1993). *Against borders: Promoting books for a multicultural world.* Chicago, IL: ALA Books / Booklist Publications.

Shannon, P. (1994). I am the canon: Finding ourselves in multiculturalism. *Journal of Children's Literature, 20* (1), 1-5.

Sims Bishop, R. (1992). Multicultural literature for children: Making informed choices. In V. Harris (Ed.), *Teaching multicultural literature in Grades K–8.* Norwood, MA: Christopher-Gordon.

Sims Bishop, R. (1994). A reply to Shannon the canon. *Journal of Children's Literature, 20* (1), 6-8.

Sims Bishop, R. (1997). Selecting literature for a multicultural curriculum. In V. Harris (Ed.), *Using multiethnic literature in the K-8 classroom* (pp. 1-20). Norwood, MA: Christopher-Gordon.

Smith, K. P. (1993). The multicultural ethic and connections to literature for children and young adults. *Library Trends, 41* (30), 340-353.

West, C. (1993). *Race matters.* Boston: Beacon Press.

Willis, A. I. (1997). Exploring multicultural literature as cultural production. In T. Rogers and A. O. Soter (Eds.), *Reading across cultures: Teaching literature in a diverse society* (pp. 135-160). New York: Teachers College Press.

Yamate, S. S. (1997). Asian Pacific American children's literature: Expanding perceptions about who Americans are. In V. Harris (Ed.), *Using multiethnic literature in the K-8 classroom* (pp. 95-128). Norwood, MA: Christopher-Gordon.

Books for Children and Young Adults

Ammon, R. (1989). *Growing up Amish*. New York: Atheneum.

Ancona, G. (1994). *The piñata maker*. San Diego, CA: Harcout Brace.

Brown, A. (1986). *Piggybook*. New York: Alfred A. Knopf.

Bruchac, J. (1995). *The boy who lived with the bears and other Iroquois stories*. New York: HarperCollins.

Burnett, F. H. (1987). *The secret garden*. New York: Bantam.

Collier, J. L., and Collier, C. (1981). *Jump ship to freedom*. New York: Delacorte.

Doreen, R. (1988). *The Boston coffee party*. New York: Harper & Row.

Edward, S. (1972). *When the world's on fire*. New York: Coward, McCann Geohegan.

Kingston, M. H. (1989). *The woman warrior: Memoirs of a girlhood among ghosts*. New York: Vintage.

Louie, A. (1982). *Yeh-Shen: A Cinderella story from China*. Ill. by E. Young. New York: Philomel.

Ringgold, F. (1991). *Tar Beach*. New York: Scholastic.

Rylant, C. (1991). *Appalachia: The voices of sleeping birds*. Ill. by B. Moser. San Diego, CA: Harcourt Brace Jovanovich.

Soto, G. (1991). *Taking sides*. San Diego: Harcourt Brace Jovanovich.

Taylor, M. D. (1976). *Roll of thunder, hear my cry*. New York: Dial.

Waddell, M. (1992). *Farmer duck*. Cambridge, MA: Candlewick.

Young, E. (1989). *Lon Po Po: A Red-Riding Hood story from China*. New York: Philomel.

2

Classifying Multicultural Literature

Despite the controversy over its definition, it is generally acknowledged that multicultural literature can play an important role in fulfilling the need for multicultural education. Books depicting experiences of non-mainstream cultures can help children from those cultures develop cultural identity and pride in their cultural heritage. The inclusion of such books in the curriculum can boost these children's self-esteem and enable them to experience successes in school. Furthermore, multicultural literature provides opportunities for all students to understand and appreciate different cultures, thus learning to respect each other and live in harmony (Austin amd Jenkins, 1973; Miller-Lachmann, 1992; Yokota, 1993; Norton, 1999; Cullinan and Galda, 2002). As the United States is becoming more and more culturally diverse, it is hoped that multicultural literature can help us find an answer to a fundamental question: "How do we create space for pluralism in ourselves and our lives?" (Dyson and Genishi, 1994, p. 11).

Great expectations have been placed on multicultural literature as an instrument to reach the goals of multicultural education. This instrument is powerful because "literature does more than change people's minds; it changes people's hearts. And people with changed hearts are people who can move the world" (Rasinski and Padak, 1990, p. 580). In the first chapter I tried to clarify the controversy over what is multicultural literature and to outline its pedagogical implications for teachers and teacher educators. In this chapter I examine ways in which multicultural literature can be classified and the uses of different types of multicultural literature for the purposes of multicultural education.

Publisher's lists of multicultural literature contain a wide variety of books, including stories set in countries around the world, translations of folktales, poems, and contemporary realistic fiction from other languages; books comparing different cultures, fiction and nonfiction works that portray the experiences of racial and ethnic groups in the United States, and so on. Although the number of these multicultural books is relatively small—about 5 to 6 percent of the total output of children's books (Barrera et al., 1997)—the variety is impressive. Sorting out the available multicultural books will facilitate evaluating and selecting them for different educational purposes.

To treat multicultural literature simply as literary creation, we can classify it as we do with literature in general, into different genres: folktales, modern fantasy, historical fiction, contemporary realistic fiction, and so on. If we look at multicultural literature, not just as literary creation, but also as a special category of books set aside to serve the purposes of multicultural education, we need to consider other ways of classification. In the following, I discuss three classifications of multicultural books: by content and intended audience, by cultural specificity, and by geographical and cultural boundaries. I also discuss the uses of different types of multicultural literature.

CLASSIFICATION BY CONTENT AND INTENDED AUDIENCE

In her landmark work *Shadow and Substance,* Sims (1982) surveyed 150 books of contemporary realistic fiction about African Americans published between 1965 and 1979. She classified these books into three categories: "Social conscience," "melting pot," and "culturally conscious" (p. 16). This classification is based on the content analysis of the sample with regards to three issues associated with African American children's literature:

(a) Who is the primary projected audience for books about Afro-American children? (b) How is the concept of a unique Afro-American experience defined and dealt with? (c) From what socio-cultural perspective have the books been written? (Sims, 1983, p. 22)

Sims's analysis shows how the author's socio-cultural perspective plays a key role in defining and interpreting the African American experience and in determining the aims of creating these books for the projected audience. Her analysis also assesses the thematic significance and quality of the books. What follows is a brief explanation of the three categories.

Social Conscience Books

Social conscience books are intended to help develop social conscience in white children, which should motivate them to empathize and sympathize with African American children. The stories usually have a plot line that involves the conflict between blacks and whites, often over desegregation in schools or neighborhoods, and a theme that advocates integration as the solution for racial problems. Most of the books in this group were written from an ethnocentric, non-African American perspective, which views the African American experience as "exotic, 'different,' or humorous" (Sims, 1983, p. 22). The projected audience for social conscience books is basically white children. For example, *The Empty Schoolhouse* (Carlson, 1965) is intended to arouse sympathy in white readers for black children who encounter racist violence in newly desegregated schools in the South. After racist attacks and threats of violence, all the children except Lullah Royall, a "Negro girl," have stopped attending a desegregated parochial school in Louisiana. Lullah ends up being shot in the ankle. The cruelty inflicted on the little girl awakens the local people's sense of justice. Order is restored, school is resumed, and hope for racial integration rekindled.

Melting Pot Books

Melting pot books refer to books that portray all characters as "culturally homogeneous" (Sims, 1983, p. 22). The only differences between black and white characters are in racially related physical appearance. Since the majority of the books are picture books, the physical differences are seen only in the illustrations. Without the illustrations, the reader cannot tell from the text whether the story features a black or white child. Melting pot books deal with such universal themes and topics such as friendship, family relationships, and everyday experiences. Many of them have a plot line that centers on interracial relationship. While celebrating human universality, most melting pot books ignore the uniqueness of African American experiences and shy away from racial problems. Written mostly by white authors from an assimilationist perspective and for an integrated audience, melting pot books convey the message of racial integration just as social conscience books do, but from a different vantage point. An example can be found in the picture book *Miss Tizzy* (Gray, 1993). Miss Tizzy is an elderly black woman who is like a grandmother to children of varied ethnic backgrounds in her neighborhood. She spends a lot of time with them, playing games, putting on puppet shows, baking cookies, and doing other fun activities. When Miss Tizzy falls ill, the children, in turn, show loving care for her. Interracial harmony is obviously the theme of this melting pot story.

Culturally Conscious Books

Culturally conscious books refer to books that seek to depict the unique experience of African Americans. The stories, usually set in an African American home or community, portray African Americans as the main characters and cover a wide range of themes, from celebrating the African American heritage, urban living, growing up African American to surviving racial oppression. They capture the characteristics of African American culture, including its language, traditions, behaviors, and worldview. They are presumably intended to help African American children understand their history and cultural heritage. Culturally conscious books that are written by African American authors are usually more successful than those written by ethnocentric outsiders in portraying African American experience (Sims, 1982). Take Christopher P. Curtis's (1995) *The Watsons Go to Birmingham—1963*, for example. It is story about the unique experiences of African Americans told from their perspective. The Watson family travels "down south" to leave the rebellious elder son, Byron, in the hands of his strict, yet loving, grandmother and in an environment away from the influence of gangs in the city of Flint, Michigan, where they live. During their brief stay in Birmingham, the family witnesses the bombing of the grandmother's church, which kills four black girls. This tragedy deeply affects the children. After overcoming their initial shock at the deaths and destruction, they become more mature and Byron begins to behave like a big brother.

The classification scheme that Sims constructed on the basis of her analysis is, to some degree, evaluative. Culturally conscious books are valued over social conscience and melting pot books. The label melting pot has pejorative connotations, recalling the assimilationist theory by the same name. Although Sims notes that there are a few well-written books in the social conscience and melting book categories, most commendable books fall in the category of culturally conscious books.

In her study, Sims applied her taxonomy to literature about African Americans only. However, it later gained popularity and has been used to classify literature about other ethnic groups. Recently, for example, Leu (2001) used Sims's classification in her analysis of Asian Pacific American children's literature published in the 1990s. Let us apply Sims' taxonomy to three books about Asian Pacific Americans. *Grandfather's Journey* by Allen Say (1993) is a culturally conscious book because it depicts the unique cross-cultural experience of Japanese Americans, who feel torn between two worlds, the United States and their native Japan. Say's *The Lost Lake* (1989), which deals with the universal theme of a father and son relationship, is a melting pot book. Although the illustrations feature Japanese Americans, we can replace them with characters of any other racial or ethnic background without affecting the content of the story. Kidd's (1991) juvenile novel *Onion Tears* can be classified as a social conscience book. It is about a young Vietnamese girl who tried to adjust to her new life as a refugee in Australia. There is tension between her and her classmates, but with the help of her teacher and foster mother, she eventually makes new friends. This book urges the intended white audience to sympathize with the Vietnamese refugees.

CLASSIFICATION BY CULTURAL SPECIFICITY

In 1992 Sims Bishop (formly Sims) formulated another taxonomy based on cultural specificity reflected in multicultural books. She classified three types of multicultural literature: "culturally specific," "generically American," [1] and "culturally neutral." This classification reflects two ways to approach an individual culture in literature: to focus either on peculiarities that are unique to an individual culture or on similarities that are shared by other cultures. Culturally specific books use the first approach, whereas generically American and culturally neutral books take the second. The classification is concerned with characteristics specific to a particular culture as portrayed in the book.

This new classification is a further development of Sims's 1982 classification. There are differences and similarities between the two. The new classification encompasses books about all non-white cultural groups, not just African Americans. Generically American and culturally neutral books are similar to melting pot books in their focus on human universals, but the category covers a wider range of books. Culturally specific books are similar to culturally conscious books in that both types of books portray the unique experience of nonwhite cultural groups, but culturally specific books do not target only black children as the projected audience. The category of social conscience books was dropped in the new classification, perhaps because of its narrow range of coverage. In the next section, I will discuss the definition and uses of the three categories of multicultural books in Sims Bishop's new classification in greater detail.

Culturally Specific Books

"A culturally specific children's book illuminates the experience of growing up a member of a particular, non-white cultural group" (Sims Bishop, 1992, p. 44). Such a book often details specific cultural aspects of the group, such as lifestyle, linguistic traits, religious beliefs, family relationships, social mores, attitudes, values, and behaviors. In addition to informing the reader on these aspects of a culture, some books in this category may also deal with issues of racism, discrimination and oppression—issues that only the so-called minority groups experience.

Picture books such as Garza's (1990) *Family Pictures/cuadros de familia* and Ringgold's (1991) *Tar Beach* fall into this category. The first book represents, in striking illustrations, many aspects of the daily family life in rural Mexican American Texas, including religious practices, traditional family outings, and games. It also acquaints the reader with a few Spanish terms, such as *faire* (fair) and *posadas* (visits to the shrine of the Virgin of San Juan). The second book portrays an African American girl's imaginative flight across the sky above New York City. The story reflects African Americans' aspiration to break away from any bondage, and its illustrations showcase their folk art of quilt making. This book is in the African American tradition of fighting for freedom, as represented in folktales adapted by Hamilton in *The People Could Fly: American Black Folktales* (1985). Both books contain "cultural markers" (Sims Bishop, 1992, p. 45) about the cultures represented in them.

Some picture books that fall into this category are culturally specific only in the artwork, which is subtly different in style from the artwork of the mainstream culture, or in other cultural markers such as "the names of the characters, the form of address for a parent, the values or attitudes of the characters, and the description of the skin color" (Sims Bishop, 1992, p. 45). These subtle cultural markers in the illustrations and text distinguish these picture books from the next category: generically American books. Greenfield's *Grandpa's Face* (1988) exemplifies this type of book. It is a story about an African American girl's close relationship with her grandfather, who is an actor. She especially loves her grandfather's face, which can express rich feelings and emotions. Even when he is mad with her, she knows from his facial expression that he loves her. But one day she sees him make a mean face in the mirror while he is rehearsing. She fears that he will show her that face until he reassures her that he will love her forever. The theme of love between granddaughter and grandfather is universal.

What is culturally specific about this book is the characters' African-American names, the description of the Grandpa's face as "sturdy brown," the extended family with the grandpa living in the same house, and other details.

Generically American Books

Generically American books present members of so-called minority groups, "but they contain few, if any, specific details that might serve to define those characters culturally" (Sims Bishop, 1992, p. 45). In other words, these characters are indistinguishable from their white counterparts except for their physical features. In picture books, it is usually the illustrations that show the racial identity of the characters. These books reflect generic experiences that are shared by all Americans. Because of "the homogenized cultural content" (Miller-Lachmann, 1992, p. 12), characters of color in this type of books could have been converted to white characters without affecting the story. Picture books like Williams's *A Chair for My Mother* (1982) and Fox's *Sophie* (1994) fall into this category. The first story portrays a Latino family. After a fire burns up all their furniture, a girl and her grandmother save dimes to buy her waitress mother a comfortable chair. This moving story has a universal theme: family love. The theme of the second story is also universal: the cycle of life and death. It shows how a little African American girl named Sophie grows into an adult while her grandfather ages and dies. These two books are culturally generic because they identify the characters racially, not culturally, and detail no specifics of African American culture.

Culturally Neutral Books

Culturally neutral books "feature people of color but are fundamentally about something else" (Sims Bishop, 1992, p. 46). These are generally informational picture books that feature people from diverse cultural backgrounds engaged in activities related to the topic but reflecting neither their culture nor their life. *Eating Fractions* (McMillan, 1991) is a typical example of this type. As Sims Bishop states, it features children of different ethnic background but does not detail any of their cultural characteristics. It is "fundamentally about something else," that is, about doing fraction problems. Another example is *My Best Shoes* (Burton, 1994), a concept book about various types of shoes, with a multicultural cast of characters. The so-called minority characters act as models to display different types of shoes worn by people from all cultural backgrounds. However, if the shoes were unique to some cultures, this book would be classified as culturally specific.

The generically American books and culturally neutral books do not give the reader insights into an individual culture, but rather highlight cultural similarities, which make up the "cultural common ground" of the United States (Wilson, quoted in Sims Bishop, 1992, p. 45). In this sense, they are like the melting pot books. Publishing such books has been a major trend in juvenile publication

(Miller-Lachmann, 1992). The positive side of this trend is that it begins to rectify the serious underrepresentation of parallel cultures in children's literature. "The writers and illustrators of these books make a strong statement about valuing diversity" (Sims Bishop, 1992, p. 46). People of color are recognized as part of the American society, so that their children can find their images reflected in the books they read. They can also help undo some stereotypes of people of color. But if these types of books far outnumber culturally specific books, the trend can be a cause for concern, because, like melting pot books, they may create an illusion that all Americans, regardless of cultural background, share the same experiences and values (Sims 1982).

Ignorance and prejudice are two main stumbling blocks to mutual understanding and appreciation among different ethnic groups. To remove these blocks we need more culturally specific books that give readers insights into cultures other than their own. In addition to providing cultural information, a well-written culturally specific book successfully depicts feelings, emotions, desires, aspirations, hopes, and other human qualities universal to all cultures. It shows a human drama played out in a unique cultural context that intensifies its aesthetic impact. It can touch the hearts of readers from various cultures and help them to sympathize and empathize with characters of different cultural backgrounds portrayed in the book.

The goal of multiculturalism is not to dissolve cultural identities so that all cultures merge into one homogeneous culture. The "melting pot" theory has been proven, not only deficient, but also detrimental to the culturally diverse society. Culturally specific books should be given a prominent place in multicultural curricula because they promote the understanding of different cultures.

CLASSIFICATION BY GEOGRAPHICAL AND CULTURAL BOUNDARIES

Classification by geographical and cultural boundaries, which was proposed by Cai and Sims Bishop in 1994, divides multicultural literature into three categories: world literature, cross-cultural literature, and parallel culture literature. Defined in simplified terms, world literature refers literature from and about cultures outside the United States; cross-cultural literature deals with interrelationships between cultures; and parallel culture literature is literature by authors from parallel culture groups about their own culture. Detailed explanation of each category follows.

World Literature

In Cai and Sims Bishop's taxonomy (1994), "world literature" [2] refers to literature from or about non-Western cultures outside the United States, the so-called root cultures of the nonmainstream ethnic groups. It includes translations, retellings, and adaptations of literature from those cultures and literature by American authors set in those cultures. Examples of the first type are Young's (1989) adaptation of a popular Chinese folktale, *Lon Po Po: A Red Riding Hood story from China* and Snyder's (1988) retelling of a Japanese trickster tale, *The Boy of the Three-Year Nap*. Examples of the second type include Staples' (1989) young adult novel, *Shabanu: Daughter of the Wind*, which is set in Pakistan; Temple's (1995) story of modern Haiti, *Tonight, by Sea*; and Haugaard's (1991) historical novel, *The Boy and the Samurai*, which reflects Japanese experience in the midst of a civil war during the sixteenth century, told from an orphan boy's perspective.

The term "world literature" as Cai and Sims Bishop (1994) use it, has a narrower scope of reference than when used by others. In *Our Family, Our Friend, Our World: An Annotated Guide to Significant Multicultural Books for Children and Teenagers*, Miller-Lachmann (1992) includes books from Western countries, such as those from Great Britain and Canada, as multicultural literature. According to Cai and Sims Bishop's taxonomy, only books from and about countries outside the Western dominant culture are classified as multicultural literature that falls into the category of world literature. If we adhere to the distinction between dominant and dominated cultures in the pedagogical definitions of multicultural literature, we would not classify literature about any cultures in the world as multicultural literature. The reason for limiting the reference of the term is clear: literature from and about dominant Western cultures is hardly underrepresented in the literature curriculum. If we count these books as multicultural literature, then are *Little Mermaid, Peter Pan,* and *Pinocchio* multicultural literature, too? Perhaps a better term for this category than world literature is root culture literature, which may distinguish this kind of multicultural literature from what is usually classified as world literature or international literature.

What is generally referred to as world literature or international literature takes up only a very small percentage of book production in the United States. It accounts for only 1 percent of about 4,500 titles published each year in the United States in the 1990s. Most of these books are from and about dominant Western cultures (Tomlinson 1998, 1999). Only a small number of books are from or about non-Western cultures outside the United States. However, these books are very useful in helping children of parallel cultural background understand their cultural roots and build pride in their cultural heritage. For example, *Mufaro's Beautiful Daughter* (Steptoe, 1987) is a Zimbabwean tale, which is imbued with beliefs and values central to the African tradition, such as "retribution for wrongdoing and reward for charity" (Afolayan et al., 1992, p. 428). Since this tale bears some resemblance to the Cinderella tale and is sometimes called the African Cinderella tale, African American children could be proud of a tale comparable to Cinderella that features black characters. Educators who are committed to the inclusion of literature about the underrepresented ethnic groups in the curriculum would value world literature from or about the root cultures of those groups more than from or about the dominant Western cultures.

A large body of world literature is made up of retellings and adaptations of folktales from other cultures. An issue involved in these works is authorship. If authors retell or adapt a tale from another country, it is their duty to indicate clearly that it is a retelling or adaptation and also to tell the reader its origin. Many authors, however, do not give their exact source. For example, the reteller of *The Magic Tree* (McDermott, 1973) says that the tale is adapted from the Bakongo tribe of the Congo River basin in Africa but falls short of providing information on its source. He does not tell the reader from which book or from whom he obtained the story. Authors who retell or adapt folktales from other cultures are cultural messengers. To transmit accurate message, the integrity of the culture from which they take their tales should be respected and reserved. Hearn (1993) stressed the importance of citing the sources for folklore:

We can ask for source citations and more critical reviews; we can compare adaptations to their printed sources . . . and see what's been changed in tone and content; we can consider what context graphic art provides for a story; we can make more informed selections, not by hard and fast rules, but by judging the balance of each book. . . We can, in short, educate ourselves on the use and abuse of folklore at an intersection. (p. 37)

Another issue is the disproportionate publication of folklore from root cultures as compared to literature reflecting contemporary experience. Although folklore may portray the heritage of a cultural group and its common bond with other groups, it does not inform readers about the group's modern-day experience. The information it provides on that culture may be incomplete or outdated. However, there is a reason behind the current trend in publishing folklore, whether originated in the United States or outside. As Hopkins and Tastad (1997) point out, "folk literature tends to avoid political correctness issues and censorship by focusing on social and cultural history of ethnic groups" (p. 401).

Cross-Cultural Literature

The second category of multicultural literature in Cai and Sims Bishop's (1994) taxonomy is cross-cultural literature that reflects intercultural relationships. This label indicates that in the world, there exit cultural gaps to be crossed and, more importantly, that there may be gaps between authors' own cultural perspective and the cultural perspective of the people they portray in their works. This category of books contains two subcategories:

1. Literary works explicitly about interrelationships among people of different cultures without apparent focus on the unique experience of any one culture;
2. Those about people from a given culture written by a writer from another culture. (Cai and Sims Bishop, 1994, p. 63)

A large amount of cross-cultural literature falls into the first subcategory. Much of it compares and contrasts ways of life in different cultures, with a view to fostering the acceptance of cultural diversity or illuminating human universals among different cultures. The following are some typical examples: *This Is the Way We Go to School* (Baer, 1990), and its sequel, *This Is the Way We Eat Our Lunch* (Baer, 1994); *Hopscotch around the World* (Lankford, 1992) and its sequel, *Dominoes around the World* (Lankford, 1998), *All in a Day* (Anno, 1986), and *Everybody Cooks Rice* (Dooley, 1991). This kind of book shows how children live and play differently in other cultures and countries. Although they may offer interesting information about cultural diversity and human universals, they usually do not address issues of interrelationships resulting from cultural differences.

Another type of book in this subcategory directly deals with interracial or intercultural relationships. Some of these books portray interracial friendship or marriage. *Mrs. Katz and Tush* (Polacco, 1993), for example, presents a friendship between an African American boy and an elderly Jewish American woman. Another example is *Dancing with the Indians* (Medearis, 1991), a story of an African American family's friendship with Seminole Indians. An example of interracial dating and marriage is *How My Parents Learned to Eat* (Friedman, 1984), which tells how a child's American father and Japanese mother learn to accommodate each other's lifestyle. He learns to eat with chopsticks, and she, with a knife and fork. Interracial dating and marriage are dealt with in greater depth in some young adult novels, for example, Woodson's (1998) young adult novel *If You Come Softly,* which features a black boy and a white girl who fall in love and have to cope with the reactions of their parents, relatives, and classmates and of people in the community.

Some other books that fall into this subcategory address issues of interracial tension or conflicts. Interracial tension is usually dealt with in novels, but to a lesser extent, it is also presented in some picture books, for example, *Angel Child, Dragon Child* (Surat, 1989), which is about an immigrant Vietnamese girl who has unpleasant experiences in school because she appears different. As characteristic of children's literature, books concerning interracial tension usually end happily, in reconciliation. Whether presenting conflicts or friendships, this type of cross-cultural book may help children reflect upon issues of interracial relationships and learn how to deal with them. Although they may vary in the scope and depth with which they address issues on intercultural relationships, this type of book provides perspectives and insights that cannot be found in books that only compare and contrast different cultures. Unfortunately, not many books of this type are available. It can be hoped that more authors will face the reality of cultural diversity and take on issues of intercultural conflicts in their literary creation.

The second subcategory of cross-cultural literature, for the most part, contains works written by white authors about people of other racial backgrounds. These authors attempt to depict the unique experience of those people, but they do not always succeed in truthfully presenting it. Because these authors did not grow up in the culture they try to portray, they usually do not think and feel like the people from that culture. In terms of sensibility and perspective, there are cultural gaps between the authors and the cultural group they try to portray. They have to cross those gaps before they can write authentically about other cultures. Failure to cross the gaps often results in misrepresenting the reality of another culture. Many cross-cultural books in this subcategory have been criticized by insiders for the misrepresentation or distortion of their experiences. For example, the widely circulated picture book, *Knots on a Counting Rope* (Martin and Archambault, 1987), is marred by the author's ignorance of, and bias against, the Native American cultures. Many details in the story are inaccurate: the "primitive and poetic" language (e.g., a "wild" storm and a "wounded wind"), the boy protagonist's constant interruption of his grandfather's storytelling, and the boy's name ("Boy-Strength-of-Blue-Horses"). The illustrations of the clothing, hairstyle, headdress, and dwellings are either inauthentic or mix up different tribes. For the Native reader, *Knots on a Counting Rope* is repulsive. "The romantic imagery of this book is no less a white fantasy than the bloody savages of more overtly racist titles" (Slapin and Seale, 1999, p. 184). Books such as this may be put on lists called "books about American Indian experience," but they are not American Indian literature. Similarly, books about black and other minority experiences by white authors may also be listed as books about the black experience, Latino experience, or Asian American experience, but realistically, they should be called a white interpretation of minority experience (Tate et al., 1970). Cross-cultural books in this subcategory should be chosen with caution. The ethnicity of the authors and artists is an important factor to consider, but this does not mean that white authors and artists cannot create culturally authentic works about people of color. In Chapter 3 we will discuss the issue of whether an "outsider" can write about a culture authentically.

Parallel Cultural Literature

The third category, parallel cultural literature, refers to "literature written by authors from parallel cultural groups to represent the experience, consciousness, and self-image developed as a result of being acculturated and socialized within those groups" (Cai and Sims Bishop, 1994, p. 66). A good example is Louise Erdrich's (1999) *The Birchbark House,* which depicts the life of the Ojibwa in Lake Superior in the mid-nineteenth century from the point of view of Omaka-yas, a young girl of seven winters. Based on her own family history and writing with an American Indian sensibility, the famous Ojibwa author truthfully and vividly captures the American Indian experience during that historical period.

Parallel cultural literature is similar to culturally conscious books in that both types try to portray the characteristics of a culture and the unique experience of its people, usually from a vintage point within that culture. It differs from culturally conscious books in that only books written by authors from parallel cultural groups about their own cultures fall into this category. It includes culturally conscious books written by insiders, but not those written by outsiders. Parallel cultural literature is not just *about* a culture but also *of* the culture, that is, an essential part of a people's cultural heritage, like their language and art. For example, *Goodbye, Vietnam* (Whelan, 1993) can be classified as a culturally conscious book because it depicts the unique experiences of Vietnamese refugees, but it cannot be classified as a parallel cultural book because it is written by an author outside Vietnamese culture.

Parallel cultural literature is the most important component of multicultural literature. If we really want to understand and appreciate a parallel culture, we should respect and value the literature written by authors from that culture. Moreover, authentic literature of a culture, in most cases, comes from so-called insiders, namely, members of that culture. "Writers create best the landscape that they know—in their minds or in their hearts" (Silvey, 1993, p. 133). With the movement of multicultural literature has come forth a galaxy of brilliant writers from parallel cultures. When we want to read about parallel cultures, their works should be our first choice. To learn about the uniqueness of the African American experience, for example, we should go to such great African American writers as Virginia Hamilton, Walter Dean Myers, Mildred Taylor, Eloise Greenfield, and Elizabeth Howard and such prominent illustrators as Jerry Pinkney, Brian Pinkney, Pat Cummings, Floyd Cooper, and Carole Byard, to name only a few.

By extensively reading literature by insiders, we can construct a frame of reference to check the authenticity of cross-cultural literature written by outsiders. Sims Bishop (1992) makes the following comments on this point: "Reading the literature of insiders will help teachers learn to recognize recurring themes, topics, values, attitudes, language features, social mores—those elements that characterize the body of literature the group claims as its own" (pp. 46-47). With truthful reflection of reality and portrayal of characters, well-written parallel culture literature helps to correct misrepresentation of parallel cultures and undo negative stereotypes of people from those cultures.

Parallel culture literature is important also in terms of political equity. Its publication represents a change in the power structure of book publishing for children and indicates that parallel cultures are beginning to develop a literature for children. Children of parallel cultures take pride in successful works of authors that they consider their own. For example, when the movie version of Amy Tan's *The Joy Luck Club* was shown in Chinese American communities, many Chinese American boys went to see it even though the story is believed to be about mother-daughter relationships. They went to the movie because they were proud of the Chinese American author's success, which her nationwide recognition. In an "all white world of children's books" (Larrick, 1965, p. 63), children of parallel cultures could not see their images reflected in the books they read and, moreover, authors of parallel cultures also could hardly get their works published. In the past three decades the works by both established authors and new talents of parallel cultures have gradually found their way into the world of children's books (Kruse et al., 1997). But the number of these works is still small and disproportionate to the population of the parallel cultural groups. According to Hopkins and Tastad (1997), works by African American writers or illustrators still number little more than fifty to seventy-five children's literature titles among the more than four thousand published each year. Although it is encouraging to see that in the 1990s, more and more people of color are telling their own stories (Kruse et al. 1997), a large number of multicultural books are still created by white authors who choose to write about cultures other than their own. Hopefully, parallel culture literature will grow and flourish in the next century so that the voice of people who have been historically silenced will be heard loud and clear. As Miller-Lachmann (1992) points out, "Authentic treatments required participation by minority authors themselves; social justice demanded it" (p. 8).

In this chapter we have examined three ways of classifying multicultural literature and also discussed different types of multicultural books in each classification. Central to the rationale for making the classifications is the belief that multicultural literature is an instrument for multicultural education. To use it effectively, it is important to classify it into different categories and understand the characteristics and function of each type. While overlapping each other in some ways, the three kinds of classification are different in focus and serve different purposes. The classification by geographical and cultural boundary maps out the domains of multicultural literature and differentiates it from literature in general. It also draws a clear-cut line between books written by outsiders and those written by insiders and thus foregrounds the power struggle over the creation of multicultural literature. The other two classifications, by content and intended audience and by cultural specificity, focus on the content of multicultural books and their expected effects on their audience. They are more obviously evaluative than the classification by geographical and cultural boundary, especially the first type, which examines issues of representation such as perspective, character, conflict, and conflict resolution.

The three classifications have great implications for the publication, selection, and classroom use of multicultural literature. They provide lenses through which to examine trends in the publication of multicultural literature and means to evaluate the collections of multicultural literature in libraries and classrooms. Although all types of multicultural literature, if well written, may serve the purposes of multicultural education, each type has its own characteristics and function. They all should be included in publication plans, library purchase lists, and school curricula, but more importantly, there should be a balance among the different types. Balance does not mean equal share of each type, but rather proportioning different types of multicultural books according to the requirements of multicultural education.

NOTES

1. It is interesting to note that the term "generically American" is often changed to "culturally generic" (e.g., Taylor, 1997; Temple et al., 1998). Perhaps one reason for the change is that "culturally generic" parallel the other two labels in word collocation and is a mnemonic aid.

2. Linda Pratt and Janice J. Beaty (1999) use the term "transcultural children's literature" to refer to what I term "world literature" here. However, they "believe that children's books about people and cultures existing outside the reader's culture and geographic location constitute a body of children's literature different from multicultural literature" (p. 3).

REFERENCES

Afolayan, M., Kuntz, P., and Naze, B. (1992). Sub-Saharan Africa. In L. Miller-Lachmann (Ed.), *Our family, our friend, our world: An annotated guide to significant multicultural books for children and teenagers* (pp. 417-441). New Providence, NJ: Bowker.

Austin, M. C. and Jenkins, E. (1973). *Promoting world understanding through literature, K–8.* Littleton, CO: Libraries Unlimited.

Barrera, R. B., Thompson, V. D., and Dressman, M. (Eds.). (1997). *Kaleidoscope: A multicultural booklist for grades K–8.* Urbana, IL: National Council of Teachers of English.

Cai, M., and Sims Bishop, R. (1994). Multicultural literature for children: Towards a clarification of the concept. In A. H. Dyson & C. Genishi (Eds.), *The need for story: Cultural diversity in classroom and community* (pp. 57–71). Urbana, IL: National Council of Teachers of English.

Cullinan, B. E. and Galda, L. (2002). *Literature and the child* (5th ed.). Belmont, CA: Wadsworth Thomson Learning.

Dyson, A. H., and Genishi, C. (Eds.). (1994). *The need for story: Cultural diversity in classroom and community.* Urbana, IL: National Council of Teachers of English.

Hearn, B. (1993, August). Respect the source: Reducing cultural chaos in picture books, Part Two. *School Library Journal, 33-37.*

Hopkins, D., and Tastad, S. A. (1997). Censoring by omission: Has the United States progressed in promoting diversity through children's books? *Journal of Youth Services in Libraries, 10* (4), 399-404.

Kruse, G. M., Horning, K. T., and Schliesman, M. (1997). *Multicultural literature for children and young adults.* Madison, WI: Cooperative Children's Book Center.

Larrick, N. (1965, September 11). The all-white world of children's books. *Saturday Review,* 63-65.

Leu, S. (2001). Reimagining a pluralistic society through children's fiction about Asian Pacific American immigrants, 1990–1999. *The New Advocate, 14* (2), 127-142.

Miller-Lachmann, L. (Ed.) (1992). *Our family, our friend, our world: An annotated guide to significant multicultural books for children and teenagers.* New Providence, NJ: Bowker.

Norton, D. E. (1999). *Through the eyes of a child: An introduction to children's literature* (5th ed.). Columbus, OH: Merrill.

Pratt, L., and Beaty, J. J. (1999). *Transcultural children's literature.* Columbus, OH: Merrill.

Rasinski, T., and Padak, N. D. (1990). Multicultural learning through children's literature. *Language Arts, 69,* 576-580.

Silvey, A. (1993). Varied carols. *The Horn Book Magazine, 69* (2), 132-133.

Sims, R. (1982). *Shadow and substance: Afro-American experience in contemporary children's fiction.* Urbana, IL: National Council of Teachers of English.

Sims, R. (1983). Strong black girls: A ten year old responds to fiction about Afro-Americans. *Journal of Research Development in Education, 16* (3), 21-28.

Sims Bishop, R. (1992). Multicultural literature for children: Making informed choices. In V. Harris (Ed.), *Teaching multicultural literature in grades K–8* (pp. 37–54). Norwood, MA: Christopher-Gordon.

Slapin, B., and Seale, D. (1998). *Through the Indian eyes: The Native experience in books for children.* Los Angeles: American Indian Studies Center, University of California.

Tate, B., et al. (1970). Authenticity and the black experience in children's books: In house and out house. *School Library Journal, 16* (10), 3595-3598.

Taylor, G. S. (1997). Multicultural literature preferences of low-ability African American and Hispanic American fifth-graders. *Reading Improvement, 34* (1), 37-48.

Temple, C., Martinez, M., Jokota, J., and Naylor, A. (1998). *Children's books in children's hands: An introduction to children's literature.* Boston: Allyn and Bacon.

Tomlinson, C. M. (Ed.). (1998). *Children's books from other countries.* Lanham, MD: Scarecrow.

Tomlinson, C. M. (1999). Children's books from and about other countries. *Journal of Children's Literature, 25* (1), 8-17.

Yokota, J. (1993). Issues in selecting multicultural children's literature. *Language Arts, 70,* 156-167.

Books for Children and Young Adults

Anno, M. (1986). *All in a day.* Ill. by R. Briggs. New York: Philomel.

Baer, E. (1990). *This is the way we go to school: A book about children around the world.* Ill. by S. Bjorkman. New York: Scholastic.

Baer, E. (1994). *This is the way we eat our lunch: A book about children around the world.* New York: Scholastic.

Burton, M. R. (1994). *My best shoes.* Ill. by J. E. Ransome. New York: Tambourine.

Carlson, N. S. (1965). *The empty schoolhouse.* New York: Harper and Row.

Curtis, C. P. (1995). *The Watsons go to Birmingham—1963.* New York: Delacorte.

Dooley, N. (1991). *Everybody cooks rice.* Ill. by P. J. Thornton. Minneapolis, MI: Carolrhoda.

Erdrich, L. (1999). *The Birchbark House.* New York: Hyperion.

Fox, M. (1994). *Sophie.* Ill. by A. B. L. Robinson. San Diego, CA: Harcourt Brace.

Friedman, I. R. (1984). *How my parents learn to eat.* Ill. by A. Say. Boston: Houghton Mifflin.

Garza, C. L. (1990). *Family pictures/Cuadros de familia.* San Francisco: Children's Book.

Gray, L. M. (1993). *Miss Tizzy.* Ill. by J. Rowland. New York: Simon & Schuster.

Greenfield, E. (1988). *Grandpa's face.* Ill. by F. Cooper. New York: Philomel.

Hamilton, V. (1985). *The people could fly: American Black folktales.* New York: Knopf.

Haugaard, E. C. (1991). *The boy and the Samurai.* Boston: Houghton Mifflin.

Kidd, D. (1991). *Onion tears.* New York: Orchard.

Lankford, M. D. (1992). *Hopscotch around the world.* Ill. by K. Milone. New York: Morrow.

Lankford, M. D. (1998). *Dominoes around the world.* Ill. by K. Dugan. New York: Morrow.

Martin, B., and Archambault, J. (1987). *Knots on a counting rope.* New York: Holt.

McDermott, G. (1973). *The magic tree: A tale from the Congo.* New York: Holt, Rinehart and Winston.

McMillan, B. (1991). *Eating fractions.* New York: Scholastic.

Medearis, A. S. (1991). *Dancing with the Indians.* Ill. by S. Byrd. New York: Holiday House.

Polacco, P. (1993). *Mrs Katz and Tush.* New York: Philomel.

Ringgold, F. (1991). *Tar beach.* New York: Crown.

Rylant, C. (1991). *Appalachia: The voices of sleeping birds*. Ill. by B. Moser. Orlando, FL: Harcourt Brace Jovanovich.

Say, A. (1989). *The Lost Lake*. Boston: Houghton Mifflin.

Say, A. (1993). *Grandfather's journey*. Boston: Houghton Mifflin.

Snyder, D. (1988). *The boy of the three-year nap*. Ill. by A. Say. Boston: Houghton Mifflin.

Staples, S. F. (1989). *Shabanu: Daughter of the wind*. New York: Knopf.

Steptoe, J. (1987). *Mufaro's beautiful daughter*. New York: Lothrop, Lee and Shepard.

Surat, M. (1989). *Angel child, dragon child*. Ill. by V. Mai. New York: Scholastic.

Temple, F. (1995). *Tonight, by sea*. New York: Orchard.

Whelan, G. (1993). *Goodbye, Vietnam*. New York: Random House.

Williams, V. B. (1982). *A chair for my mother*. New York: Mulberry Books.

Woodson, J. (1998). *If you come softly*. New York: Putnam's.

Young, E. (1989). *Lon Po Po: A Red Riding Hood story from China*. New York: Phiomel.

Part II

Issues Related to the Creation and

Critique of Multicultural Literature

3

Imagination, Ethnicity, and Cultural Authenticity

The debate over who can create valid books about a particular culture has been raised intermittently since the late 1960s. For a time, the debate centered around some widely circulated books about African Americans written by white authors, such as *Sounder* (Armstrong, 1969), *Words by Heart* (Sebestyen, 1979), *A Girl Called Boy* (Hurmence, 1982), *Ben's Trumpet* (Isadora, 1979), and *Jake and Honeybunch Go to Heaven* (Zemach, 1982), which have been criticized for containing negative images and even racist overtones. More recently, an editorial of *The Hornbook Magazine* rekindled the debate (Silvey, 1993; Aronson, 1993; Stolz, 1993; Murphy, 1993). Some claim that only an insider can write culturally authentic literature, while others counter that through imagination, outsiders can also succeed in capturing ethnic experiences (Sims Bishop, 1992). An outsider may be defined as one who does not belong to the ethnic group about which he/she writes. On the other hand, an insider is one who is a member of the ethnic group about which he or she writes. Anita Silvey (1993) of the *Horn Book Magazine* observes:

On the one hand there are those who fight for artistic freedom and license. No one should prescribe what a writer or illustrator attempts, and creative genius allows individuals to stretch far beyond a single life and to write about lives never lived or experienced. On the other side are those who argue with equal conviction that only those from a particular culture can write about that culture or can write valid books about it. (p. 132)

This insider versus outsider debate is not only a verbal battle over the question of who can portray cultural authenticity in literary creation, it also involves a power struggle over whose books get published. Books by outsiders such as those mentioned here have been published and defended on the basis of their literary merits and quality of imagination, no matter how they distort the reality and stereotype people of the culture they attempt to represent (Sims, 1984). In the name of literary excellence, cultural imposition has been perpetuated by the publication of these "pseudo-multicultural" books. It is an irony that literary excellence is posed against cultural authenticity as if falsifying reality and stereotyping characters did not violate basic principles of literary creation. This kind of literary evaluation emanates from a mentality that regards marginalized cultures as nonentities— something worthless to be toyed with or trampled underfoot. The evaluation seems to be done in nonpolitical form, but actually "furthers certain political uses of literature all the more effectively" (Eagleton, 1983, p. 209). Implicitly or explicitly, the literary and social-political aspects of the insider versus outsider issue are interrelated.

In the following discussion I will attempt to deal with a literary question: Can we cross cultural gaps on the wings of imagination? The power of imagination has been used as a protective umbrella, even for blatantly biased or poorly researched multicultural works. It also has been drawn upon as a source of inspiration for outsider authors who wish to venture into unfamiliar cultures. Thus, the function of imagination in the creation of multicultural literature is an issue central to the insider versus outsider debate. If we can clarify this issue, we can shed some light not only on a literary question, but also on the social-political side of the debate.

THE CRUX OF THE ISSUE

In terms of literary creation the crux of the insider versus outside issue is not the relationship between authors' ethnic background and literary creation but rather the relationship between imagination and experience—a time-honored issue.

The realities reflected in multicultural literature are culturally specific realities experienced by ethnic groups. Ethnic literature is usually defined on the basis of its focus on the unique experiences of an ethnic group. For example, Asian American literature is literature that reflects the experiences of Asian Americans (Norton, 1999; Yokota, 1993). Ethnic literature is therefore culturally specific (Sims Bishop, 1992).

Cultural authenticity is the basic criterion for evaluating multicultural literature. "The purpose of authentic multicultural literature," as Howard (1991) puts it, "is to help liberate us from all the preconceived stereotypical hang-ups that imprison us within narrow boundaries" (p. 92). If we agree with Howard, we will accept cultural authenticity as a major criterion. Departing from the reality of ethnic culture, imagination leads to nothing but misrepresentation or distortion of reality in multicultural literature. Lack of imagination may result in uninspired, insipid writings, but misrepresentation of reality is even worse; it perpetuates ignorance and bias and defeats the purpose of multicultural literature. Cultural authenticity is the basic criterion in the sense that no matter how imaginative and how well written a story is, it should be rejected if it *seriously* violates the integrity of a culture.

Cultural authenticity, it should be reaffirmed, is the basic criterion for realistic literature, not a demand for "literature-as-propaganda." To put the criterion of authenticity first does not mean to neglect other criteria for literary excellence, to which we subject all kinds of literature. We should collapse the dichotomy between the good and the authentic story. As Taxel (1986) points out, "demands for realistic, nonstereotyped characters, and for historical and cultural accuracy and authenticity in writing . . . need not conflict with the demand for literary excellence" (p. 249). Those who believe only insiders can write valid literature about ethnic experiences hold a determinist view of the relationship between the author's ethnicity and creation of authentic multicultural literature. According to this view, the reality of ethnic culture is inaccessible to any outsiders even if they have plenty of direct and indirect experience of that culture. Gates, Jr. (1991) repudiates this determinist view in an article on *The Education of Little Tree* (Carter, 1976): "No human culture is inaccessible to someone who makes the effort to understand, to learn, to inhabit another world." *The Education of Little Tree* is an example of a book written by an outsider and accepted as culturally authentic by insiders (Gates, 1991, p. 27). This novel is about the life of a Native American orphan who learned the ways of his culture from his Cherokee grandparents in Tennessee. When recently reprinted it was an instant success, highly acclaimed by critics in general and well accepted by some Native American reviewers. Then, suddenly, it became a cause of controversy, an embarrassment to those who praised it, as the author's true identity was revealed. Forrest Carter turned out to be a pseudonym for a racist now deceased. The irony is that the author was not only an outsider but also a racist. Although this is an atypical example, it makes it impossible to insist that only insiders are able to write culturally authentic literature about ethnic experiences.

On the other hand, those who argue that through imagination, outsiders can also write culturally authentic books overestimate the power of imagination to cross cultural gaps. In her debate with B. Hurmence, the author of *A Girl Called Boy*, on the issue of perspectives, Sims (1984) cogently argued that white authors fail to truthfully reflect black experience in their books because they have not been socialized into the ways of living, believing, and valuing that are unique to Black Americans. She emphasized the difficulty for an outsider to acquire the perspective of an ethnic culture. Those who believe in the omnipotence of imagination do not seem to recognize the difficulties involved in crossing cultural gaps and tend to be carried away by their imagination. This view abets the publication of books that distort ethnic realities and stereotype ethnic people. It should command the serious attention of everybody who sincerely supports multiculturalism.

CULTURAL BOUNDARIES

People who believe in the outsiders' power of imagination to cross cultural gaps have raised questions about the uniqueness of ethnic realities, cultural identities, and the cultural specificity of ethnic literature. For example, in the 1993 July/August issue of *The Horn Book Magazine*, Aronson states in his letter to the editor:

No modern culture arose alone and "belongs" solely to a particular people . . . In modern America, it is very difficult to say where one ethnic group ends and another begins . . . Since we live in a shared society, and since we all grew up in worlds which are inflected with the accents of other cultures . . . we can all claim an "authentic" connection with many different cultures. (pp. 390-391)

It is true that every ethnic group in modern American society, be it Asian American or African American, has a mixed cultural heritage, part of which is their traditional root culture and part of which is the American mainstream culture. But the duality of this cultural heritage, the influence of the mainstream culture or other cultures, has not obscured the distinction between the cultures of different ethnic groups. As there are no autonomous regions for ethnic groups in the United States, geographically it is hard to say where one ethnic group ends and another begins. But in terms of tradition, customs, attitudes, beliefs, values, and experiences, each ethnic group has defining features, which are culturally specific. If we map the cultural characteristics rather than the locations of people of different ethnic backgrounds, we see the distinct parameters of each culture, which belong solely to that ethnic group. As August Wilson points out:

We share certain mythologies. A history. We share political and economic systems and a rapidly developing, if suspect, ethos. Within these commonalities are specifics. Specific ideas and attitudes that are not shared on the common ground. These remain the property and possession of the people who develop them. (quoted in Sims Bishop, 1992, p. 41)

As Banks (1979) states, in America, there exist "ethnic subsocieties which contain cultural elements, institutions, and groups which have not become universalized" (p. 247). If we deny this, then we deny the existence of ethnic cultures and ethnic literature.

Multiple acculturation, or mutual influence among cultures, enables all of us to claim some connection with many different cultures. But the key issue is how strong and authentic that connection is. Banks (1979) proposes a four-level hierarchy of cross cultural competency, which provides us with a yardstick to test one's "authentic connection" with another culture:

Level I The individual experiences superficial and brief cross-cultural interactions
Level II The individual begins to assimilate some of the symbols and characteristics of the "outside" ethnic group
Level III The individual is thoroughly bicultural
Level IV The individual is completely assimilated into the new ethnic culture. (p. 251)

If an author's cross-cultural competence is only at Level I, for instance, having visited a Chinatown, eaten some Chinese food, and read a couple of books about Chinese culture, can such an author claim "authentic connections" with the Chinese culture and therefore be considered qualified to write a book about Chinese Americans? If most of us had achieved a high level of cross-cultural competence and could claim really "authentic connections" with different cultures, then there would be true mutual understanding between different ethnic groups. Cultural rapport would have resulted and racial tension would have been greatly reduced. To overestimate people's cross-cultural competence is to lower the goal for multicultural education and to lose sight of the difficulties involved in the creation of multicultural literature.

ETHNIC PERSPECTIVE

A difficult task confronting writers who try to truthfully reflect the reality of an ethnic culture, whether or not they are from that culture, is to grasp the perspective of that culture in order to provide culturally authentic literature for the readers. An ethnic perspective is "a world view shaped by an 'ideological difference with the American majority'" (Sims, 1984, p. 148). This perspective is reflected in culturally specific ways of living, believing, and behaving. The key is to take on the group's perspective "like actors who take on a role so thoroughly that they come to be identified with it (and occasionally act it out in real life)" (Miller-Lachmann, 1992, p. 17).

Consider *The Happy Funeral* (Bunting, 1982), for example. The story reflects a Chinese belief that a person who lives a happy and long life is considered to have good luck when dying. In the funeral service for such a person, there will be elements associated with celebration of happy events, such as births and weddings. For example, the color red, a symbol of happiness, may be used along with the color white, a symbol of mourning. Mourners may be given candies wrapped in red paper to sweeten their sorrow. The children of the Chinese American family in this story do not quite understand this belief at first, but gradually they begin to understand and accept it. Bunting has written a sensitive and touching story reflecting this particular belief, but to call the funeral a "happy funeral," striking as it is, is too bluntly direct and misleading. The Chinese concept of seeking consolation from the longevity of the deceased cannot be translated into "happy funeral." It would have been better to leave it implied than to explicitly state it. The misnomer shows that the author has not yet completely taken on the Chinese perspective.

To introduce concepts from one culture to another is a very challenging task, if not an impossible mission. Robert Frost defines poetry as "what is lost in translation" (quoted in Barry, 1973, p. 159). In a similar way, we may define culture as "what is lost in translation." Authors of multicultural literature are acting as cultural messengers, but they may unconsciously impose their cultural beliefs and values on the culture they try to recreate, exhibiting what Nodelman (1988) called "cultural arrogance." As an example of unconscious "cultural arrogance," he cited the translation of an oriental tale in a collection called *Best-Loved Folk Tales of the World* (Cole, 1982). The story is about a woman who believes she is fated to marry a specific man. But the man proposes too late and dies of remorse. On the day of her wedding to another man, she stops by the grave of her true lover and says, "If we are intended to be man and wife, open your grave three feet wide" (Cole, 1982, p. 5365). The grave opens instantly, and she jumps into it. Finally, the couple turns into rainbows. This story reflects a cultural belief that relationships among people, be it lovers or friends, are determined by fate. But the title of the story is mistranslated as "Faithful Even in Death," which, as Nodelman (1988) comments:

distorts the story in order to accommodate non-Oriental cultural assumptions: it implies that the woman's faithfulness is a matter of choice on her part, and therefore, a virtue that is being rewarded, whereas the story itself makes it clear that the woman had no choice but to love he whom she was meant to love, and that the situation has nothing to do with virtue or reward. Only someone whose conception of story derived from European fairy tale could have distorted this tale making the moral health of the characters the driving force behind the events of the plot. (p. 232)

Another example of cultural arrogance, whether conscious or unconscious, is provided by Zhihui Fang et al. (1999). They show us how, in its English retelling, a traditional Chinese tale, *Meng Jian Nu,* is transformed, into *The Journey of Meng,* a "quest" story that fits not only the Western cultural concept but the Western literary form as well. The original story tells of a woman who journeys to the north to look for her husband at the construction site of the Great Wall, only to find him dead. Her heart-rending cries bring down a section of the wall. The author of the English version gives a twist to the plot line of the original story. After the Great Wall tumbles down, the emperor demands that the woman marry him as a reprisal. In defiance, she kills herself by jumping into the sea. The central theme of the story is fidelity to one's husband, but in the retelling, it becomes rebellion against sexual oppression. In the original story, Meng is an ordinary country woman, whereas in the retelling, she becomes "a sex object" and "a symbol of courage and defiance against male tyranny" (p. 262).

The subtleties and nuances of cultural beliefs and behaviors can be elusive to an outsider. In order to give authentic representation to an ethnic culture, an author must make the effort to enter the world of that culture, which cannot be entered simply on the wings of imagination, no matter how imaginative the author. Insiders who want to write about their own ethnic cultures have great advantages over outsiders, but they also need to observe and learn. An ethnic group's perspective is not inherited through genes, but acquired through direct and indirect experiences. "Just as authors from outside a group can write convincingly about that group, being a member of the group is no guarantee that an author's perspective will be with the group" (Miller-Lachmann, 1992, p. 18).

In "A Chinese Sense of Reality," Lawrence Yep (1987) talks about his experience of creating *Dragonwings* (1975). It took him six years of research in libraries and universities to find the information needed to reconstruct a picture of what life was like in the Chinatown of the 1900s. He had tried to understand the background that shaped him and "to develop a special sense of reality, a Chinese sense rather than an American sense" (p. 488). This "special sense of reality" is an equivalent of an ethnic perspective. It is this "special sense of reality" plus his powerful imagination that distinguishes Yep's works from those that stereotype the Chinese. Some multicultural books fail, not because the authors are unimaginative but because they have not acquired the culturally specific perspective.

BRUTE FACTS

If a member of an ethnic group has to make great efforts to develop the group's special sense of reality, a nonmember who is unfamiliar with the ethnic culture has to make double efforts to get that sense. There is no denying that imagination is a creative power, but imagination is not the master of reality. On the contrary, it can be limited by reality. As the critic Rabinowitz (1987) points out, "brute facts" impose great constraints and limitations on the author's imagination, especially in historical fiction. This is also true of multicultural literature. Cultural differences are "brute facts" that limit the author's imagination and put constraints on his or her literary choices.

An author writing about the Chinese dragon dance, for example, must work within the restraints of cultural conventions and represent the facts of the dance authentically. The picture book *Chin Chiang and the Dragon Dance* (Wallace, 1984) features the dragon dance, but the dance is confused with the lion dance. In the dragon dance, the head and tail of the dragon are held up with poles rather than directly by the hands, as in the lion dance. This flaw mars the portrayal of the Chinese culture.

Even insider artists sometimes misrepresent cultural facts, perhaps because they are negligent or have not done the necessary research. In *How My Parents Learned to Eat* (Friedman, 1984), the award-winning artist Allen Say depicts a Japanese girl in school uniform dating an American sailor, also in uniform, publicly. This could be a sensational scandal during that period of time in the story, but other characters in the illustration pay no attention to them (Yokota, 1993). A recently published picture book *The River Dragon* (Pattison, 1991), illustrated by two Chinese American artists, contains ludicrous misrepresentation of cultural facts. For example, it shows ancient Chinese people eating fortune cookies and swallow meat and a dragon chasing the reflection of a moon to its death. Many people know that the fortune cookie is an American invention, but do not know that Chinese people eat the nest that a special species of swallow makes with secretion from its mouth rather than swallow meat. The notion of the dragon chasing the moon is alien to Chinese culture and the god of the river would not die in the river. If the two artists had taken their job seriously and done some research, they would have refused to illustrate this brazenly inaccurate book.

Sometimes insider authors may also present inaccurate cultural information. The well-known Chinese American author Amy Tan, for example, misrepresents some cultural details in her novel *The Kitchen God's Wife*. For the most part, the story takes place in China during World War II, and on the whole, the book truthfully recaptures that period in Chinese history from an insider's perspective. Nevertheless, it does contain minor inaccuracies. For example, a fortuneteller in the story brags that "she had the luckiest fortune stick" for her customers (p. 121). This would immediately betray the fortuneteller as an impostor. A fortuneteller may boast of prophesying accurately with his fortune sticks but will never promise good fortune for his customer. Some Chinese words in the text are misinterpreted: *tang jie* does not mean sugar sister, "the friendly way to refer to a girl cousin," (p. 154). The first Chinese character *tang* in the word *tang jie* ("cousin") is confused with its homonym *tang* ("sugar"). A Chinese person would never refer to a girl cousin as "sugar sister," perhaps except in jokes. *Sau nai-nai*, meaning "young mistress of the house," is mistranslated as "milk nurse" (p. 258). By the mistranslation, the

author has promoted the social status of the "milk nurse." A more serious instance
of inaccuracy occurs in the plot line, when the protagonist and narrator is jailed,
having been falsely accused by her husband (p. 387), and her aunt comes to her
rescue by telling the Kuomintang officials that they have imprisoned a relative of a
high ranking Communist leader. Since the Communists are soon coming to take
over, they had better release her. This is historically false. The Communists and the
Kuomintang were sworn enemies. Although they formed a united front twice
against common enemies—once against the imperial rulers and another time
against the Japanese invaders—they were fundamentally antagonistic toward each
other. In the civil war period that followed World War II, they were again engaged
in cut-throat battles. Before the Kuomintang fled to Taiwan, they killed many
Communists being held in prison. What the aunt says could only endanger her
niece's life. Two chapters earlier, some characters are talking about the enmity between the two parties: "All this talk about unity among all the parties—nonsense. If
the Kuomintang find out we have a daughter who is a Communist—ssst!—all our
heads could be rolling down the street" (p. 338). The inaccuracies in the novel
show that the American-born and -raised Chinese writer has not completely
grasped the realities in the land of her ancestors.

Cultural "brute facts" are not only visible facts in the external reality but also
invisible facts in the internal reality. The invisible "brute facts" are even more difficult to grasp. True, authors can write about lives never directly experienced, but
they need at least indirect experience as a basis for their imagination to take off.
Imagination, as Samuel Coleridge defined it, has two functions. In terms of human
perception, the function of imagination enables us to "grasp the forms first and then
to visit and revisit them in our mind's eye thereafter" (quoted in Warnock, 1976, p.
204). In terms of literary creation, imagination enables the author to recreate
"something out of the materials which we have acquired from perception" (Warnock, 1976, p. 92). Imagination "dissolves, diffuses, dissipates, in order to re-
create" (Coleridge, quoted in Leask, 1988, p. 136). Coleridge's theory states that
poetic imagination is a faculty to re-create, rather than to create, experience.

Ethnic experiences can never be accessed by imagination without any direct or
indirect perception. For example, in *Children of the River* (Crew, 1989), we read
that the Cambodians believe that if you ruffle a child's hair, you may scare away his
intelligence or soul and that if you step over a person lying on the ground, it is bad
luck for him (Chinese also share this belief). If the author has not read about or
heard her Cambodian friends on her farm talk about those culturally specific facts,
can she get to know them by sheer imagination? One may imagine the fears of losing one's intelligence or soul, because they are common to human sensibility, but
one definitely cannot imagine the culturally specific situations in which the fears
occur.

Some authors, however, believe that they need only common human experiences
to help them write about other cultures. Salisbury (1998), for example, contends
that to access the experience of other cultures, all you need is your humanities:

Does one have to be Hawaiian to know and love an island, an ocean, the jungles and valleys, the hearts and minds of dogs, the sun, the surf, the sand? Does one have to be Hawaiian to write about how rich all that natural life feels? No.

Does one have to be Japanese to know and write about how it feels to lose someone you love? To be mistrusted and mistreated? To be removed? No.

Well then what does one have to be?

Human. That's all. Just human. (p. 8)

Other authors believe that common human experience alone is not enough. When the author of *A Distant Enemy* (1998), Deb Vanasse, discussed writing about Yup'ik Indians as an outsider, she emphasized the importance of "cultural immersion." To develop cultural sensitivity, authors must immerse themselves in the culture they want to depict. Vanasse had immersed herself in the Yup'ik culture before she wrote the novel. She lived and taught in the Yukon-Kuskokwim area in southwestern Alaska for many years. To the question, "What right do I have to write about the experiences of another people?" her answer is: "An author can write about whatever she chooses. But to write well, to write responsibly, the writer must always be sensitive, walking as it were in the shoes of others, seeing the world through different eyes" (p. 21). In her article "Who Can Tell My Story," the African American author Woodson (1998) also emphasizes the importance of experience, including common human experiences as well as culturally specific experiences. She starts with the difficulty for an outsider to understand black English. To understand her grandmother's language, she says, one does not need to be part of her family, but one does need to have been part of her family's experience. By extension, to understand another culture, one needs at least indirect experience of that culture. Drawing upon her experience of writing *If You Come Softly* (see Chapter 2), she talks about how she weaves her experiences of being black woman who has an interracial relationship with a Jewish man into the creation of the Jewish girl in the story. Although she cannot directly experience a Jewish girl's life, she can still successfully develop a believable Jewish character because she bases her artistic creation on her experiences, especially stepping "inside the house" of her Jewish partner's experience (p. 37). For Woodson, being "inside the house" of a culture is crucial. She hopes that "those who write about the tears and the laughter and the language in my grandmother's house have first sat down at the table with us and dipped the bread of their own experience into our stew" (Woodson, 1998, p. 38).

To access culturally specific reality, authors cannot rely only on imagination. Direct or indirect experience of that reality is a must. One of Ernest Hemingway's aesthetic principles provides a balanced view of the relationship between imagination and reality. According to Jeffrey Meyers (1985), Hemingway believed that "fiction must be founded on real emotional and intellectual experience and be faithful to actuality, but also be transformed and heightened by imagination until it becomes truer than mere facts" (p. 138). Faithfulness to truth is the essence of this principle. When engaged in writing, Hemingway "liked to know how it really was; not how it was supposed to be" (cited in Meyers, 1985, p. 138). To create an imaginary world of another culture, authors should never start with "how it was supposed to be."

If one elevates the power of imagination to unlimited heights, one may end up distorting reality. In our postmodern era, as Kearney (1988) points out, the romantic dream that imagination is able to transcend reality to create a realm "in the full liberty of aesthetic play" (Schiller, quoted in Kearney, p. 186) has collapsed before the onslaught of realities. It may sound anachronistic to make extravagant claims for imagination.

A COMPARATIVE STUDY OF TWO NOVELS

Historical fiction is often used as an example of imagination's power to harness experience (e.g., Sims, 1984; Aronson, 1993). We can never experience what those who lived before us experienced but, relying on research and imagination, we can still write historical fiction. None of the people living now met Christopher Columbus personally, but many write about him. If it were imperative to write from direct experience, then there would be no historical fiction. Imagination can synthesize the bits and pieces of information into an artistic representation of him, and where information is not available, imagination will be relied on to restore the damaged tapestry of history (Fleishman, 1971).

The question is: who presents the real historical figure, the real Columbus? Whose work is true both to the facts and spirit of that historical period? Look at all the biographies of Christopher Columbus and you will see that we get as many images of Columbus as the perspectives from which he has been portrayed. If a historical novel distorts the facts and spirit of the past, does it succeed or fail? Of course, it fails, no matter how imaginative the author is. Authenticity is the first criterion for historical fiction, and for multicultural literature as well.

To achieve authenticity, the author's ability to take on the perspective of other people living in the past or in other cultures is crucial. Comparing books on the same subject may shed some light on this point. The Chinese involvement in the construction of the U.S. transcontinental railway is the subject matter for many novels. Yep (1993) recently published a novel on this topic, titled *Dragon's Gate*. Let us briefly compare it with *The Footprints of the Dragon* by Vanya Oakes (1949).

The Chinese workers made tremendous contributions to the construction of the railway by working under trying conditions unthinkable to us. Both books imaginatively represent the trials and tribulations the Chinese experienced and the courage and tenacity they demonstrated in overcoming the obstacles in their way. But there are some major differences between the two books.

In Oakes's book, all the white railroad bosses treat the Chinese workers nicely. The only villains in the book are a Chinese foreman named Lee and his friend Mosquito. Whereas the white bosses are all kindly and benevolent, Lee acts like a slave driver. This is a thorough falsification of history intended to cover up the brutal exploitation of the Chinese. Can you imagine that in that historical period there was no racial discrimination and oppression against the Chinese?

All the Chinese workers, especially the main character, Yip Wo, are presented as workaholic, accepting the inhuman working conditions with very little complaint; on the contrary, they are exhilarated in meeting the challenges of their work, no matter how dangerous they are. For example, when battling against a severe snowstorm, a group of Chinese workers is buried beneath an avalanche. what is the reaction of their fellow workers? They are stunned with horror, but no one complains, and certainly no one protests. Hip Wo rationalizes, "In such a great task as this there are always some who must perish" and urges the others to continue working: "Come, there is work to be done. . . . There is nothing to be done for them" (p. 176). Neither he nor the other Chinese workers say anything about having a decent burial for the dead. The images of Chinese presented here are typical stereotypes.

In striking contrast, Yep's *Dragon's Gate* presents historical facts and realistic portraits of Chinese workers. It shows that the Chinese workers were not only subjected to harsh living conditions and a dangerous working environment, but also victimized by the white bosses. The arch villain in Yep's book is a white foreman, called Kilroy. Another villain, the Chinese interpreter, Shrimp, is only a hatchetman working for Kilroy. The foreman treats the Chinese as subhumans, relentlessly driving them to work under dangerous circumstances. He whips anyone who dares to defy him. He never calls a Chinese person by his name; instead, he addresses every Chinese as John—someone with no identity. He prohibits his son, Sean, from befriending the Chinese boy, Otter, who is the narrator of the story. When he finds Sean having a meal together with Otter, Kilroy yells at Otter: "I said go, you filthy little heathen. You eat with your own kind" (p. 154). In *The Footprints of the Dragon*, you do not even find this kind of racist slur, let alone any mention of racist oppression.

Unlike the submissive and workaholic stereotypes in Oakes's book, the Chinese workers in Yep's book voice their grievances and fight for their rights when they can no longer put up with the inhuman treatment. After the workers are buried by the avalanche, the Chinese workers refuse to go on working and insist that they look for the bodies in the snow. "We not send bodies home, their ghosts not happy" (p. 223) one of them argues. Yep's treatment of this incident is not only realistic but also culturally authentic. The Chinese believe that if the dead are not buried in their hometown, their ghosts will wander the world, howling all the time. In the end of the story, the Chinese workers stage a strike, demanding basic human rights. As Yep points out in the Afterword, the strike is historically real. But it was ignored both by the media during that period of time and later by authors like Oakes, who wrote about the Chinese builders from a white perspective. The author's perspective determines what will be included in the book. As Joel Taxel (1992) points out, "narratives are value-laden selections from a universe of possibilities and that different selections tell different stories" (p. 22). Omission can be a form of distortion, just as fabrication is.

Yep not only selected historical facts that are ignored or covered up by authors who hold an outsider's perspective but also included details that recapture the way the Chinese workers looked at the things and people around them. In the new world, the Chinese workers experienced the novelty of a different culture, or cultural shocks, if you will. They perceived the alien world from a Chinese perspective. Listen to them talk about time: "Westerner will waste most anything—food, money, land—but not time. One T'ang hour makes two of theirs. They sliced up the hours into finer and finer portions . . . into minutes and minutes into seconds" (p. 92). This shows how the Chinese workers try to understand the Western concept of time. Here are two more examples that show how the Chinese see things differently from the Westerners: When Otter first sees Sean eat with a fork, his first reaction is "How do you keep from hurting yourself with that thing?" It looks like a "miniature metal rake" to him (p. 149). When two white men are fighting, Otter and other Chinese workers are puzzled as to why they do not use their feet. "Don't they know they have feet," Otter asks (p. 159). Clearly, the author is able to see through the Chinese workers' eyes and write about them from the inside out. In Oakes's book, there is little description of the Chinese workers' reaction to cultural differences because the author neither inhabits the characters nor cares much about their feelings. As a result, the characters appear to be two-dimensional.

Both Oakes and Yep demonstrate considerable power of imagination to evoke scenes of the past, which neither of them directly experienced. However, Yep's insider's vision, coupled with careful research, led him to include historical facts that undo the stereotypes of Chinese laborers. If, without imagination, authors "would have been manipulating stick figures across a historical landscape" (Aronson, 1993), without basing their work on historical facts, authors create phantoms in a realm of fantasy. The same holds true for multicultural literature.

The comparison between *The Footprints of the Dragon* and *Dragon's Gate* is diachronical as well as synchronical. There is a span of forty-five years between the publication of the two novels. Time has changed people's perspectives. An author of today would view the Chinese experiences during that period from a perspective very different from that commonly held in the past. Now nobody except racists would view Chinese laborers as subhumans or, as one correspondent did in 1867, make fun of their demand for an eight-hour work day (Yep, 1993). Even people from parallel cultures have changed their self-perception, liberating themselves from the influence of the dominant culture that once degraded and demeaned them. As people's perspective changes, their presentation of reality changes, too. This shows that perspective, rather than imagination, is the commanding factor in the creation of historical novels or multicultural literature.

CONCLUDING THOUGHTS

Before authors try to write about another culture, they should ask themselves whether they have acquired the specific perspective of that culture, in other words, whether they have developed a culturally specific sense of its reality. To help their readers cross cultural gaps, authors should cross them first. If an author makes persistent efforts to understand a culture, he or she may finally be able to look at the world from the perspective of that culture and write about it as authentically as insider authors. If the author is able to do so, he or she should be considered an insider.

A good example of an author who makes earnest efforts to get inside a culture is Suzanne F. Staples, the author of *Shabanu* (1989), a powerful book about desert people in Pakistan. She studied their language, did research on their culture, mingled with them as much as she could, and was able to identify with them, "laughing at the same things very spontaneously as they did." She had lived in Asia for about twelve years and was familiar with much of the culture. As she puts it, to write about another culture, a writer should not only be a better observer and listener, but also be more empathetic, with a desire to "be under somebody else's skin" (Staples, quoted in Sawyer and Sawyer, 1993, p. 166). We hope outsiders make similar painstaking efforts to take on another culture's perspective before they write about that culture. If they still believe that they can fly across cultural gags on the wings of imagination, what Silvey (1993) predicts may be inevitable despite the fact that some people do not agree with the prediction: "The great writers and illustrators for children of parallel cultures will, on the whole, come from members of those cultures" (p. 133) in the coming thirty years as they did in the past thirty years.

The goal of the multicultural literature movement is to give voice to those who have been historically silenced, to represent those who have been underrepresented, to give true faces back to those whose images have been distorted. But unfortunately, in the name of multiculturalism, some authors and artists from the mainstream culture are doing disservice to the movement by turning out books that perpetuate stereotypes or present inaccurate cultural information. If authors and artists, along with publishers from mainstream culture, have truly praiseworthy motives to represent parallel cultures, they should closely examine the social effects their books have produced and listen attentively to criticism from the people whom they portray. One cannot help questioning the motives of those who become wrapped up with the power of imagination and ignore the fact they are imposing their perspectives on the experiences of other ethnic groups.

NOTE

An earlier version of this chapter was published in the Winter 1995 issue of *The New Advocate*. Reprinted by permission of *The New Advocate*.

REFERENCES

Aronson, M. (1993). Letter to the editor. *The Horn Book Magazine, 69* (4), 388-389.

Banks, J. (1979). Shaping the future of multicultural education. *Journal of Negro Education. 68*, 237-252.

Barry, E. (1973). *Robert Frost on writing.* New Brunswick, NJ: Rutgers University Press.

Eagleton, T. (1983). *Literary theory: An introduction*. Minneapolis: University of Minnesota Press.

Fang, Z., Fu, D., and Lamme, L. L. (1999). Rethinking the role of multicultural literature in literacy instruction: Problems, paradox, and possibilities. *The New Advocate, 12* (3), 259-276.

Fleishman, A. (1971). *The English historical novel*. Baltimore, MD: John Hopkins University Press.

Gates, H. L., Jr. (1991, November 24). "Authenticity," or the lesson of Little Tree, *New York Times*, pp. 1, 26-30.

Howard, E. F. (1991). Authentic multicultural literature for children: An author's perspective. In M. Lindgren (Ed.), *The multicolored mirror: Cultural substance in literature for children and young adults* (pp. 91–100). Fort Atkinson, WI: Highsmith.

Kearney, R. (1988). *The wake of imagination: Toward a postmodern culture*. Minneapolis: University of Minnesota Press.

Leask, N. (1988). *The politics of imagination in Coleridge's critical thought*. New York: St. Martin's Press.

Meyers, J. (1985). *Hemingway: A biography*. New York: Harper and Row.

Miller-Lachmann, L. (Ed.). (1992). *Our family, our friends, our world*. New Providence, NJ: Bowker.

Murphy, B. (1993). Letter to the editor. *The Horn Book Magazine, 69* (4), 389.

Nodelman, P. (1988). Cultural arrogance and realism in Judy Blume's *Superfudge*. *Children's Literature in Education, 19* (4), 230-241.

Norton, D. E. (1999). *Through the eyes of a child: An introduction to children's literature* (5th ed.). Columbus, OH: Merrill.

Rabinowitz, P.J. (1987). *Before reading: Narrative conventions and the politics of interpretation*. Ithaca, NY: Cornell University Press.

Salisbury, G. (1998). Island blood. In J. E. Brown and E. C. Stephens (Eds.), *Cultural sensitivity: Using multicultural young adult literature in the classroom* (pp. 3-8). Urbana, IL: National Council of Teachers of English.

Sawyer, W. E., and Sawyer, J. C. (1993). A discussion with Suzanne Fisher Staples: The author as writer and cultural observer. *The New Advocate, 6* (3), 159-169.

Silvey, A. (1993). Varied carols. *The Horn Book Magazine, 69* (2), 132-133.

Sims, R. (1984). A question of perspective. *The Advocate, 3*, 145-156.

Sims Bishop, R. (1992). Multicultural literature for children: Making informed choices. In V. J. Harris (Ed.), *Teaching multicultural literature in grades K-8* (pp. 37–54). Norwood, MA: Christopher-Gordon.

Stolz, M. (1993). Letter to the editor. *The Horn Book Magazine, 69*, (5), 516.

Taxel, J. (1986). The black experience in children's fiction: Controversies surrounding award winning books. *Curriculum Inquiry, 16* (3), 245-281.

Taxel, J. (1992). The politics of children's literature: Reflections of multiculturalism, political correctness, and Christopher Columbus. In V. Harris (Ed.), *Teaching multicultural literature in grades K-8* (pp. 1-36). Norwood, MA: Christopher-Gordon.

Vanasse, D. (1998). Cultural sensitivity. In J. E. Brown and E. C. Stephens (Eds.), *Cultural sensitivity: Using multicultural young adult literature in the classroom*. Urbana, IL: National Council of Teachers of English.

Warnock, M. (1976). *Imagination*. Berkeley: University of California Press.

Woodson, J. (1998, Janurary/February). Who can tell my story. *The Horn Book Magazine*, 34-38.

Yep, L. (1987). A Chinese sense of reality. In B. Harrison and G. Maguire (Eds.), *Innocence and experience* (pp. 485-489). New York: Lothrop.

Yokota, J. (1993). Asian and Asian American literature for children: Implications for classroom teachers and librarians. In S. Miller and B. McCaskil (Eds.), *Multicultural literature and literacies: Making space for difference* (pp. 229–246). Albany: State University of New York Press.

Books for Children and Young Adults

Armstrong, W. (1969). *Sounder*. New York: Harper and Row.

Bunting, E. (1982). *The happy funeral*. Ill. by Vo-Dinh Mai. New York: Harper and Row.

Carter, F. (1976). *The education of Little Tree*. New York: Delacorte.

Cole, J. (1982). *Best-loved folktales of the world*. Garden City, NY: Doubleday.

Crew , L. (1989). *Children of the river*. New York: Delacorte.

Friedman, I. R. (1984). *How my parents learned to eat*. Ill. by Allen Say. Boston: Houghton Mifflin.

Hurmence, B. (1982). *A girl called Boy*. New York: Ticknor and Fields.

Isadora, R. (1979). *Ben's Trumpet*. New York: Greenwillow.

Oakes, V. (1949). *The footprints of the dragon*. Philadelphia, PA: John C Winston.

Pattison, D. (1991). *The river dragon*. Ill. by J. Tseng and M. S. Tseng. New York: Lothrop, Lee and Shepard.

Sebestyen, O. (1979). *Words by heart*. New York: Bantam.

Staples, S. F. (1989). *Shabanu: Daughter of the wind*. New York: Knopf.

Tan, A. (1991). *The kitchen god's wife*. New York: G. P. Putnam's Sons.

Wallace, I (1984). *Chin Chiang and the Dragon's Dance*. Atheneum, NY: Margaret K. McElderry.

Woodson, J. (1998). *If you come softly*. New York: Putnam's.

Yep, L. (1975). *Dragonwings*. New York: HarperCollins.

Yep, L. (1993). *Dragon's gate*. New York: HarperCollins.

Zemach, M. (1982). *Jake and Honeybunch go to heaven*. New York: Farrar, Straus & Giroux.

4

Reader Response Theory and the Author's Role in Multicultural Literature

In the discussion of multicultural children's literature, critics and educators often debate whether a work is an authentic reflection or a distortion of ethnic experiences, whether it presents truthful portraits or stereotypes of an ethnic group, and whether it exhibits any racial prejudices. A closely related question is the author's role in creating these textual features. Contrary to belief in the "death of the author," or the banishment of the author from the interpretation of the text, many hold that the author's perspective has tremendous impact on the outcome of the literary creation, and the autho's ethnic identity, in turn, has great bearing on his or her perspective (e.g., Sims, 1982; Sims Bishop, 1992; Harris, 1992; Silvey, 1993; Yokota, 1993). At present, the "battle about books" is still very much a "battle about author . . . as social constituency" (Gullory, cited in Gates, 1991, p. 26).

The focus of the debate over the author's role in multicultural literature is whether the author's or the illustrator's cultural identity and perspective have any significant impact on the outcome of their artistic creation. This debate entails many complicated issues, such as the relationship between imagination and experience, authors' social responsibilities (Noll, 1995), and censorship. In the last chapter, I discussed the relationship between imagination and cultural experiences. In this chapter I attempt to justify the concern with the author's cultural identity and perspective in terms of reader response theory.

The current concern with the author's influence on the text of multicultural literature seems to run counter to the assumptions of reader response theory, which has shifted the focus of literary criticism from the author and the text to the reader. To some critics, emphasis on the author's identity and perspective appears to be outmoded and perhaps is a kind of atavism. In "Authenticity, or the Lesson of Little Tree," the noted African American critic Henry Louis Gates, Jr., argued against a preoccupation with authenticity and the author's identity, lamenting that the "assumptions" that "ethnic or national identity finds unique expression in literary forms . . . hold sway even after we think we have discarded them." He went on to say, "After the much-ballyhooed 'death of the author' pronounced by two decades of literary theory, the author is very much alive" (p. 26).

Is the concern with the author's or illustrator's identity and perspective a legitimate one? Is it "politically correct" but literarily incorrect? Does it violate any principle of the presently prevailing reader response theory? This chapter attempts to justify the concern with the author's identity and perspective in terms of reader response theory. I try to answer these questions by first examining the basic principles of reader response theory regarding the text and author and then, in light of these principles, justifying the concern with the author's cultural identity and background.

THE ROLE OF THE AUTHOR IN READER RESPONSE THEORY

The role of the author in literature is played out through the text that he or she creates. From the reader response perspective, "the communication with the author becomes in fact a relationship through the text" (Rosenblatt, 1978, p. 76). An overview of the position on the status of text taken by various perspectives theorists will shed light on the extent to which they accept the author's role in the process of reading.

It should be noted that reader response criticism "is not a conceptually unified critical position, but a term that has come to be associated with the work of critics who use the words 'reader,' 'reading process,' and 'response' to mark out an area for investigation" (Tompkins, 1980, p. ix). Varied as they are, all branches of reader response theory, however, do share a basic assumption, namely, that reading is an action, an event, or an experience. The text is not a physical object, the container of a message to be extracted like a nut from a shell. Rather, it is an occasion for action on the part of the reader. All brands of reader response theories recognize the reader's contribution to the making of meaning. The controversy centers on the statue of text and the role of its creator—the author—in the meaning-making process. While emphasizing the reader's role, most reader response theories, to varying degrees, also acknowledge the role of the text and author. Their position on the role of the text and author as well as the reader in the process of meaning making distinguishes them from New Criticism, the predecessor of reader response theory, which repudiates the analysis of the author's intention as "intentional fallacy" and the study of the reader's response as "affective fallacy" (Wimsatt and Beardsley, 1958a, 1958b).

Uniaction, Interaction, and Transaction

Positions on the relation between the reader and text, in my view, can be classified into three categories: uniactional, interactional, and transactional. The root *action* in the three terms can be operationally defined as the contribution of the agent (reader or text) to the making of meaning. The extreme uniactional view admits only the action of one of the two coordinates or elements in literature, namely, either the text or the reader alone has a role to play in the making of meaning.

E. D. Hirsch's theory of validity (1967) is a variant of reader response theory in the sense that it accepts the fact of the text's openness, that is, the text can have different significations. Yet his theory is uniactional because it rejects the notion that there can be more than one valid interpretation for a text. For him, the only acceptable meaning of a text is the meaning the author encoded in it. What the individual reader reads into the text is not meaning but "significance." Therefore, a text can have a constant "meaning," as intended by the author, but shifting "significances" (p. 213), as decoded by the reader.

Stanley Fish's theory (1980), which claims that all the meaning is supplied by the reader, is uniactional on the other extreme; it is actually a theory of "reader action" instead of reader response. Fish claims that "the interpreters do not decode poems; they make them" (p. 327). The epistemological assumption beneath this assertion is: "It is not that the presence of poetic qualities compels a certain kind of attention but that the paying of a certain kind of attention results in the emergence of poetic qualities" (1980, p. 326). As the author's text has become a nonentity, literature exists only in the reader, whose interpretive strategies can mold the text like plasticine into any desired shape. From this theoretical perspective, the author is driven totally out of the scene.

David Bleich's "subjective criticism" (1978) is also a uniactional model of reading. He considers the text as a series of symbols, the meaning of which entirely depends upon the reader's mental activity in constructing it. The reader becomes the independent self and the sole agent in the reading process. He rejects the active nature of the text—the guidance and constraints that a text might give to the reader.

Holland's (1968) psychoanalytical approach borders on the uniactional theory. He sees the relationship between reader and text as between the self and the "other." He admits that the text as the "other" exists prior to the reader's experience of it and puts constraints on the reader's interpretation. However, his main concern and interest center on the function of the reader's identity. Holland later defines interpretation as "a function of identity" (1980, p. 123). Reading becomes a process of re-creating the text in terms of the reader's personal identity.

In contrast to the uniactional theories are the interactional and transactional theories, which incorporate both the reader and text as significant contributors to the reading experience but do not assign a central intended meaning to the text as the universal criterion for validity of interpretation. Both interactional and transactional theorists view the reading process as a reciprocal one, rather than a uniactional one in which a passive reader is acted on by the text or a passive text is acted on by the reader. However, the transactional theory (Rosenblatt, 1978, 1995) collapses the traditional subject/object dichotomy. The transaction between the reader and text is not a process of the subject (reader) responding to the stimuli of the object. Rather, it is a "highly complex ongoing process of selection and organization" (1978, p. 49) that results in the evocation of the literary work as distinguished from the text, which is a sequence of verbal symbols. It is important to point out that Rosenblatt does not exalt the reader's creativity as Fish does. As she notes, "the view that the reader in re-creating the work reenacts the author's creative role superficially seems more reasonable" (1978, p. 49). Nor does she deny the text's constraints on the reader's re-creation.

Robert Scholes's (1985) dialectic view of the relation between reader and text is compatible with Rosenblatt's. He believes that the reader is engaged in three kinds of activity: "reading, interpretation, and criticism . . . In reading, we produce text within text; in interpretation we produce text upon text; and in criticizing we produce text against text" (p. 24).

Iser's (1974, 1978) phenomenological theory carries some similar assumptions. Like Rosenblatt, who sees meaning making as experiential, Iser holds that "meaning is no longer an object to be defined, but is an effect to be experienced" by the reader (1978, p. 10). A literary text itself does not formulate the meanings, but "initiates performances of meaning" (p. 27). It is this nature of indeterminacy that brings about the text-reader interaction. While the text contains "gaps" (i.e., what is only implied) that stimulate the reader to "concretize" (p. 21) them with their projections so as to synthesize an aesthetic object, it also provides instructions and conditions for the production of that object.

Jonathan Culler's (1975) structuralist reading theory is primarily concerned with literary conventions, the knowledge of which enables a reader to understand literature. The literary conventions are a system of rules governing the operation of literary discourse, like the grammar of a language. Both author and reader have internalized this "grammar of literature" (p. 114), which makes literature intelligible. Reading, metaphorically, is a rule-governed game played by both the author and reader on the court of the text.

Rosenblatt's transactional theory and the interactional theories of Iser, Scholes, Culler, and others acknowledge the text's constraints on, and guidance of, the reader, albeit from different theoretical perspectives. These theories justify the investigation of the "textual power" (Scholes, 1985) of literature and the role of the author, who infuses the text with that power. Rosenblatt admits the author into the scene of literary experience in this way: "He [the reader] will be conscious always that the words of the author are guiding him; he will have a sense of achieved communication, sometimes, indeed, with the author" (1978, p. 50). In some works, the author intrudes into the text with open comments; in others the author withdraws behind the characters. The author-reader relationship has evolved down through the literary history. Yet, whether in the traditional "closed" texts or more modern "open" texts—in Barthes's terms, "readerly" or "writerly" texts (1970, p. 4)—the author is always there. In children's literature, especially, the author's voice always speaks out loud, conveying attitudes, values, and assumptions that shape the younger reader's mind and heart, even though such literature is no longer as openly didactic as in the past.

Fish and Bleich's uniactional theories and Holland's near-uniactional theory not only put the reader at the center of the stage of literary criticism, but they have also pushed the author and text off the stage. Their theories constitute the most subjectivist trend in the reader response movement. In terms of influence, however, they by no means represent the mainstream of the movement. And the most often quoted critic in the educational research is Rosenblatt, not Fish or Bleich. The widely accepted reader response theories have not declared the death of the author or banished the author from the criticism of literature.

In reading, as Terry Eagleton (1983) suggests, readers do not merely engage textual objects, but involve themselves in "forms of activity inseparable from the wider social relations between writers and readers" (p. 206). Although it is an outdated notion to view the author's intention as the objective of reading, the dynamics of reading certainly lie in the interaction between the author and the reader. This occurs through the latter's reaction to the text, especially when there are discrepancies between the author's and reader's beliefs, assumptions, and values, as frequently happens with multicultural literature. According to one feminist view of reader response (Schweickart, 1986), "literature—the activities of reading and writing—[is] an important arena of political struggle" (p. 39). In the case of a female reader reading a male-authored text, she asserts herself against the control of the text. As Schweickart points out, "the reader taking control of the text is not, as in Iser's model, simply a matter of selecting among the concretizations allowed by the text." It means "reading the text as it was not meant to be read, in fact, reading it against itself" (p. 50). The reader then becomes a "resisting reader" (Fetterley, quoted in Schweickart, 1986, p. 42). If the author were dead and his voice silent, there would be nothing to resist and there would be no literary criticism.

Just as female readers resist male-chauvinistic texts, readers from nonmainstream culture resist literature showing racial bias and prejudice. The well-known author Milton Meltzer's (1987) response to the stereotyping of Jews in many literary masterpieces by major writers in history, such as Sir Walter Scott in *Ivanhoe*, Charles Dickens in *Oliver Twist*, and William Shakespeare in *The Merchant of Venice*, offers a typical example of reader resistance to authorial sensibilities. Although he liked these works in his early years, he tried to ignore anti-Semitism "references to Jews as usurers, liars, hypocrites, as covetous, contemptible, inhuman" (p. 493), and was "anxious to get on to passages less painful to me as a Jewish child" (p. 494). Meltzer speaks for all those who feel strongly about racial bias and prejudice encountered in literature.

These authors of classic literature—many of them were great humanitarians— may not have been aware of the anti-Semitism in their works. As their perspectives were shaped and conditioned by their times, they may have unconsciously reflected in their works the prevalent prejudices of their times. The prejudices may have been implied rather than intended. This is also the case with some authors of multicultural literature of our times. In whatever age, authors do not live in a social vacuum; their consciousness is determined by their social existence. In short, authors are social beings. If we were to accept the notion that "the author is dead," we would do nothing less than excuse authors from their social and ethical responsibilities. A more realistic view is that authors no longer wholly determine the meaning of their texts. We cannot deny the social nature of writing and reading; fiction and other forms of literature are "a contract designed by an intending author who invites his or her audience to adopt certain paradigms for understanding reality" (Foley, 1986, p. 43). It is up to the reader to decide whether they will accept the author's contact. Meltzer found the invitation to view Jews disparagingly presented by the authors of the classics to be unacceptable and therefore rejected the contract.

THE REAL AUTHOR AND THE IMPLIED AUTHOR

Some reader response theories have not only acknowledged the author's role in the reading process but also developed a new perspective with which to look into the author's presence in the literary work. Iser (1974), for example, maintains that every literary work has two poles: the artistic creation (the text) by the author and the aesthetic realization (the reading) by the reader. The literary work lies halfway between the two poles. The author's presence is only implied in the artistic creation. These theorists also provide new terms to deal with the concept of the author's role, such as "implied reader" (Iser, 1974), "authorial audience" (Rabinowitz, 1987), and "implied author" (Booth, 1961). All these terms point to the author's presence in the text and acknowledge his or her role in the event of reading.

While reader response theories reject the author's intended meaning as the objective of interpretation, reading the author's intended meaning, or "authorial reading," provides a basis for critical reading from "some perspective other than the one called for by the author" (Rabinowitz, 1987, p. 32). Rabinowitz's theory dovetails with Scholes's theory of "producing text against text."

The author's intention may not be realized by the text that he or she created. There may exit a discrepancy between the actual author and his or her implied image in the text. Booth's (1961) concept of implied author addresses this discrepancy. It refers to the implied presence or version of the author as the "implied author," as distinguished from the real author who wrote the book. Booth is not generally regarded as a representative reader response theorist, but his concept of implied author wa endorsed by Wofgang Iser, one of the leading reader response theorists. Iser (1974) stated that "we should distinguish, as Wayne Booth (1961) does in his *Rhetoric of Fiction,* between the man who writes the book (author) and the man whose attitudes shape the book (implied author)" (p. 103).

According to Wayne Booth (1961), the author's presence is implied in his or her artistic creation. Different from the real author who writes the book, the implied author is the real author's "second self." A real author has "various official versions of himself" in different works that he or she creates:

Just as one's personal letters imply different versions of oneself, depending on the differing relationships with each correspondent and the purpose of each letter, so the writer sets himself out with different air depending on the needs of particular works. (Booth, 1961, p. 71)

The implied author is not to be identified with the speaker in the work, often referred to as "persona," "mask," or "narrator," who is only one of the elements created by the implied author. The narrator could be a dramatized character in the work, but the implied author cannot. "The 'implied author' chooses, consciously or unconsciously, what we read. . . . [He] is the sum of his own choices" (pp. 74-75). The reader can always get a clear picture of the implied author, no matter how impersonal the real author tries to be when writing the work. In fiction, some aspects of the implied author may be inferred from the style and tone of the work, "but his major qualities will depend also on the hard facts of action and character in the tale that is told" (p. 74).

In an article on cultural politics, the renowned children's author Katherine Paterson (1994) talks about how her presence is always in the text that she creates, no matter how hard she tries to erase it. The reader can sense her presence from the choices she makes:

As carefully as I research, as sensitively as I try to write, as hard as I try not to impose my own beliefs on the story, there is no way I can eliminate myself entirely—the over middle-aged, middle-class, somewhat liberal, white, American, Presbyterian female who has lived in China, Japan, Virginia, West Virginia, North Carolina, Tennessee, New York, New Jersey, Maryland and now lives in Vermont. I will be present not only in the original choice of subject but in all the choices which flow from it. That can't be helped. I am the author. The reader is warned. My name and bio are on the book. (p. 89)

Paterson's remarks corroborate Booth's theory of implied author from an author's perspective.

Booth's concept of implied author is endorsed by Iser, who paraphrases the term in simple words: "the man [sic] whose attitudes shape the book" (1978, p. 103). But Iser is more concerned with the process of reading than the ethics of literature. His phenomenological explication of the reading process centers on how the implied author exerts control or provides guidance for the reader's act of reading. The implied author's attitudes that shape the book are equivalent to what he termed "schematized views," a concept Iser borrowed from Roman Ingarden. The "schematized views" are not plainly stated, but hinted at by various perspectives offered by the text. In the novel, for example, "there are four main perspectives: those of the narrator, the characters, the plot, and the fictitious reader [the intended reader]" (1978, p. 35). As the reader tries to use these perspectives to relate the "schematized views" to one another, he or she brings the text to life; their meeting place, which the reader finds at the end, is his or her experienced meaning of the text. Different readers may find different meeting places. However, the network of perspectives predisposes the reader to read in certain ways.

Iser's term for the series of perspectives, the "network of response-inviting structures," is "implied reader" (p. 34). The term seems to be opposite to Booth's implied author, but in fact they refer to essentially the same thing, although from different perspectives. Both are theoretical constructs formulated to designate the conditioning force that the real author builds into the text when creating the literary work. Both denote the "perspective view of the world put together by (though not necessarily typical of) the author" (Iser, 1978, p. 35). The similarity of the two concepts is footnoted by these remarks of Booth's: "The author creates, in short, an image of himself and another image of his reader; he makes his reader, as he makes his second self" (1961, p. 138). An example may help to make these terms less abstract. In 1984, there was a debate between Sims (1984) and Belinda Hurmence (1982), author of *A Girl Called Boy,* in the *Advocate.* According to Sims, Hurmence's book presents a white perspective that perpetuates stereotype of African Americans, even though it is a well-intended attempt to depict their experiences. She bases her argument on the sum of choices the author made, consciously or unconsciously, choices of details to include, of words in the descriptions of things and people, of what to emphasize or deemphasize. For example, while mentioning the cruelties of the slave system throughout the book, according to Sims, the author also emphasizes the benevolence of some slave owners and the slaves' ambivalent attitude toward them. Implied in her literary choices is the author's perspective, or, in Iser's terms, "schematized views" on the reality presented in the book. The reader, such as Sims, would create from the author's choices the implied author— the image the real author created of herself when she created the book. According to Sims's reading, the implied author is a person who is sympathetic to black Americans but is not yet able to look at the world through their perspective. One may argue that Sims's inference about the implied author in the text is inaccurate and that one may then create from the text another, very different implied, author. Different inferences of the implied author are possible and natural, which explains why there is controversy over a multicultural literary work. Sometimes it is possible to get opposite readings of the same book. It may be criticized by one reader as racist while praised by another as an excellent example of multicultural literature. In a sense, the implied author may also be termed the *inferred author.* The implied author, as the name indicates, is not portrayed by the author in definite terms; it has to be inferred by the reader from the literary choices the author made. The reader's inference, however, is a "structured act" (Iser, 1978, p. 35), not a random guess. The literary choices that the author made sketch a contour of his or her image in the text. The reader then fills in the blanks with shade and color to form a clear picture of the implied author. Figure 4.1 illustrates the relationship among the actual author, the implied author, and the reader.

Despite her laudable intention to contribute to the representation of black experience in children's literature, the author of *A Girl Called Boy* implies in her choices an author whose perspective is not acceptable to some black readers. Here a tension arises between the actual reader's and implied author's attitudes. Translated into Iser's (1978) terms, the tension is between the "role offered by the text and the real reader's own disposition." This tension is ever-present in any process of reading, because it is "a precondition for the processing and for the comprehension that follows it" (p. 37). This tension is particularly conspicuous in reader response to multicultural literature because, being conditioned by cultural differences, the gap between the actual reader's and the implied author's perspectives is often very wide. When the implied author and the real author are different, the perspective of the world represented in the text, as Iser (1978) notes, is not necessarily typical of the real author. An author who writes about a culture other than his or her own may take on the alien beliefs and values of that culture. In some cases, he or she may give an authentic presentation of the alien culture in his or her works. The implied author, or the second self that the real author creates, may be accepted by readers from that culture. *The Education of Little Tree* (Carter, 1976) is a typical example of the gap between real author and implied author. If a racist like Carter can write an authentic book about a minority group, one may ask, why do we need to concern ourselves with the real author's perspectives and ethnic identity?

Figure 4.1
The Real Author, the Implied Author, and the Reader

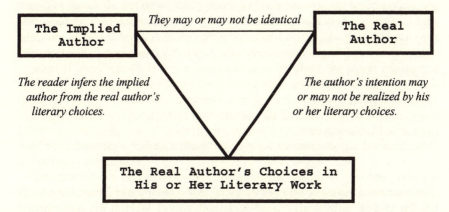

We may counter that question with another question: how many racists have written books like *The Education of Little Tree*? It is only rarely that a racist is willing and able to write an authentic book about the experiences of an ethnic group. Although some authors may be able to create an implied author that is completely different from them, others may not. This is especially true in multicultural literature. In many cases, the implied author and the real author are not two utterly different persons. In creating a literary world, the real author cannot put a complete view of reality into it, and instead has to choose what to include. The choices the author makes often consciously or unconsciously reflect his or her experiences and perspectives of the real world. It is not easy, as Staples put it, "to be under somebody else's skin" (Sawyer and Sawyer, 1993, p. 166), or as Yep (1987) states, to become an "invisible man," erasing all the features on your own face, so that it becomes "a blank mirror reflecting other people's hopes and fears" (p. 485).

The distinction between the real author and the implied author makes it possible to explain the existence of such books as *The Education of Little Tree*. The relation between the real author's identity and his or her literary creation is not one of determinism (Gates, 1991). It is possible for authors of the mainstream culture to write authentic books about minority experiences. Among the numerous works of cross-cultural literature, there are well written ones. Outsiders are not doomed to failure when they write about cultures other than their own. The lesson—if there is one—that we may draw from *The Education of Little Tree* is not that the standard of cultural authenticity should be discarded or that the author's ethnic identity is no longer significant, but rather that, while emphasizing the influence of an author's cultural background on his or her works about another culture, we should not claim an absolute causal relationship between the two. How can we do so if Forrest Carter, "a Ku Klux Klan terrorist," succeeds in creating a second self "who captures the unique vision of Native American cultures" (Gates, 1991, p. 26)?

Authors' experiences (direct and indirect) and imagination may help them surmount cultural barriers and create an implied author acceptable to the reader from a specific culture, but the gaps are not as easy to cross as one might imagine. Relying on imagination alone may end up in making a laughing stock rather than a respectable self-image of the author. One example is the implied author in *Knots on the Counting Rope* (Martin and Archambault, 1987), which contains so many cultural inaccuracies. This is how the critics might infer ignorant, irresponsible implied authors from the text:

"I know! I know! He's an Indian! A *blind* Indian!"

"Oh, wow, perfect!. . . but wont' we hafta do a lot of research? I mean, I don't know very much about Indians, do you?"

"Oh, sure, I've got all these rugs my old man bought from the Navajos back in the 'forties—said he got 'em for a song." (Seale, 1998, p. 134)

This scenario probably has not happened and the authors may be well-intentioned, but the results of their literary creation implies they have little knowledge of American Indian culture and merely jumped on the bandwagon of creating multicultural literature.

From the standpoint of ethical criticism, Booth (1961) holds that the actual writer should create for his or her work an implied author that represents a wise ethos. This often means "giving up a beloved fault or taking on an alien virtue" (p. 128). We can apply Booth's notion of an implied author representing a wise ethos to multicultural literature. In doing so, I suggest that the actual writer should create in his or her work an implied author that represents the attitudes, beliefs, and values—in short, the perspective—of the culture he or she tries to portray and is thus identified with the reader from that culture. An outstanding example of such an author is Paul Goble, a non-American Indian who has created many picture books that, in striking contrast with *Knots on the Counting Rope*, authentically reflect American Indian culture. His works are highly acclaimed for their authenticity and distinct artistic style. His success has been attributed to his long-term relationship with American Indian culture (Noll, 1995).

THE AUTHOR'S CULTURAL IDENTITY IN MULTICULTURAL LITERATURE

Reader response theory shifts the focus of critical attention from the text as the sole locus of meaning to the reader as an important constituent of meaning. This shift does not entail the death of the author. Although uniactional theories deny the role of the text in literary interpretation, interactional and transactional theories recognize the text as a constraining and guiding force and also recognize the author's participation in the reading event. These theories justify the concern with the author's cultural identity and perspective, as reflected in the text of multicultural literature.

The concept of implied author in particular defines the author's presence in the text: the literary choices the actual author makes combine to form an image of the author or a second self. This concept also explains possible discrepancies between the real author and the implied author—between the author's intention and the actual effects of his or her literary creation. This has two significant implications, among others, the creation of multicultural literature.

First, an author can write about a different culture and create a "second self" that shares the perspective of the people from that culture, even if he or she has not become one of its members. While we emphasize the influence of an author's cultural background on his or her works about another culture, we should not hold a deterministic view that claims an absolute causal relationship between the two.

Second, a well-intentioned author may create a literary work about an ethnic culture that proves unacceptable to its people. The author's cultural identity and background may adversely influence his or her literary choices without the author knowing it. From the perspective of social progress, multicultural literature is intended to inform people about other cultures, to liberate them from the bondage of stereotypes, to foster respect for one's own cultural heritage as well as that of others, and to promote cross-cultural understanding. Many authors who write multicultural literature for children may be motivated by these lofty purposes, but good intentions do not guarantee that the implied author in their books will achieve the desired effects. Instead of insisting on good intentions, authors would be better off turning an eager ear to readers' responses to their work and taking responsibilities for the social effects their works may have produced. As promoters and gatekeepers, publishers share some of this responsibility with authors.

The battle over the role of the author will continue in the political arena of multicultural literature. The mainstream reader response theories are on the side of those who uphold the relevance of the author's cultural identity and perspective regarding the creation of multicultural literature.

NOTE

An earlier version of this chapter was published in Theresa Rogers & Anna O. Soter. (Ed.). (1997). *Reading across Cultures: Teaching Literature in a Diverse Society*. New York: Teachers College Press. Reprinted by permission of Teachers College Press.

REFERENCES

Bleich, D. (1978). *Subjective criticism*. Baltimore, MD: Johns Hopkins University Press.
Booth, W. (1961). *The rhetoric of fiction*. Chicago: University of Chicago Press.

Booth, W. C. (1988). *The company we keep; An ethics of fiction*. Berkeley: University of California Press.

Culler, J. (1975). *Structuralist poetics: Structuralism, linguistics and the study of literature*. Ithaca, NY: Cornell University Press.

Eagleton, T. (1983). *Literary theory: An introduction*. Minneapolis: University of Minnesota Press.

Fish, S. (1980). *Is there a text in this class?* Cambridge, MA: Harvard University Press.

Foley, B. (1986). *Telling the truth: The theory and practice of documentary fiction*. Ithaca, NY: Cornell University Press.

Gates, H. L., Jr. (1991, November 24). "Authenticity," or the lesson of Little Tree. *York Times Book Review*, pp. 1, 26-30.

Harris, V. J. (Ed.). (1992). *Teaching multicultural literature in grades K–8*. Norwood, MA: Christopher-Gordon.

Hirsch, E. D., Jr. (1967). *Validity in interpretation*. New Haven, CT: Yale University Press.

Holland, N. (1968). *The dynamics of literary response*. New York: Oxford University Press.

Holland, N. (1980). Unity identity text self. In J. Tompkins (Ed.), *Reader response criticism: From formalism to post-structuralism* (pp. 118–134). Baltimore, MD: Johns Hopkins University Press.

Iser, W. (1974). *The implied reader: Patterns in communication in prose fiction from Bunyan to Beckett*. Baltimore, MD: John Hopkins University Press.

Iser, W. (1978). *The act of reading: A theory of aesthetic response*. Baltimore, MD: Johns Hopkins University Press.

Meltzer, M. (1987). A common humanity. In B. Harrison and G Maguire (Eds.), *Innocence and experience* (pp. 490–497). New York: Lothrop.

Noll, E. (1995). Accuracy and authenticity in American children's literature: The social responsibility of authors and illustrators. *The New Advocate, 8* (1), 29-43.

Paterson, K. (1994). Cultural politics from a writer's point of view. *The New Advocate, 7* (2), 85-91.

Rabinowitz, P. J. (1987). *Before reading: Narrative convention and the politics of interpretation*. Ithaca, NY: Cornell University Press.

Rosenblatt, L. M. (1978). *The reader, the text, the poem: Transactional theory of the literary work*. Carbondale: Southern Illinois University Press.

Rosenblatt, L. M. (1995). *Literature as exploration* (5th ed.) New York: The Modern Language Association.

Sawyer, W. E., and Sawyer, J. C. (1993). A discussion with Suzanne Fisher Staples: The author as writer and cultural observer. *The New Advocate, 6* (3), 159-169.

Scholes, R. (1985) *Textual power: Literary theory and the teaching of English*. New Haven, CT: Yale University Press.

Schweickart, P. P. (1986). Reading ourselves: Toward a feminist theory of reading. In E. B. Flynn and P. P. Schweickart (Eds.), *Gender and reading* (pp. 31–62). Baltimore, MD: John Hopkins University Press.

Seale, D. (1998). Book reviews. In B. Slapin and D. Seale (Eds.), *Through the Indian eyes: The native experience in books for children*. Los Angeles: American Indian Studies Center, University of California.

Silvey, A. (1993). Varied carols. *The Horn Book Magazine, 69* (2), 132-133.

Sims R. (1982). *Shadow and substance*. Urbana, IL: National Council of Teachers of English.

Sims R. (1984). A question of perspective. *The Advocate, 3*, 145-156.

Sims Bishop, R. (1992). Multicultural literature for children: Making informed choice. In V. J. Harris (Ed.). *Teaching multicultural literature in grades K-8*, pp. 37-54.

Tompkins, J. (Ed.) (1980). *Reader-response criticism: From formalism to post-structuralism*. Baltimore, MD: The Johns Hopkins University Press.

Wimsatt, W. K. & Beardsley, M. (1958a). Intentional fallacy. In W. K. Wimsatt (Ed.), *Verbal icon* (pp. 5-18). New York: Noonday Press.

Wimsatt, W. K. & Beardsley, M. (1958b). Affective fallacy. In W. K. Wimsatt (Ed.), *Verbal icon* (pp. 21-38). New York: Noonday.

Yep, L. (1987). A Chinese sense of reality. In B. Harrison and G Maguire (Eds.), *Innocence and experience* (pp. 485-489). New York: Lothrop.

Yokota, J. (1993). Issues in selecting multicultural literature. *Language Arts, 70* (3), 156-167.

Books for Children and Young Adults

Carter, F. (1976). *The education of Little Tree*. New York: Delacorte.

Hurmence, B. (1982). *A girl called Boy*. New York: Clarion.

Martin, B., and Archambault, J. (1987). *Knots on the counting rope*. New York: Holt.

5

Stereotyping and the Politics of Representation

Of all the controversial issues relating to multicultural literature, stereotyping is probably the most sensitive. None other than stereotyping sparks off anger, indignation, and frustration in the oppressed cultural groups that are misrepresented in literature. And more than anything else, it also touches off vehement debates. Heated exchanges have been raging for a long time with regard to stereotypes in books for children and young adults published in the past, such as *The Story of Little Black Sambo* (Bannerman, 1899, 1923), *The Five Chinese Brothers* (Bishop, 1938), and *The Indian in the Cupboard* (Banks, 1980). The re-appearance of an old stereotype in a new book can add fuel to the fire. It sometimes incurs a barrage of strong protests from the cultural group that is stereotyped, just as a person would cry out if a new injury reopened an unhealed wound.

A recent example is the picture book *Nappy Hair* (Herron, 1997), which portrays a black girl named Brenda, who has "the kinkiest, the nappiest, the fuzziest" hair. She and her family take pride in her hair, sporting it as an object of beauty created by God. A white teacher in Brooklyn read this story to her third-grade class and suddenly found herself caught in the cross-fire of a racial battle. Lynette Clemetson reported in the December 14, 1998 issue of *Newsweek*: "Some parents thought a white teacher had no business raising such a culturally sensitive subject. . . . Others say they would have objected to any teachers—white or black—talking to children about the topic, which they consider offensive" (p. 38). A protest was staged in the neighborhood and the teacher ended up leaving the school. Clemetson noted that, "ironically," only one of the people who protested had a child in the class, and most of them had not read the book. She went on to say that "all sides are trying to figure out how a book about hair could tear a school apart" (pp. 38-39).

There is no easy answer to the question, but one thing is clear: the representation of racial and ethnic minorities is not simply a literary issue, but a serious social-political issue. Nappy hair is historically part of the stereotypical description of African Americans' physical appearance and a symbol of discrimination and humiliation for years. Details of nappy hair as an object of ridicule frequently occurred in nineteenth- and early twentieth-century musical minstrel shows and plantation songs authored and performed by whites (Lester, 1999). The renowned African American Poet Maya Angelou offered historical evidence of racial discrimination relating to nappy hair:

A hundred years ago . . . there were churches in Philadelphia, in Virginia and in New Orleans which had a pine slab on the outside door of the church and a fine-tooth comb hanging on a string. And when you tried to go into the church you had to be able to stand beside that pinewood and be no darker than that, and take that fine-tooth comb and run it through your hair without snagging. That's how you get into the church. (quoted in Lester, 1999, pp. 171-172)

This demeaning and dehumanizing negative image has hurt African Americans so deeply that its reappearance naturally infuriated them. The African American parents' emotional explosion over the book *Nappy Hair* is understandable if it is viewed in the historical context of the battle over representation in literature. Whether the book stereotypes African Americans is open to discussion (I will come back to it shortly), but the incident of boycotting *Nappy Hair* indicates that we should be more sensitive to the delicate issue of stereotyping. Innocent people with good intentions but lacking the necessary knowledge and strategies may tread a political minefield. As the African American commentator Leonard Pitts, Jr. (1998), points out, the teacher "wasn't wrong in thinking this is a good book to share with children. Her only error, if you want to call it that, was in her naiveté, her evident unfamiliarity with the politics of black hair" (pp. 1g-2g).

Stereotyping in multicultural literature is not only a sensitive, but also a complicated, issue, which deserves close scrutiny. This chapter is an attempt to look into various aspects of stereotyping in order to shed some light on its nature and ramifications, with the hope that the controversy may be clarified, if not resolved.

DEFINITION OF STEREOTYPE

The word "stereotype" was coined in 1798 to describe the use of fixed casts of type in the printing process (Ashmore and Del Boca, quoted in Stroebe and Insko, 1989, p. 4). By using the stereotype, the typesetter could avoid recasting type. The term was introduced into the context of social and political ideas by American journalist Walter Lippman in 1922, as a metaphor for the pictures in our heads of various social groups. From the beginning, the term has had derogatory connotations. Generally speaking, it "imposes a rigid mold on the subject and encourages repeated mechanical usage" (Enterman, 1996, p. 9). In the representation of social groups, "it implies undesirable rigidity, permanence, and lack of variability from application to application" (Stroebe and Insko, 1989, p. 4).

In terms of literary creation, Miller-Lachmann (1992) defines stereotyping as follows: "[W]hen an author assigns general characteristics to a group particularly if those characteristics have long been attributed to the group rather than exploring its members' diversity and individuality, it can be said that the author has engaged in stereotyping" (p. 16). Whether used in literary criticism or in sociological studies, *stereotype* is a pejorative term that denotes an oversimplified generalization that trivializes individual differences and complexities. "Stereotypes are like masks put on individuals. Masks cover up individual characteristics and make the people wearing them look alike" (Cai, 1992a, p. 108). Stereotyping also converts real persons into constructed, artificial people (Enterman, 1996, p. 10).

Because of the economy of effots, however, authors often use stereotypes as a sort of artistic shorthand (Goebel, 1995). When viewed as a literary technique of representation, stereotypes seem to be as ideologically neutral as other literary devices of characterization, such as *type*, *archetype*, and *prototype*. For example, in folktales there are the stereotypes of the big, bad wolf, and the wicked stepmother; in contemporary realistic fiction for young adults, there are the stereotypes of the manipulative mother, the perfect sister, the self-conscious teen in love, and so on. (Coyle, 1991). When examined in a social-historical context of representation, however, many stereotypes immediately take on ideological and social implications. From a feminist perspective, the traditional stereotype of the beautiful, virtuous princess, who often has to be rescued by the handsome, valiant prince is a symbol of prejudice against women. From the perspective of critical multiculturalism, the stereotype of the "inscrutable" Oriental makes a political statement that labels Asian Americans as mysterious, dangerous aliens. In cultural criticism, stereotypes are defined more by their social-political function than by their aesthetic function.

THE SOCIAL-POLITICAL NATURE OF STEREOTYPE

Representation in literature is never a purely literary issue, for literary works are both aesthetic and social constructs. Such representation reflects the values, beliefs, and attitudes of those who produce the literature (Eagleton, 1983; Taxel, 1992). The politics of representation has been playing out for decades in the imaging of oppressed groups. The dominant culture has constructed a version of the subjugated groups that is designed to meet its own ideological needs (Said, 1978). Notorious stereotypes have been created to influence the popular consciousness and thus serve the agenda of the dominant culture.

Historically, the stereotypes of American Indians, either as "noble savage" or as "ignoble savage," were created to justify the displacement of the Native inhabitants. This stereotype reflects the white perception of American Indians, that, "akin to primitive children in a rude state of nature they are nobly innocent, but when crossed they will turn wild and uncontrollable" (Bird, 1996, p. 3). The Sambo stereotype of the African American as happy, docile, and imbecile was created to justify the slavery of African Americans. It is derived from the racist notion of black inferiority. Blacks are seen by white supremacists as "biologically less than a person, occupying a lower position on the chain of being than whites. . . . [As] culturally stunted in heathen Africa, the race needed to be cared for by white Christian masters" (Cassuto, 1997, pp. 134-135). On the other hand, African Americans were also stereotyped as dangerous and violent pagans who would benefit from the civilizing influence of Christian slaveholders. The purpose for this kind of representation is the same as for the Sambo stereotype, to provide an excuse for Anglo enslavement of African Americans (Martindale, 1996).

The politics of image making is not only reflected in the dominant culture's stereotyping of oppressed groups in the United States but also in its stereotypical representation of people in other countries. For example, Arabs have long been the object of stereotyping in this country. They are often portrayed as "Moslem fanatics" who are "diabolically clever," hostile, and violent, or as "terrorists" who scheme to infiltrate into the United States (Frankel, 1996). When the federal building in Oklahoma City was bombed On April 19, 1995, the media initially reported that three suspects driving a pickup truck were spotted in the scene, two of them said to be Middle Eastern men with black hair and beards. In the end, however, two European Americans were arrested for the crime (Jackson, 1996). After the September 11, 2001 terrorist attack on the United States, it is even more critical to avoid the stereotype. To label all Moslems as fanatics or terrorists will undermine the campaign against terrorism because it confuses friends and foes. Another example is the representation of Asian women by the movie industry in accordance with the United States' foreign policy towards Asian countries. In Hollywood movies set in during World War II, when China was an ally of the United States, Chinese women, including peasant women, were portrayed positively as independent, socially progressive, and politically conscious. But during the Cold War, when China was an ally of the Soviet Union, the image of Chinese women became conservative and vicious. However, Japanese women were portrayed favorably—their images were very different from those represented during World War II—because Japan had become an ally with the United States (Wang, 1997).

There are numerous stereotypes of the oppressed groups in the United States and of people in the Third World countries. There is no need to list them all to illustrate the social-political nature of stereotypes. Unless one is prejudiced against the oppressed groups and nations, it is impossible to miss the politics of image making.

THE DETRIMENTAL EFFECTS OF STEREOTYPES

From their experience of being victimized culturally and politically, members of the oppressed groups are acutely aware of what the stereotypical representation of them in literature and art can inflict upon their lives. As Dyer (1993) remarks, "how we are seen determines in part how we are treated. . . . [S]uch seeing comes from representation" (p. 1). Stereotyping leads to political discrimination and persecution against the oppressed groups. For example, the stereotyping of Asian Americans as "foreigners" has resulted in the deprivation of their civil rights and even in murder. Historically, the internment of thousands of Japanese Americans during World War II was in part due to the "foreigner" stereotype. If the stereotype, deep seated in the collective psyche of the nation, had not played a role, the Government would also have put Americans of German or Italian ancestry in interment camps. More recently, in 1980, Chinese American Vicent Chin, mistaken for a Japanese American, was beat to death by two unemployed men in Detroit, who believed Japanese economic success had caused them to lose their jobs (Yamate, 1997).

Stereotypes not only impact how stereotyped groups are treated but also how they see themselves. When commenting on the detrimental effects of negative images of Latinos, author and poet Pat Mora (1998) writes:

Certainly Latinos are keenly aware of that myth when we reflect on what is reported in the media about us. Now we are often the stars of bad news about drugs, dropouts, and delinquents; while in images of the Old West, we are poor, sleepy, and thieving. Only one to two percent of media images are about us, and most of those are negative, villainized, and romanticized: the hot senorita, the childish, happy servant. How a media depicts a group affects how a group sees itself, such is the power of images, the power of words. (p. 281)

Stereotypes not only injure dominated cultural groups mentally, but also breed ignorance and prejudice in children of the mainstream culture. The stereotypical image of American Indians, for example, has been a steady diet dished out to non-Indian children through children's books, television, movies, comics, advertisements, games, toys, cards, clothing, food packages, and so on. It permeates their consciousness and spawns skewed perception of American Indians. A survey of 238 kindergarten and 239 fifth grade children conducted by the League of Women Voters in 1975 found that the majority of the children had misperceptions about American Indians. A full "76 % of the kindergarten students had an image of American Indians dressed in feathers; and 43 of them thought an Indian was a hostile enemy with which to contend" (League of Women voters, quoted in Hirschfelder, Molin, and Wakim, 1999, p. 12). A majority of the fifth graders responded to some of the survey questions with information about Indians of the past, even though the questions were phrased in the present tense. While they provide more information about contemporary American Indians in the interviews than the kindergarten students, many fifth grade students held the negative image of American Indians as people who get stuck in the past, living by hunting and dwelling in tepees. A more recent study, by McElmeel (1993), also showed how pervasive the distorted image of American Indians among non-Indian school children. In the study, 250 elementary school children were asked how they would know if an Indian walked into the room. The most common responses were "They'd be wearing feathers," "They'd have war paint on," and "They'd be carrying a tomahawk" (p. 39). Rejection by society is often followed by self-rejection by American Indian children. American Indian parents and communities find it difficult to raise their children with positive information about their cultural heritage (Hirschfelder and Singer, 1992).

Not only negative stereotypes injure people who are stereotyped, so-called positive stereotypes can also have a detrimental impact. For example, Asian Americans are labeled as "model minority." This stereotype appears to be positive and complimentary, but in essence it is pernicious and dangerous. As E. San Juan, Jr., (1992) observes: The positive minority myth privileges "only a few successful individuals but ignores the large number of disadvantaged underclass . . . and thus legitimizes the prevailing system of racially based economic inequality underpinning the powerlessness of people of color" (p. 135). Stacy Lee's (1996) ethnographic study at a high school on the East Coast, *Unraveling the "Model Minority" Stereotype*, reveals the harmful influence of the positive stereotype on Asian American students. It causes identity crises, silences their voices, and sets them against other minority groups.

Debates over representation in multicultural literature have been part of cultural wars that are concerned not only with literary criticism of presentation but also with the control over the right to represent reality in a stratified society. The phrase "cultural wars" refers to ideological battles between different social and ethnic groups, especially between the dominant and the dominated. In the arena of literature, according to Eagleton (2000), it "suggests pitched battles between populists and elitists, custodians of the canon and devotees of *difference*, dead white males and the unjustly marginalized." Eagleton goes on to say that the clash, however, "is a matter of actual politics, not just academic ones" (p. 51). In essence cultural wars are political battles over equal rights between the political conservatives and advocates of multiculturalism in literature, education, and other areas.

THE CULTURAL WAR OVER IMAGE MAKING

The cultural war over the representation of minority groups has been fought for decades and is still going on. One of the earliest battles was waged in the mid nineteenth century between the southern proslavery writers, on the one hand, and the abolitionist writer Harriet Beacher Stowe and the first African American novelist William Wells Brown, on the other. The literary depiction of slavery had long been controlled by apologists for slavery and therefore permeated with racist Sambo stereotypes. Stowe's *Uncle Tom's Cabin* and Brown's *Clotel* entered the battlefield to rebut the stereotypical representation of slaves. Their challenge to the dominant culture immediately met with counterattack from the proslavery writers, who churned out more proslavery novels (Cassuto, 1997).

The Story of Little Black Sambo replicates the Sambo stereotype in children's literature. Although African Americans have voiced strong resentment about the book, it continues to be published long after slavery was abolished. Today it is not only in print but also sells very well. In addition, the Sambo image is exported to other countries in the world (Harris, 1995). Recently, African American author Julius Lester and illustrator Jerry Pinkney (1996), created *Sam and the Tigers,* which eliminates the Sambo stereotype in the text and illustration of the original picture book. It represents an effort to directly counteract the age-old Sambo stereotype.

Historical stereotypes of other cultural groups have also persisted to the present time. The derogatory image of the American Indian as a plaything, for example, is a demeaning and dehumanizing stereotype that denies the dignity of American Indians. As the well-known American Indian writer Michael Dorris points out, it relegates them to the "special property of children." It is "the worst of all" stereotypes of American Indians (Dorris, 1994, p. 120). Nevertheless, this obnoxious stereotype is accepted and abetted by the dominant cultural industry. Many children's books containing this stereotype have been published, such as *Ten Little Rabbits* (Grossman, 1998), which has cute little rabbits dressed up like Indians for children to count, and *The Indian in the Cupboard* (Banks, 1980), which features a plastic Indian figurine for a white boy to toy with in his fantasy world. In addition to books, this stereotype appears in various kinds of cultural artifacts, from toys to postcards to TV commercials. It has also become an artistic shorthand that many artists, use consciously or unconsciously. Books like Iona Opie and Rosemary Well's highly acclaimed *My Very First Mother Goose* (1996) and Mary Hoffman and Caroline Binch's *Amazing Grace* (1991) are flawed by this stereotype. In the former, the illustration for the rhyme "Up the Wooden Hill" shows bunnies wearing feathers and headbands selling blankets outside a teepee. In the latter, the main character, Grace, is role-playing Hiawatha, who is portrayed as wearing face paint and a headband with feathers, a time-worn stereotypic image of the American Indian.

The continued publication and popularity of books stereotyping oppressed groups carry the unmistakable message that the tradition of prejudice and racism is deep-rooted in the collective conscious of the dominant culture and entrenched in the cultural industry of children's literature. For the oppressed groups, stereotypes are symbols of age-long cultural oppression. Their strong reactions to stereotypes, however, are not yet heeded by many people of the dominant culture. The cultural war over image making will not be over soon.

As Dyer (1993) observes, "Stereotypes express particular definitions of reality, with concomitant evaluations, which in turn relates to the disposition of power within society. Who proposes the stereotype, who has the power to enforce it, is the crux of the matter." (p. 14). Pat Mora (1998) also points to the power struggle that lies beneath the representation of images: "Why do society place different values on different groups? The issue isn't inherent inferiority; it's power. Who controls the economic resources and who controls the images, the words? . . . Images matter, words matter, visibility matters" (p. 281). Many studies (e.g., Broderick, 1973; Hirschfelder et al., 1999; MacCann and Woodard, 1985; Slapin and Seale, 1998) reveal that historically, the dominant culture has been able to enforce blatantly racist stereotypes in children's literature. More subtle stereotypes of oppressed groups are still being perpetuated and circulated in society and schools because the dominant culture enforces them through the institutions it controls. Every racial or ethnic stereotype has a history behind it and carries a social-political message. To fully understand stereotypes, it is imperative to view them in the social-historical context of the cultural war over representation.

STEREOTYPES AS PARTIAL TRUTH

When stereotypes in books for children and young adults are criticized, a typical argument put forward in their defense is: Aren't some people in real life like that? It implies that if the images exist in reality, it is then legitimate to present them in literature. For example, while discussing the selection of books about diversity, Hopkins and Tastad (1997) state:

Jack and Honeybunch Go to Heaven, a delightful picture book that depicts blacks in heaven eating spareribs and listening to jazz, has been criticized for being too stereotyped. Why? Some African Americans do like jazz and spareribs. Ezra Jack Keat's books about Peter have been accused of being derogatory because the mother portrayed is a large black woman. What is wrong with that? Some African American mothers are large women. (p. 402)

The same questions, "What is wrong with that?" and "Aren't some people are just like the characters portrayed in the book?" can be asked of many other stereotypic images in literature. This defense mechanism can be used to counter criticism of virtually every stereotype. When the stereotype of Mexican Americans as a fun-loving people or of Chinese Americans as a workaholic people is criticized, one may object that it is true of *some* Mexican Americans or *some* Chinese Americans.

It should be acknowledged that stereotypes are partially true, but partial truth is not the whole truth. I think the "mouse moral" of the fable *Seven Blind Mice* (Young, 1992) best illustrates the point: "Knowing in part may make a fine tale, but wisdom comes from seeing the whole" (n.p.). The problem with stereotypes is that they present limited, partial truth as the whole truth, just as six of the seven blind mice in the story touch a part of an elephant and believe it is a pillar, snake, cliff, spear, fan, and a rope. Nothing could be farther from the truth. The blind act results in the distortion of reality by omission. Examples of this kind of distortion are abundant. A few will suffice to show how stereotyping distorts reality. Hispanic Americans are stereotyped as poor migrant farm workers. True, some of them work in the rural areas, but the majority of them, more than 90%, lives in cities or suburban towns (Chávez, 1996). African Americans are often maliciously portrayed in literature and the media as poor, immoral, and violent. For example, a longitudinal study of leading newspapers' coverage of African Americans found that many of the stories about prisons, drug use, crime, drug and alcohol addicts, AIDS patients, the homeless, and welfare recipients were illustrated mostly by photos of African Americans, as if few Anglos fall into these categories. Yet statistics indicate that "not all—not even most—of the people in the above categories are African Americans" (Martindale, 1996, p. 23). When the media ignores the fact that Anglos have the same problems as African Americans, it falsifies reality through passing off partial truth as the whole truth.

Because they can be partially true, as Durbin (1998) points out, "confronting stereotypes has always been a far trickier proposition than trafficking in them." Stereotypes, Durbin goes on to say, "form around a core of recognizable facts, borrowing fact's credibility even as they distort its truth" (p. 13).

Limited, partial truth becomes the delusion of reality, not in an instance, but through repetition. It is imposed on people's perception again and again until it gives the false impression of being the whole truth. This is the cumulative nature of the stereotype—the overgeneralized characteristics are applied to a social group repeatedly without variation. If only one author or illustrator portrayed a fat black woman, that would not be a stereotype. But when this image appears repeatedly, in many books while other images of black women are rendered invisible, then we have a negative stereotype. The image of Hiawatha in *Amazing Grace* would not be a stereotype if it appeared only in a few picture books, but it is a historically overused symbol of American Indians, and hence a stereotype. If *The Five Chinese Brothers* (Bishop, 1938) had been published in China, it might not have been accused of stereotyping Chinese there. In the social context of the United States, however, the illustrations of the book's cartoon-style caricatures of Chinese characters, as all looking the same, with yellow skin, slanted and slit eyes, long pigtails, and wearing coolie clothes have been repeated so many times that they have become "part and parcel of the perception of Asian Americans and their descendants as subhuman creatures" (Schwartz, 1977, p. 6). In China, Chinese are not represented repeatedly in the same disparaging manner, and there are other images that would counterbalance the caricature. Therefore, the images of Chinese in this picture book might not be considered stereotypes there. The images would be simply caricatures, without social-political implications.

The reason why partial truth can be imposed as reality is because the people who impose it hold the power over representation through control of the media and the publishing industry. The social groups who are stereotyped do not have the power to present their version of the story and images of their people. Theo Goldberg (1993) argues that questions about representations in racial discourse, such as stereotypes, should not focus on how true they are, but on how they "draw their efficacy from traditions, conventions, institutions, and tacit modes of mutual comprehension" (p. 46). To truly understand the nature of stereotypes, we would do better to examine them in a social-historical context than stress that they may be partially true. Only after we realize how well-worn those stereotypes are and how they serve particular social-political agendas will we begin to replace, or at least counteract, them with new, fresh images.

VIEWING IMAGES IN THE BIG PICTURE

The nature of stereotypes as partial truth makes the distinction between stereotype and realistic portrayal very difficult. If showing African Americans eating fried chicken, watermelon, or spareribs is a stereotype, does it mean it is a taboo to detail this in any story? The same question can be asked of other stereotypes, such as showing Mexican Americans as migrant workers, Chinese Americans as workaholics, or Native Americans as being tied to the past. To complicate the matter further, some of these images occur in award-winning books by minority authors. For example, in the picture book *Tar Beach* (Ringgold, 1991), the African American family is shown eating fried chicken and watermelon on "Tar Beach," that is, the tar-covered roof of the building. How do we explain this?

Nobody accused Ringgold of stereotyping African Americans. What would have happened if a white illustrator had done this? He or she might have been subjected to criticism for stereotyping African Americans. One explanation seems to be that it is not right for white authors to detail anything that can be interpreted as stereotypical. In criticizing *Ben's Trumpet* (Isadora, 1979), which portrays a musically talented black boy from a dysfunctional family, Hade (1997) makes this statement: "And surely there are African Americans who enjoy eating watermelon. But if a white illustrator shows African Americans eating watermelon, that person would justifiably be accused of using a stereotypical image of African Americans" (p. 242).

This argument implies that, because we live in a racialized society and everyone's race becomes a sign, any white author who touches upon the negative side of African Americans or other people of color would automatically show a discriminatory attitude and justifiably be accused of racial prejudice. White authors should never cross the racial line and intrude into the "internal affairs" of the people of color. To illustrate his point, Hade compares *Ben's Trumpet* with another picture book *Charlie Parker Played Be Bop* (Raschka, 1992), also written and illustrated by a white author. Both books feature African Americans and deals with the same topic of making music. But the author of the latter focuses solely upon the theme of music and stays away from "racializing" the book. It is wise for Raschka and any other white authors and illustrators not to "use race" negatively, otherwise their books are doomed to draw protests and criticism from people of color.

While refuting the argument that the stereotype is a partial truth, Hade poses a basically deterministic theory on the issue of white authors using stereotypical images of racial minorities. Nevertheless, this theory does reflect the strong reaction of many people of color toward the politically sensitive issue of stereotype. There seems to be zero tolerance of stereotypes, especially if the author is white. If white authors are puzzled by criticism of books like *Ben's Trumpet* by people of color and may feel a double standard is being applied, they may understand the issue better if they view the controversial images in the big picture of the historical cultural war over presentation, rather than dwell on how true they may be to some facts.

Hade's theory addresses the social-political aspect of the issue, but in terms of literary representation, it does not answer the question of why the same images are considered stereotypical in some works but not in others, notwithstanding the author's racial background. When criticizing the stereotypes in *Ben's Trumpet*,

Hade does suggest a criterion for determining whether an image is stereotypical: any negative image is stereotypical unless the author offers some comments to counteract its negative impression on the reader. *Ben's Trumpet* fails the test of the criterion because the negative image of Ben's dysfunctional family is not balanced with any positive comments by the narrator. This criterion somewhat modifies Hade's deterministic theory and provides some maneuvering room for white authors. The problem with this criterion is that the literary quality of a work may be jeopardized if the narrator has to make some corrective comments each time a negative image occurs. Narrators' comments may be one literary technique to counteract the negative images, but it is not the only one. What is most important is to assess the effect of the whole story. A book makes an ideological statement implicitly, not just through the choice of narrative stance, but also through the plot structure, characterization, point of view, language, tone, and other devices (Pinsent, 1997). All these elements combine to form a "systematized view" (Iser, 1978) that the reader gets from the whole book. Therefore, a better way to determine whether a book stereotypes a social group is to view the images in the context of the whole story. Although *Tar Beach* includes images of a black family eating fried chicken and watermelon, it does not stereotype African Americans. This is so, not because the author is an African American, but because the story as a whole reveals the discrimination against African Americans in the 1930s and celebrates their aspirations for emancipation and happiness.

Negative images may take a vilifying or somewhat innocuous form. Unlike the negative image of eating fried chicken and watermelon, *Ben's Trumpet* contains a viciously negative image—a dysfunctional black family, with the parents drinking, smoking, gambling, and totally ignoring their children. This image is foregrounded in the illustration, if not in the text, and it is not tempered with the narrator's comments or other literary devices. The story is not without a positive side. It portrays a talented black boy, who, with the help of a nameless black musician, realizes his dream of becoming a musician, against the odds of poverty. The positive portrayal of the boy, however, does not redeem the negative effects of picturing an unfeeling, uncaring black family. As Moore (1985) points out, Ben "falls helplessly into the presumptive stereotype of the exceptional Black having to disavow and throw off the drag-down atmosphere of Black family and community in order to succeed" (p. 187). The positive aspect of the book is outweighed by its negative aspect. A comparison can be made with the notorious *Little Black Sambo*. Like Ben, Sambo is an intelligent black boy who is able to trick the tigers. But this positive aspect pales in comparison with the racist stereotypes. Like *Little Black Sambo, Ben's Trumpet* is severely flawed by a vilifying stereotype.

This brings us back to the controversy over the picture book *Nappy Hair*. People are understandably outraged at the reappearance of a damaging stereotype—"nappy" or "inky" hair—in a picture book for children in the 1990s—it is a stereotype of physical appearance as devastating as those in *Little Black Sambo*. But does the book really perpetuate the stereotype? Viewed in isolation, the negative image seems to be a repeat of the old stereotype. Viewing it in the context of the whole story, however, we can argue that the book is actually an attempt to convert a negative image created by white supremacists to a positive image of black beauty and pride. The message it conveys to the reader is that nappy hair is God's creation: "One nap of her hair is the only perfect circle in nature" (n.p.).

Since the issue of stereotype is extremely sensitive and complicated, we need to view the negative images in the context of the whole story to see if they are a repeat of old stereotypes. Oversimplified criticism looks at negative images in isolation and labels every one a stereotype.

STEREOTYPES AND HISTORICAL REALISM

Many controversial books that stereotype minority groups are historical fiction. Some of them are highly acclaimed award winners, such as *Sounder* (Armstrong, 1969), *The Cay* (Taylor, 1969), *Slave Dancer* (Fox, 1973), and *Words by Heart* (Sebestyen, 1979). Because it is set in the past, historical fiction poses a challenge to the authors. They have to present history accurately, without perpetuating stereotypes. This is a very difficult task, if not an impossible one. Joann Mazzio, an author of adolescent literature, remarks on her experience of writing historical fiction: "In writing *Leaving Eldorad* [I was] always walking a tightrope in trying to present history accurately and, at the same time, making sure that I wasn't perpetuating negative stereotypes of the cultures my characters represent" (quoted in Noll, 1995, p. 38). On the other hand, as Diane Stanley cautions us, authors "must be careful not to create new myths and falsifications in our zeal to get rid of old stereotypes and bias" (quoted in Sipe, 1997, p. 250). If we impose contemporary social and moral standards on the past, we falsify history to suit our social-political needs.

Many authors of historical fiction about minority groups fail to present history accurately without perpetuating stereotypes, not because they are not good writers, but because their perspective on history is skewed by racial bias and prejudice. History has always been interpreted and reinterpreted from the author's point of view. Theis perspective is the commanding element in historical fiction (Cai, 1992b). In the "selective tradition," authors select the subject to write about and historical facts to include in the book. They consciously or unconsciously select facts that are consistent with their beliefs while omitting those that contradict them (Taxel, 1986).

Joel Taxel (1981) studied children's novels about the American Revolution that were published between 1899 and 1976 and found that an overwhelming majority of them contain negative stereotypes of black characters. They are described as "carefree, indolent," and "incapable of thinking and fending for themselves," as if they were "unconcerned and did little to advance their own freedom" (p. 5). Do these images authentically reflect historical reality? Taxel notes that in that historical period, most blacks were conscious of the issue of freedom for themselves. Actually, they took advantage of the Revolutionary War to gain freedom. He quotes a study of the American Revolution by A. F. Young: Of the approximately 500,000 blacks in the colonies, the majority "voted with their feet against either side, that is, they fled to freedom under whatever circumstances they could" (p. 9). Taxel concludes that the stereotypical descriptions of blacks in these early books reflect the authors' own perspective more than historical reality and are consistent with the prevalent societal attitudes toward blacks during the periods when they were written.

White authors may have good intentions to write an antiracist book but thanks to their white perspective end up stereotyping minority groups. *Sounder* (Armstrong, 1969), *Words by Heart* (Sebestyen, 1979), and *The Cay* (Taylor, 1969) can be classified as social conscience books (Sims, 1982, see Chapter 2 of this work for a definition of the term), which, in a sense, deal with the guilty conscience on the whites and aim to develop sympathy for blacks. While to some extent these books expose the inhuman treatment of blacks in history, they also perpetuate stereotypes of blacks, not unlike those in the books about the Revolution that Taxel (1981) criticized. The adult black protagonists in the first two books—the father in *Sounder* and Ben Sills in *Words by Heart*—fit Sims's (1985) description of "the good Negro—hard-working, Bible-quoting, understanding, passive, loving and forgiving towards whites, and willing to wait on the Lord until whites are ready to accept his family" (p. 126). Timothy in *The Cay* is also a "good Negro" of the same type except that he does not have a family (for a more detailed analysis of *The Cay,* see the next chapter). All three "noble" black men suffer racist oppression silently, maintain no ties to other black people, and die in the end. Timothy dies while protecting a white boy from a hurricane; Ben is shot by a white racist but insists that his daughter first save his murderer, who has fallen off his horse; and "the father in *Sounder* dies in prison, crushed, not by the mean prison guard, but by a chance act of God " (Schwartz, 1985, p. 149). All three stereotypical characters are created to embody the spirit of "overcoming evil with good." However, as Sims (1985) observes, in a world where "racial differences *do* count, when the responsibility for loving, forgiving, and overcoming evil with good lies solely with the book's Black characters, the action takes on racist overtones" (p. 128).

Historically, it is true that not all blacks directly confronted, and revolted against, the slave system. Under the terrifying racial oppression, many of them might become resigned to their fate and coped as best as they could (Taxel, 1986). The characters in the three novels may bear some resemblance to real people in life. As a matter of fact, the author of *Sounder* claimed in his Author's Note that the story was that of a real black teacher. In defense of his novel, the author of *The Cay* also argued that the fictional story was based on fact and the characters drawn from real life. He cited as evidence the fact that he lived in the Caribbean for a while and mingled with West Indian sailors there (Taylor, 1975). Admittedly, the characters in their books are partially true, but this does not exonerate them from stereotyping blacks. Two questions can be asked of the characterizations in these books. First, why did the authors choose to portray these types of black characters? Why did they choose to put so much emphasis on

some traits of these people—their passiveness and pessimism, being forgiving
and loving to whites—that their characters are twisted and distorted to the point
of becoming unreal and unbelievable (Sims, 1985; Taxel, 1986). The answer to
the questions lies in the fact that it is the authors' white perspective that, consciously and unconsciously, led them to make these literary choices, and as a
result perpetuate stereotypes of blacks. They failed to "develop characters whose
ethnic, social, cultural, and personal experience mesh in all the complex ways
they do in real life" (Thomas and Woodard, 1985, p. 47).

In the debate over historical fiction about parallel cultural groups, a frequently
used argument is that to portray history accurately, it is unavoidable for authors
of historical fiction to include negative images, biases, prejudices, and other unpleasant facts of the past in their books. This is true, but the question is: Are
these negative aspects included as an essential part of an accurate, objective description of history or are they used to constitute a demeaning view of the minority groups being portrayed? It is not easy to make the distinction.

Some critics try to distinguish the two different uses of negative images in historical fiction. For example, in an article about the portrayal of American Indians
in children's literature, Noll (1995) addresses the relationship between historical
fiction and multiculturalism, especially the issue of negative images of minorities
in historical fiction. She compares two novels about American Indians, *Little
House on the Prairie* (Wilder, 1953) and *The Return of the Indian* (Banks,
1986). Both books have been criticized for stereotyping American Indians as
wild savages. Noll argues that the demeaning statements about American Indians
made by white settlers in Wilder's book are reflective of white people's fear of
American Indians and racist attitudes in the time period in which the story is set.
So "Wilder's description is an accurate representation of her childhood experiences" (Noll, 1995, p. 38). Wilder also provides an alternative perspective view
that somewhat mitigates the pejorative view of American Indians when Laura
wonders why the American Indians should have to move from their territory to
create settlements for the whites. In contrast, "the distorted and demeaning cultural images in Bank's book have no historical justification and in no way improve the overall literary quality" (Noll, 1995, p. 38).

It should be noted that there is another major difference between these two
books. Wilder's story is a contemporary account of life in the pioneer years,
whereas Bank's story is one by a contemporary author set in the past. Bound by
the limitations of her time, Wilder might not have been able to break through the
boundary of racist ideologies that prevailed in her society. But Bank wrote in a
time when racist ideas were repudiated and egalitarian views of ethnic cultures
were advanced. Therefore, presenting demeaning stereotypes of American Indians is inexcusable in Bank's book.

Another controversial historical novel is *The Slave Dancer* (Fox, 1973), an
account of a thirteen-year-old white boy's experience on a slave ship told
through his point of view. The boy witnesses horrifying, inhuman treatment of
blacks on the journey from Africa to America. The book has been criticized for
historical inaccuracy and negative images of blacks. In its defense, Joel Taxel

(1986) contends that the negative images of African Americans in *The Slave Dancer* do not constitute a pejorative view of African Americans. He states:

It is difficult to believe that anyone who carefully reads *The Slave Dancer* can be unsure about Fox's attitude toward the events she describes. While there are no explicit diatribes against the [slave] trade, comments throughout the book point to its unquestioned evil. (p. 269)

He goes on to say that the potentially negative effects of the images are mitigated by "consideration of the work as a whole" and by "the central image of the slave trade as a monstrous crime against humanity" (p. 271). One criticism of *The Slave Dancer* is that members of the white crew make blatantly racist statements about the Africans and no one on board the ship counters them. Taxel contends that these statements can be justified as a realistic report by the narrator, the innocent white boy, Jesse, who himself is a captive on the ship. Although the terrified Jesse does not speak for the Africans, he shows "remarkable compassion" to them and develops a tenuous friendship with Ras, an African boy. Taxel also argues that since this story is told from Jesse's point of view, to put in a character as spokesman for the captives would violate the literary integrity of the story. While the ugly racist words are not directly countered, Taxel further points out, the muted suffering of the Africans produces a powerful artistic effect that contrasts and counteracts the "coarseness and brutality" of the white crew. Taxel's point-to-point rebuttal of the criticism of *The Slave Dancer* shows that determining whether the inclusion of negative images and other historical unpleasantries results in a demeaning view of the cultural group being portrayed needs to be done by examining the effect of the story as a whole. Taxel's method of determining whether the negative images result in perpetuating negative attitudes toward African Americans is through scrutinizing the negative images in the context of the whole story and assessing the total artistic effect of various literary elements. Taxel makes a strong case that the negative images in the novel are tempered with alternative perspectives.

Whether Noll and Taxel succeeded in their defense of these controversial books is open to discussion. Nevertheless, one thing is certain: the negative images in historical novels should not be taken out of context during evaluation. It is important to view them in the whole context of the story as well as in the social historical context of the time in which the story is set.

CONCLUDING THOUGHTS

The issue of stereotypes is very complicated, and it is sometimes hard, as in the case of *Nappy Hair,* to determine whether an image is a demeaning stereotype. This issue's complexity is compounded by the social political struggle over representation and educational concerns with exposing children to negative images. Stereotyping in multicultural literature is never a purely literary issue. First and foremost, it is a social-political issue. Stereotypes are created by the dominant culture to distort the images and destroy the dignity of the dominated cultures. Writers who perpetuate stereotypes may deny that they serve the political agenda of the dominant culture, but because they do not live in social political vacuum their writing is likely to implicitly reflect their cultural prejudices and serve the interest of the dominant culture.

In creating, critiquing, and using multicultural literature, great efforts must be made to detect and dissect stereotypes. On the one hand, old and new stereotypes that serve the social political agenda of the dominant culture must not be allowed to creep into multicultural literature. On the other, special caution should be taken to ensure that realistic portrayals of the dominated cultural groups are not mistakenly considered stereotypes. Keeping a balance between the two require-ments is a fine line to walk, but it is the only correct course of action.

REFERENCES

Bird, E. (1996). Introduction: Constructing the Indian, 1830s-1990s. In E. Bird (Ed.), *Dressing in feathers: The construction of the Indian in American popular culture* (p. 1-12). Boulder, CO: Westview.

Broderick, D. (1973). *Image of the Black in children's fiction.* New York: Bowker.

Cai, M. (1992a). A balanced view of acculturation: Comments on Laurence Yep's three novels. *Children's Literature in Education, 23* (2), 107-108.

Cai, M. (1992b). Values and valuables in historical fiction for children. *The New Advo-cate, 5* (4), 279-291.

Cassuto, L. (1997). *The inhuman race: The racial grotesque in American literature and culture.* New York: Columbia University Press.

Chávez, R. (1996). The Mexican Americans. In P. M. Lester (Ed.), *Images that injure: Pictorial stereotypes in the media* (pp. 327–344). Westport, CT: Praeger.

Clemetson, L. (1998). Caught in the cross-fire: A young star teacher finds herself in a losing racial battle with parents. *Newsweek, 132,* 38-39.

Coyle, L. R. (1991). The creative use of stereotypes in the short stories of Norma Fox Mazer. *The Alan Review, 18* (1), 7-8.

Dorris, M. (1994). *Paper trail: Essays.* New York: HarperCollins.

Durbin, K. (1998, June 21). A new, if not improved, stereotype. *New York Times,* 24.

Dyer, R. (1993). *The matter of images: Essays on representations.* London: Routledge.

Eagleton, T. (1983). *Literary theory: An introduction.* Minneapolis: University of Min-nesota Press.

Eagleton, T. (2000). *The idea of culture.* Malden, MA: Blackwell.

Enterman, W. F. (1996). Stereotyping, prejudice, and discrimination. In P. M. Lester (Ed.), *Images that injure: Pictorial stereotypes in the media* (pp. 9-14). Westport, CT: Praeger.

Frankel, E. R. (1996). Bias and stereotypes in the portrayal of Palestinian-Arabs in American juvenile trade fiction, 1957-1985: An analysis of a selected bibliography. *Multicultural Review, 3* (30), 48-52.

Goldberg, D. T. (1993). *Racist culture.* Oxford, England: Blackwell.

Goebel, B. (1995). Expanding the literary canon and reading the rhetoric of "race." *Eng-lish Journal, 85* (4), 42-48.

Hade, D. D. (1997). Reading multiculturally. In V. Harris (Ed.), *Using multiethnic litera-ture in the K–8 classroom* (pp. 233-256). Norwood, MA: Christopher-Gordon.

Harris, V. (1995). "May I read this book?" Controversies, dilemmas, and delights. In S. Lehr (Ed.), *Battling dragons: Issues and controversies in children's literature* (pp. 275–283). Portsmouth, NH: Heinemann.

Hirschfelder, A., Molin, P. F., and Wakim, Y. (1999). *American Indian stereotypes in the world of children: A reader and bibliography* (2nd ed.). Lanham, MD: Scarecrow.

Hirschfelder, A. B., and Singer, B. R. (1992). Harsh realities. In A. B. Hirschfelder and B. R. Singer (Eds), *Rising voices: Writings of young Native Americans* (pp. 87-88). New York: Charles Scribner's Sons.

Hopkins, D., and Tastad, S. A. (1997). Censoring by omission: Has the United States progressed in promoting diversity through children's books? *Youth Services in Libraries, 10* (4), 399-404.

Iser, W. (1978). *The act of reading: A theory of aesthetic response.* Baltimore, MD: Johns Hopkins University Press.

Jackson, N. B. (1996). Arab Americans: Middle East conflicts hit home. In P. M. Lester (Ed.), *Images that injure: Pictorial stereotypes in the media* (pp. 63-68). Westport, CT: Praeger.

League of Women Voters. (1999). Children's impression of American Indians: A survey of suburban kindergarten and fifth grade children. In A. Hirschfelder, P. F. Molin, and Y. Wakim. (Eds.), *American Indian stereotypes in the world of children: A reader and bibliography* (2nd ed., pp. 3-8). Lanham, MD: Scarecrow.

Lee, S. J. (1996). *Unraveling the "model minority" stereotype: Listening to Asian American youth.* New York: Teachers College Press.

Lester, N. A. (1999). Roots that go beyond big hair and a bad hair day: *Nappy Hair* pieces. *Children's Literature in Education, 30* (3), 171-183.

MacCann, D., and Woodard, G. (Eds.). (1985). *The black American in books for children: Readings in racism* (2nd ed.). Metuchen, NJ: Scarecrow Press.

Martindale, C. (1996). Newspaper stereotypes of African Americans. In P. M. Lester (Ed.), *Images that injure: Pictorial stereotypes in the media* (pp. 21–26). Westport, CT: Praeger.

McElmeel, S. L. (1993). Toward a real multiculturalism. *School Library Journal, 39* (11), 50.

Miller-Lachmann, L. (Ed.). (1992). *Our family, our friends, our world: An annotated guide to significant multicultural books for children and teenagers.* New Providence, NJ: Bowker.

Moore, O. (1985). Picture books: The un-text. In D. MacCann and G. Woodard (Eds.), *The black American in books for children: Readings in racism* (pp. 183-191). Metuchen, NJ: Scarecrow Press.

Mora, P. (1998). Confessions of a Latina author. *The New Advocate, 17* (4), 279-289.

Noll, E. (1995). Accuracy and authenticity in American Indian children's literature: The social responsibility of authors and illustrators. *The New Advocate, 8* (1), 29-43.

Pinsent, P. (1997). *Children's literature and the politics of equality.* New York: Teachers College Press.

Pitts, L. Jr. (1998, December 5). Politics of hair speaks volumes about black pride. *Miami Herald,* pp. 1g-2g.

Said, E. W. (1978). *Orientalism.* New York: Pantheon.

San Juan, E. Jr. (1992). *Racial formations/critical transformation.* Atlantic Highlands, NJ: Humanities Press.

Schon, I. (1993). Good and bad books about Hispanic people and culture for young readers. *Multicultural Review, 2* (1), 28-31.

Schwartz, A. V. (1977). The five Chinese brothers: Time to retire. *Interracial Books for Children Bulletin, 8* (3), 3-7.

Schwartz, A. V. (1985). *Sounder:* A black or white tale? In D. MacCann and G. Woodard (Eds.), *The black American in books for children: Readings in racism* (pp. 147-150). Metuchen, NJ: Scarecrow.

Seale, D. (1998). Book reviews. In B. Slapin and D. Seale (Eds.). (1998), *Through Indian eyes: The Native experience in books for children* (pp. 85-178). Los Angeles: American Indian Studies Center, University of California.

Sims, R. (1985). Words by Heart's black perspective. In D. MacCann and G. Woodard (Eds.), *The black American in books for children: Readings in racism* (pp. 123–128). Metuchen, NJ: Scarecrow.

Sipe, L. (1997). In their own words: Authors' views on issues in historical fiction. *The New Advocate, 10* (3), 243-258.

Slapin, B., and Seale, D. (Eds.). (1998). *Through Indian eyes: The Native experience in books for children.* Los Angeles: American Indian Studies Center, University of California.

Sleeter, C. (1996). Foreword. In S. J. Lee, *Unraveling the "model minority" stereotype* (pp. vii–x). New York: Teachers College Press.

Stroebe, W., and Insko, C. A. (1989). Stereotype, prejudice, and discrimination: Changing conceptions in theory and practice. In D. Bar-Tal, C. F. Graumann, A. W. Kruglanski, and W. Stroebe. (Eds.), *Stereotyping and prejudice: Changing concepts* (pp. 3–34). New York: Springer-Verlag.

Taxel, J. (1981). The American Revolution in children's books: Issues of racism and classism. *Interracial Books for Children Bulletin, 12* (7, 8), 3-9.

Taxel, J. (1986). The black experience in children's fiction: Controversies surrounding award winning books. *Curriculum Inquiry, 16,* 245-281.

Taxel, J. (1992). The politics of children's literature: Reflections on multiculturalism and Christopher Columbus. In V. Harris (Ed.), *Teaching multicultural literature in grades K-8* (pp. 1-36). Norwood, MA: Christopher-Gordon.

Taylor, T. (1975). Letter to the editor. *Top of the News, 31* (3), 284-288.

Thomas, J., and Woodard, G. (1985). Black perspective in books for children. In D. MacCann and G. Woodard (Eds.), *The Black American in books for children: Readings in racism* (pp. 39-51). Metuchen, NJ: Scarecrow.

Trousdale, A. M. (1990). A submission theology for black Americans: Religion and social action in prize-winning children's books about the black experience in America. *Research in the Teaching of English, 24* (2), 117-140.

Wang, J. (1997). *The politics of interpretation in canonical reception of Asian American women's writing.* Paper presented at the MMLA special session: Institutions of literary reception, Iowa City, Iowa.

Yamate, S. S. (1997). Asian Pacific American children's literature: Expanding perceptions about who Americans are. In V. Harris (Ed.), *Using multiethnic literature in the K-8 classroom* (pp. 95-128). Norwood, MA: Christopher-Gordon.

Books for Children and Young Adults

Armstrong, W. H. (1969). *Sounder.* New York: Harper & Row.

Banks, L. R. (1980). *The Indian in the cupboard.* New York: Avon.

Banks, L. R. (1986). *The return of the Indian.* Garden City, NY: Doubleday.

Bannerman, H. (1899, 1923). *The story of Little Black Sambo.* New York: Harper and Row.

Bishop, C. (1938). *The five Chinese brothers*. Ill. by K. Wiese. New York: Coward-McCann.

Fox, P. (1973). *The slave dancer*. New York: Bantam Doubleday Dell.

Grossman, V. (1998). *Ten little rabbits*. Ill. by S. Long. San Francisco: Chronicle Books.

Herron, C. (1997). *Nappy hair*. New York: Knopf.

Hoffman, M. (1991). *Amazing grace*. Ill. by C. Binch. New York: Dial.

Isadora, R. (1979). *Ben's trumpet*. New York: Greenwillow.

Lester, J. (1996). *Sam and the tigers: A new retelling of Little Black Sambo*. Ill. by J. Pinkney. New York: Dial.

Opie, I. (Ed.). (1996). *My very first Mother Goose*. Ill. by R. Wells. Cambridge, MA: Candlewick.

Ringgold, F. (1991). *Tar Beach*. New York: Scholastic.

Raschka, C. (1992). *Charlie Parker played be bop*. New York: Orchard.

Sebestyen, O. (1979). *Words by heart*. New York: Bantam.

Taylor, T. (1969). *The cay*. New York: Doubleday.

Wilder, L. E. (1953). *Little house on the prairie*. New York: Harper.

Young, E. (1992). *Seven blind mice*. New York: Scholastic.

6

Cultural Correctness and the Evaluation of Multicultural Literature

The concept of multicultural literature requires that books in this category be treated, not only as literary works, but also as cultural products. Although all literature is a cultural product that reflects various cultural beliefs, values, and attitudes, the cultural aspects of multicultural literature deserve special attention, because it is a weapon used in the "cultural wars" between dominant and dominated cultures, and also because multicultural literature is an educational instrument to inform students about the interrelationships and interactions of different cultures and to inculcate in them ideas and ideals of multiculturalism. Anyone who is committed to the cause of multiculturalism will inevitably examine the social-political implications of each multicultural literary work and be very concerned with the cultural messages it conveys to children. These so-called extraliterary concerns arise from a belief that multicultural literature should be, first and foremost, evaluated as cultural product. If a piece of literature expresses racist discrimination, no matter how well written it is, it has to be rejected, because it is worse than a piece that is culturally correct but tells a mediocre story. What I term cultural correctness must be the basic criterion for evaluating multicultural literature, if we are to maintain the cultural integrity of the people represented in it. There is nothing radical about this position. Think of how we evaluate children's literature in general. It has been a widely accepted assumption that literature performs two functions: it entertains and instructs. When selecting books for children, we especially emphasize its function to instruct. Although children's books should not be moralizing tracts, we are concerned that bad books may instill immoral ideas in children's impressionable minds. Would we recommend a children's book if it demoralizes children no matter how well written it was? In this chapter I will explain the concept of cultural correctness and discuss issues in evaluating multicultural literature.

CULTURALLY CORRECT

Sims Bishop (1994) formulated the following main criteria for evaluating multicultural literature: "(1) that the book should contribute in a positive way to an understanding and appreciation of persons of color and their cultures, or (2) that the book should offer a positive vision of a diverse society and a multicultural world" (p. xv). The key word in these two criteria is "positive." In essence, Sims Bishop is saying that multicultural literature should foster a positive attitude toward other cultures and toward cultural diversity. If a piece of multicultural literature has the potential to produce that effect in the reader, we may say it is culturally correct. To foster this positive attitude does not mean that multicultural literature must portray only the positive aspects of a culture or a culturally diverse society. It does not mean that multicultural literature must always present so-called minority characters as strong characters or role models. Positive effects on the reader are *not* the same as positive presentation in a book. If we demanded that multicultural literature portray only positive aspects of a culture or a multicultural society, it would lead to positive essentializing of racial or ethnic groups, which is nearly the same as creating positive stereotypes of them (Nodelman, 1996). Under the influence of ethnic essentialism, characters in multicultural literature who are not perfect have often been taken out of context and criticized as negative stereotypes. Consequently, ethnic essentialism may lead to censorship and the imposition of restrictions on creative expression, and multicultural literature may become just political propaganda.

Some guidelines for selecting multicultural literature (e.g., Pang et. al., 1992) do recommend that teachers select books with positive portrayals of minority characters. Trousdale (1990) maintained, "The need, for black children, was for books that portrayed realistic and positive black characters, characters with whom they could identify, whose culture reflected their own, whose lives suggested possibilities for their own" (p. 118). Not only black children but all children of parallel cultures need books that fit Trousdale's description. However, there is an important distinction between selecting books for children and evaluating books in literary criticism. Racial and ethnic stereotypes have long pervaded literature for young people, so educators have good reasons to choose books with positive characters to use with students. This criterion of selection, however, should not be confused with Sims Bishop's criteria for the evaluation of multicultural literature. A book can be of great literary value and culturally correct but inappropriate for use with children or immature readers who do not have the literary competence to understand it.

Unfortunately, the concept of cultural correctness is often misunderstood, and what Sims Bishops terms "positive effect" is confused with positive presentation. For example, Nodelman (1996), misinterpreting Bishop's criteria, contends that "to insist on only *positive portrayals* is to insist on misrepresentation, [mainly because] the experience of being a person of color or living in a multicultural society isn't always a positive one—nor are members of minorities are incapable of actions that might be viewed in a negative light" (p. 133, my italics). He uses the Canadian author Carol Matas's (1993) book *Sworn Enemies* to show that members of minorities are capable of doing mean and malicious things. This novel portrays a Jewish boy as a *khapper,* who kidnaps other Jewish boys to fill the Czar's army quotas of recruits in 19th-century Russia. According to Nodelman, a school trustee in Vaughan, Ontario, requested that the book should not be added to a list of recommended reading for students. "Apparently," Nodelman comments, "the goal of tolerance was more important than the obvious truth that Jews—and blacks and Asians—are just as capable of self-seeking and malice as the rest of humanity is" (p. 133).

Whether this book is culturally correct or not should be judged on its total artistic effects, not on one negative character. A book should not be criticized just because it contains negative characters of ethnic minority backgrounds. It is a violation of the principle of realism if we insist on presenting only positive images and experience of being a person of color or living in a multicultural society. In *Sworn Enemies*, some Jews, like Zev, the *khapper*, betray their own people. To be true to reality, this author includes the *khappers* in her book, which portrays Russian Jews in that historical period. Including negative images and experiences in the portrayal of a parallel culture does not necessarily undermine a positive understanding and appreciation of it. Although *Sworn Enemies* includes negative images and experiences of Jewish people, it still meets Sims Bishop's criterion because it does contribute to a positive understanding and appreciation of Jews and their culture. It helps the reader to see how Jews were persecuted historically and how they fought hard to survive inhuman treatment. Anyone who is not prejudiced against Jews will feel sympathy for their sufferings and admiration for their courage. The negative images of *khappers* sould not adversely affect responses to Jewish people as a whole as represented in the book, because it is understandable that there are villains in any culture, including the mainstream culture, and because there are positive images of Jews in the story such as Zev's sworn enemy Aaron and his friends, who fight courageously for their survival and human dignity. To demand only positive images and experiences in literature about other cultures would turn literature into mere propaganda.

There are many award-winning multicultural books that do not shy away from portraying negative experiences and images but still contribute to a positive understanding and appreciation of other cultures, such as *Somewhere in the Darkness* (Myers, 1992), *Dragonwings* (Yep, 1975), *Parrot in the Oven* (Martinez, 1996), *The Heart of a Chief* (Bruchac, 1998), and *Bud, Not Buddy* (Curtis, 1999) to name only a few. All these books contain negative characters who are ethnic minorities and touch upon some negative aspects of reality in their cultures, but this does not impair their positive effects on the reader. For example, in *Somewhere in the Darkness,* we have an antihero rather than a hero. The protagonist, Crab, an African American, is a convicted criminal. Although he has committed some petty crimes, he is unjustly convicted of murder. Having lost any hope in the judicial system, his only wish is to prove himself innocent to his son. He runs away from the hospital, where he was being treated for a fatal disease. Before he dies he manages to show his son that he was wronged. Crab is by no means a positive character or a role model, but he makes us think about the time-honored issue of crime and punishment. The story reveals to us that Crab is a victim of a judicial system that discriminates against blacks. As we read along, our attitude toward him changes from resentment to empathy, and finally to sympathy. *Somewhere in the Darkness* is a powerful, realistic work that does not present a positive main character but still gives the reader a positive feeling about the experiences of an ethnic group.

It is a misunderstanding, or even a distortion, of the standard of cultural correctness to claim that those who uphold the standard demand nothing less than perfection in the representation of marginalized ethnic groups—"the ethnic characters must always be strong, dignified, courageous, loving, sensitive, wise" (Rochman, 1993, p. 17). It is true that some good-quality multicultural books, like Paula Fox's *Slave Dancer,* have been criticized for presenting less than perfect people of color. And many multicultural books may be culturally correct but mediocre literature. But the greatest danger is that the standard of cultural correctness may not be truly embraced and applied by authors, publishers, and critics. Many books with cultural inaccuracies, stereotypes, and a dominant culture's perspective are still being published, favorably reviewed, and widely circulated. A good example is the recently published book about the Carlisle Indian school, *My Heart Is on the Ground: The Diary of Nannie Little Rose, A Sioux Girl* (Rinaldi, 1999). This book is in the extremely popular "Dear America" series, which attempts to capture different periods of American history through fictional characters' diaries. This series is touted as the best of historical fiction for any age and has over 5 million books in print. *My Heart Is on the Ground* has received high critical acclaim from major review journals. *School Library Journal* praises the author for a clear and compassionate depiction of widely divergent cultures and claims that the book adds another "excellent volume to a popular series" (quoted in Atleo et al., 1999, paragraph 27). A review of the book in *The Booklist* (1999) states that it presents rich details about American Indian culture and customs and a realistic portrayal of "the frustrations, the joy, and the confusion of one of yesterday's children growing up in two cultures" (p. 141). With the favorable reviews and wide circulation of the book, it could have probably become the major source of information about the Indian boarding school experience for schoolchildren in the United States. Yet this book has been severely criticized by a group of nine people who are very knowledgeable about American Indian culture, including the famous critic Beverly Slapin. They found numerous distortions of historical facts, cultural inaccuracies, various stereotypes, and a white perspective in the book. They pointed out that the author ignored all the documented horrors of the "noble experiment" in Carlisle and cast the Indian Industrial School in a positive light, declaring it was Indian children's "only chance for a future" (Rinaldi, 1999, p. 177). They indignantly denounced the book for its cover-up:

Nowhere in this book is to be found the screaming children, thrown onto horse-drawn wagons, being taken away from their homes. Nowhere in this book is to be found the desperately lonely children, heartbroken, sobbing into the night. Nowhere is to be found the terrified children, stripped naked and beaten, for trying to communicate with each other and not understanding what was expected of them. Nowhere is to be found the relenting daily humiliation, in word and deed, from the teachers, matrons and staff. Nowhere is to be found the desperate runaways, lost, frozen in the snow. Nowhere to be found is the spirit of resistance. Nowhere. (Atleo et al., 1999, paragraph 108)

They concluded that "this one book epitomizes the utter lack of sensitivity and respect that has come to characterize the vast majority of children's books about Native Americans" (para. 111). If we compare their critique of the book and the favorable reviews of the book by the journals, it is not hard to see the difference between those who uphold the standard of cultural correctness and those who do not. The reviewers see only literary merits in the book but are blind to its cultural incorrectness. It has been contended that books help to dispel prejudice, not with "role models" or "noble messages," but with "enthralling stories that make us imagine the lives of people" (Rochman, 1993, p. 19). I would argue that enthralling stories and vivid characterizations of individuals alone cannot guarantee that a book will produce positive effects on the reader, it must also be culturally correct. It should be conceded that the author of *My Heart Is on the Ground* is very imaginative and tells a well-crafted story, yet it does not dispel prejudice but rather perpetuates it. For those whose life experiences are misrepresented in it, the story will not be engaging but rather repelling.

To critique a book by the standard of cultural correctness is within the purview of literary criticism. It should be emphasized that to think of cultural criticism as an imposition or, even worse, as a bane on genuine literary criticism, is a mistake. As Thomas and Woodard (1985) point out, "To judge literature in terms of the racial attitudes presented in them is actually to judge whether the writer has gone beyond and behind stereotypes, myths, and ideas about blacks" (p. 47). This statement is also true of literature about other parallel cultural groups.

While I argue that cultural correctness is the basic criterion, I do not endorse mediocre literature. There is a danger of evaluating literature only on the basis of its content, without applying other criteria. Sometimes we may be willing to accept mediocre works simply because they are multicultural in nature (Hopkins and Tastad, 1997). Mediocre literature cannot give children an engaging aesthetic experience; neither can it move their hearts or enlighten their heads. Therefore, a mediocre work, even if it is culturally correct, may not be very useful. Hopefully, there will one day be a large number of high-quality multicultural books that are also culturally correct. Unfortunately, not many are available today. When I have to choose between a mediocre but culturally correct book and one that is of high literary value but severely flawed culturally, I choose the former. I would not choose *Little Black Sambo, Five Chinese Brothers,* and *Knots on the Counting Rope,* even though they are well-crafted stories. In 1986, Stephen King compiled a listing of recommended "scary" books for children. He listed *The Story of Little Black Sambo* as the number two book, arguing that the literary merits of the book far outweighed the arguments by some African Americans (Harris, 1990). To insist that the literary merits of *Little Black Sambo* outweigh its racial prejudices reflects an indifference to the negative impact on children of books that impart racist attitudes.

POLITICALLY CORRECT

Critics who uphold the standard of cultural correctness are likely to be labeled as politically correct watchdogs or bullies, who are eager to limit the creative freedom of authors, while authors who perpetuate cultural bigotry are tolerated or even honored for the literary merits of their work. For some writers and critics, literature is a sacred sanctuary of art. How dare you sully it with social-political doctrines such as multiculturalism? How dare you invade the domain and patrol it as the "thought police"?

Debates over political correctness (PC) have been swirling in the academia for some time, and the field of children's literature is not insulated from them (Taxel, 1995). As Joel Taxel (1995) observed, "Advocates of PC are said to favor the banishment of unfavorable speech, opinions, and attitudes about women and minority groups from college campuses and from the pages of children's literature" (p. 156). The attack on political correctness is actually attack on multiculturalism. Banfield (1998) pointedly states, "The term *politically correct* has been transformed into a mocking description of vocabulary or actions used to avoid race or gender bias" (p. 17). To defend the standard of cultural correctness, we need to take on the issue of political correctness.

First, the political nature of literature and literary criticism should be made clear, because those who attack proponents of multiculturalism as politically correct watchdogs seem to be free of political interests. As Eloise Greenfield (1985) poignantly states:

It is true that politics is not art, but art is political. Whether in its interpretation of the political realities, or in its attempt to ignore these realities, or in its support of the status quo, all art is political and every book caries its author's message." (p. 20)

The aim of sociocultural criticism is to surface and criticize the underlying ideological values of the established literature that serves the political interests of the dominant culture. Racist and sexist bias, prejudice, and discrimination that have been defended or concealed by established critical discourse have to be exposed. Critics who disagree with this kind of criticism often accuse it of serving a political agenda and caricature it as "political correctness," while they see themselves as apolitical, dealing with only purely literary matters. British critic Terry Eagleton (1983) points out that "the idea that there are 'non-political' forms of theory is simply a myth which furthers certain political uses of literature all the more effectively. [Not only] political criticism [but all criticism reads] literary text in light of certain values which are related to political beliefs and practices" (p. 203). Wayne C. Booth (1988), a theorist of ethic criticism, concurs with ideological or political critics' claim that "all criticism reflects and reinforces ideologies that *can* be used to serve power" (p. 385). The reviews of *My Heart Is on the Ground* are a perfect example of seemingly nonpolitical criticism that "reflects and reinforces" the dominant culture's ideologies by wittingly or unwittingly concealing the book's misrepresentation of American Indians.

In evaluating children's books we have always have been concerned with extra-literary matters. When we put a book in a child's hand, we often ask if it coveys correct moral messages. Ever since children's literature came into existence, there have been debates over the "moral correctness" of books. People may argue over different standards for moral correctness and censor books that fail to meet the standards, but they usually reach a consensus over the basic assumption that children's books should not impart immoral ideas and practices. As Amy McClure (1995) comments in an article about censorship, the debate is not over "the problem of good versus evil but 'your' perception of good versus 'my' perception of good" (p. 4). If it is a legitimate concern about the moral message, it is also a legitimate concern about the cultural message a book sends to our children. The issue of cultural correctness is in the final analysis a moral issue. To violate a culture's integrity with distortions is an immoral act of cultural abuse. However, although "moral correctness" has seldom been questioned as a standard for evaluating children's literature, cultural correctness has been ridiculed as "political correctness."

Commenting on the historically oppressed and powerless groups' struggle against traditional educational biases, Gregory Jay (1997) makes some insightful remarks that are relevant to our discussion here: "Those who seek to tell the story differently will inevitably be accused of 'politicizing' the curriculum when in fact they are simply trying to point out the effect that politics has already had on what we study and what we value" (p. 6). What he says about curriculum reform can be applied to sociocultural criticism of literature, too. Sociocultural critics have been accused of politicizing literature when in fact they are simply exposing the political inequality and injustice in literary representation and pointing out how literature has been used to serve dominant social and political institutions.

To accuse the powerless groups of politicizing education or literature when they rise against the unjust political system is a kind of hypocrisy on the part of those who seem to champion the cause of intellectual freedom. Jay (1997) demands, with indignation:

Where were today's born-again champions of democracy, freedom of thought, and evaluation by merit during all the years when women were denied admissions to the nation's top colleges and universities? Where were they during all the years when Jews, blacks, and others were similarly discriminated against? Why were *Atlantic, Time, Newsweek, The New York Times,* and the rest of the media relatively silent during the decades when curriculum and teaching practices amount to a "thought police" on behalf of white Anglo-Saxon males? Who cried *then* about "political correctness" on campus? (p. 6)

Similar questions can be asked of those who claim that there are "politically correct bullies" attempting to impose rigid restrictions on the freedom of literary
creation. Where were the champions of democracy and intellectual freedom
when people of color were excluded from literature for young people or portrayed as ridiculous stereotypes?

Proponents of multiculturalism in education and literature are not only carica-
tured as "politically correct bullies" but also blamed for creating a PC crisis, as if
they had already taken over university campuses and created a "backlash" in the
publication of children's literature. The power and influence of proponents of
multiculturalism has been ludicrously exaggerated (Harris, 1994; Taxel, 1995;
Jay, 1997). Joel Taxel (1995) points out that "it is a distortion of current reality
[to presume that] there is an army of PC enforcers" (p. 157). Those who hold
that presumption, Taxel goes on to say, "fail to provide evidence to support their
claim that PC 'watchdogs,' 'bullies,' and 'whiners' are imposing a new censorship on children's book publishing" and also fail to situate the actions of proponents of multiculturalism in historical context of cultural wars (p. 157). If many
authors and editors show a new cautiousness in dealing with multicultural subjects and themes, Taxel notes, it stems from a "new found respect" for the historically oppressed groups. It is not a "backlash" caused by "PC bullies." If the
proponents of multiculturalism had the power over book publishing—as Harris
(1996) notes, they do not—books that have long been criticized for stereotyping
ethnic minority groups, such as *The Story of Little Black Sambo* and *The Five
Chinese Brothers*, would not have posted such large sales and good quality multicultural books, such as *Willie Bea and the Time the Martians Landed* (Hamilton, 1983) would take the place of culturally incorrect books. The fabricated PC
conspiracy is non-existent; it is a myth conjured up out of "fear on the part of the
establishment" that the marginalized groups may be winning some ground (Jay,
1997, p. 6). It is the attack on political correctness that is actually creating a
backlash in the movement of multicultural literature.

EMOTIONALLY CORRECT

In the debate over *Huckleberry Finn,* Chester B. Stevens (1999), vice-
president of the African-American Parent Coalition, said that he was strongly
opposed to using the novel in the classroom because it uses the word "nigger"
for black more than 200 times, which is emotionally devastating for African
American children. In evaluating the appropriateness of any book for classroom
use, he argued, we need to consider, not just whether it is "politically correct,"
but also whether it is "emotionally correct." "What I feel is missing in all the
discussions about this book and other contentious books unfavorable to African-
Americans," he said, "is the voice of psychology and psychiatry" (paragraph 2).

For an example of the book's devastating emotional impact on African American children, read this letter to the *New York Times* written by a reader who recalls his reactions to having the book read aloud in a predominantly white school
some years ago:

I can still recall the anger I felt as my white classmates read aloud the word "nigger." In fact, as I write this letter, I am getting angry all over again. I wanted to sink into my seat. Some of the whites snickered, others giggled. I can recall nothing of the literary merits of this work that you term "the greatest of all American novels." I only recall the sense of relief when I would flip ahead a few pages and see the word "nigger" would not be read that hour. (quoted in Henry, 1992, p. 29)

Many detractors of *Huck Finn* argue against using the book in the classroom on the grounds that black children experience painful humiliation and insults when it is read aloud. That traumatic experience cannot be erased by what defenders of the book believe is well-intended irony and satire (Henry, 1992). For them, the criterion of "emotionally correct" is an essential criterion for evaluating books about people of color. John H. Wallace (1992), for example, recommended that *Huckleberry Finn, The Slave Dancer,* and *To Kill a Mockingbird* be listed as racist books and excluded from the classroom because black parents and teachers, and students have complained about books containing the "N" word being read aloud in class. No literary analysis of these books' presumably positive artistic effects can ease the emotional sufferings of black children.

Whether *Huckleberry Finn* and the other books are favorable or unfavorable to African Americans and whether they should be listed as racist and excluded from the classroom is debatable. Yet the concern about the psychological effects of a book on children is legitimate. When we select a book to use with children, we should be concerned about whether it is developmentally appropriate. If a book is not developmentally appropriate, not matter how good it is, it either cannot be understood or can have adverse effects on children. When we want to discuss a book on a sensitive topic, for example, divorce or sexuality, we would consider how children would react to it. By the same token, we should be concerned about the psychological effects on the children, especially children of parallel cultural groups, when we share multicultural literature with them. It is very important to keep in mind that racial and ethnic minority students bring to school cultural backgrounds and experiences very different from those of students of the mainstream culture. John Fisher, former president of Columbia Teachers College, wrote about black students' burden of the history of their race:

The black American youngsters happen to be a member of a large and distinctive group that for a very long time has been the object of special, legal, and social action. . . . Every black child is the victim of the history of his race in this country. On the day he enters kindergarten, he carries a burden *no white child* can ever know, no matter what other handicaps or disabilities he may suffer. (quoted in Wallace, 1992, p. 22)

Because of their cultural backgrounds and the existing racial relations, students of parallel cultural background may be psychologically vulnerable to negative descriptions and language that may not affect students of the mainstream culture. Books to be used with children in the classroom should be selected with sensitivity. Teachers should concern themselves, not just with what a book means, but also with what a book can do to a reader (Booth, 1988). The criterion of emotional correctness should be a guideline for using multicultural books with children. Ricker-Wilson (1998) states that we need to give children what "Deanne Bogdan refers to as 'the literature of need,' literature that provides 'psychic nourishment' to its readers" (p. 71). In the past the literary canon "primarily meets the pyschic needs of a white, male, heterosexual interpretive community while it provides angst for many other readers" (p. 71). Today, the inclusion of multicultural literature makes available "the literature of need" for parallel cultural students, but not all multicultural literature may provide "psychic nourishment" to them.

Emotional correctness, however, is a criterion for selecting rather than evaluating a book. We cannot reject a book as racist because it has some offensive elements that may make reading or sharing it disturbing to parallel cultural students or parents. Even a culturally correct book might have undesirable psychological effects if it is shared in a classroom setting. Ricker-Wilson (1998) raised questions about using Alice Walker's (1982) *The Color Purple,* Toni Morrison's (1972) *The Bluest Eye,* and Zora Neale Hurston's (1969) *Their Eyes Were Watching God* with her eleventh grade class, because they all contain negative depictions of black men. The standard of cultural correctness does not demand the exclusion of negative or imperfect parallel cultural characters. However, a parallel cultural reader may feel offended by the portrayal of such characters in a book, despite the fact that its total artistic effect may "contribute in a positive way to an understanding and appreciation of persons of color and their cultures" (Sims Bishop, 1994, p. xv). As a matter of fact, readers may be offended by a book for any negative things related to race and ethnicity in it. For example, a Korean girl wrote to tell Katherine Paterson that she was offended by her *Park's Quest* (1988), because she was "embarrassed and hurt" when the white boy Park in the book calls a Vietnamese girl names (Paterson, 1994, p. 85), even though the boy changes his attitude to her in the end. A book should not be evaluated based on readers' emotional response to isolated aspects of it, but on its total artistic effect.

To give a multicultural book objective evaluation, educators and critics will do better if they do not get emotional. The criterion of emotional correctness may lead to subjective rejection of a good multicultural book as culturally incorrect. On the other hand, seemingly objective checklists for content analysis of multicultural literature may also lead to inaccurate evaluation.

ANALYZING CONTENT ANALYSIS AS A MEANS OF EVALUATION

Content analysis is a widely used instrument for scholarly research. Many thesis, dissertations, and studies use content analysis to examine the representation of cultural images in children's books and to determine how culturally authentic they are. Here are some examples of content analysis studies: "A Study of Black Characters in Caldecott and Newbery Award and Honor Books for Children" (Gary, 1984), "Issues of Ethnicity, Authenticity, and Quality in Asian-American Picture Books, 1983-1993" (Harada, 1995), "Images and Stereotypes of African

Americans and Hispanic Americans in Contemporary Children's Fiction" (Cobb, 1995), and "Are Mexican-American Females Portrayed Realistically in Fiction for Grades K-3? A Content Analysis" (Rocha and Dowd, 1993). Evaluative instruments used in many content analysis studies typically include a checklist of variables for evaluating the sample of books. To evaluate characterization of Asian Americans, for instance, the checklist could include items such as "model minority character, inscrutable, overtly polite, sneaky, exotic, and no stereotypes" (Harada, 1995, p. 142). Whether a book portrays Asian Americans accurately is largely decided by checking the items.

A problem with this evaluation instrument in content analysis is that it sometimes dissects the organic whole of a literary text into separate segments and passes judgment based on isolated textual evidence taken out of context. If isolated pieces of textual evidence are not synthesized and examined in the context of the whole story, a content analysis may degenerate into a mechanical, piecemeal approach to the evaluation of multicultural literature and result in oversimplified, unjustifiable evaluation.

Gary's (1984) study, for instance, is problematic in the way it uses the checklist to determine stereotypes. The checklist used in the study has three categories of items: physical description, language usage, and status in community. In each category there are a number of items. In the category of physical description, the following items are used to denote whether or not negative stereotyping occurred: "kinky hair, unusually wide nose, unusually big lips, fat, jolly 'mammy' type females, big feet, natural rhythm, and dress style" (p. 46). The category of language usage includes two items: sub-standard grammar and dialect. The category of status in community contains items such as "leadership," "absence of father figure in the home," "physical location of the house or structure of the house," and "negative description of the car" (p. 48). The checklist is applied to books under study to determine the frequency of occurrence of stereotypes denoted. If a character fits any item in the three category, he or she is a stereotype. This piecemeal approach results in some dubious findings. Although the study finds stereotypes in controversial books like *Ben's Trumpet* (Isadora, 1979) and *Sounder* (Armstrong, 1969), it also discovers stereotypes in some masterpieces of African American children's literature, such as *Roll of Thunder, Hear My Cry* (M. Taylor, 1976), *The Planet of Junior Brown* (Hamilton, 1971), and *M.C. Higgins, the Great* (Hamilton, 1974). According to the study, *Roll of Thunder, Hear My Cry* negatively stereotypes language usage of all the black characters and a black character's status in the community—T.J.'s stealing behavior; *The Planet of Junior Brown* shows evidence of negative stereotypes in language usage; and *M.C. Higgins, the Great* is classified as negatively stereotyped for language usage and status in the community. As the historical background, complete picture of characterization, and the artistic effect of the whole literary work are ignored in the analysis, it is not surprising for the study to come up with this kind of inaccurate, or even ridiculous, evaluation.

Another problem with content analysis is that items on the checklist may be questionable. In Cobb's (1995) study, for instance, a character analysis instrument is a list of eighty-four stereotypic adjectives such as "quiet," "cowardly," "stupid," "intelligent," "loud," "generous," "alert," "courteous," "kind," "superstitious," "very religious," "rude," "brilliant," and "honest." These adjectives are chosen to denote both positive and negative stereotypes. The author found that out of one hundred African American characters in the study, twenty-seven explicitly or implicitly show the stereotypical characteristic of being "quiet," and the stereotype "cowardly" is ascribed to twenty characters. Eight stereotypes are attributed to 10 percent or more of the African American characters. There are more positive stereotypes than negative stereotypes. Partly based on this data, the author concludes that the books in the study are generally "favorable in their treatment of the minority groups under consideration" (p. 23). No explanation is given for attributing a stereotypical characteristic trait to a specific character. It is unclear how the study coding was done. Characterization in literature is a complicated literary element. Many characters are three dimensional, not caricatures with a single characteristic trait. Furthermore, there are positive, negative, and neutral characters. These factors of characterization should be carefully considered in character analysis. How accurate is an analysis that attributes only one characteristic trait to each of one hundred characters and declare him or her a stereotype? A character may possibly fit two or more characteristics on the checklist. The possibility that two or more characteristics can be assigned to one character in a book calls into question the validity of a piecemeal analytical approach that pigeonholes characters into minutely differentiated categories.

The difficulty of assigning just one characteristic to one character is also shown in Harada's (1995) study. Her checklist for stereotyping with respect to plot development has six items, including: "Success measured by assimilation" and "Asian resolves own conflict" (p. 142). The former is an indicator of stereotyping, whereas the latter indicates nonstereotyping. Both characteristics can be attributed to the main character in a picture book included in the study, *Baseball Saved Us* (Mochizuki, 1993). The story is set in the internment camp of Japanese Americans during World War II. The main character, a Japanese boy, learned to play baseball to make life easier for himself and his family. He became highly skilled in the game and his outstanding baseball skills saved him from racist discrimination after he left the interment camp. The boy fits both the positive indicator, "Asian resolve own conflict," and the negative one, "success measured by assimilation." He solved his problem through his own painstaking efforts, but his solution is assimilation into the mainstream culture. Harada's study attributes "Asian resolves own conflict" to twenty books under study and "success measured by assimilation" to none. In discussing the findings, the author noted a stereotypical plot line in two books other than *Baseball Saved Us*. Obviously the author of the study considers the main character in *Baseball Saved Us* to be nonstereotypical.

Content analysis can appear deceivingly objective. With tabulations of figures and reported high percentages of interrater reliability, it gives the impression of objective evaluation. Actually, however, the ratings of books against a checklist, even though done by two or more evaluators, can still be subjective. Some evaluative items on the checklist may be objective indicators requiring little interpretation, such as the locale, social-economic status, profession, and education level. Other items, especially those denoting stereotypes, could be subject to various interpretations, and therefore highly subjective. In Rocha and Dowd's (1993) study, "music/dance" and "traditional Mexican hairstyle/dress" are indicators of stereotyping. Can we say any book that includes these images stereotypes Mexican Americans? Would this include Cisneros' (1994) picture book *Hair=Pelitos* or Ancona's (1995) *Fiesta*? While reporting an increase in stereotypes of music and dance, the authors of the study note that because Mexican Americans are rediscovering cultural traditions, there are more books involving music and dancing. How do we distinguish between involvement in these activities to celebrate Mexican American cultural heritage and indulgence in a propensity for amusement, which is truly stereotypical? The interpretation of the stereotypical characteristics can be controversial. In Harada's (1995) study, for another example, three picture books are cited as stereotyping Asian Americans, one for presenting a model minority character and the other two for portraying Chinese Americans as "exotic foreigners" (p. 141). The evaluation of these books is debatable. According to Yamate (1997), they do not stereotype Asian Americans. In the picture book *Nene and the Horrible Math Monster,* a Filipino American heroine is a student who excels in math. On the surface, she seems to fit the stereotype that every Asian American student excels in math, but a close look at the development of the plot shows that the story actually dispels the stereotype. Nene does not like math and is confronted with the teacher's stereotypical expectations of her as an Asian American student. Only through hard work and home tutoring does she succeed in doing well in math. Nene does not fit the stereotype of a mathematical prodigy (Yamate, 1997). The other two picture books, *Char Siu Bao Boy* and *Almond Cookies and Dragon Well Tea* feature Chinese American characters who adhere to their cultural heritage. If we identify them as "exotic foreigners," then any minority characters who try to preserve their ethnic culture also fit the stereotype. Asian Americans are often viewed as foreigners in their own countries. When the author of the study labels the characters' taste for *char siu bao* (barbecued pork bun), almond cookies, and dragon tea as exotic (Yamate, 1997), she ironically perpetuates a stereotype of Asian Americans while trying to expose it.

Content analysis is not inherently faulty as a means for evaluating multicultural literature. However, a content analysis study may be seriously flawed if its evaluation instrument is improperly designed and implemented. A potential risk lies in producing an oversimplified analysis by coding characters into predetermined categories. Inaccurate analysis may result from drawing conclusions based on the faulty data.

"OVERBURDENING" CRITICISM

In our zeal to rectify historical errors of demeaning minority cultures in literature and ensure that multicultural literature transmits culturally correct messages to children, we may unrealistically expect every multicultural book to reflect the complexity of reality or provide fundamental solutions to sociocultural issues. The imposition of unrealistic "missions" on a single multicultural book may be termed "overburdening criticism" of multicultural literature. Overburdening criticism often leads to unfair censure of multicultural books. Let us look at three popular books that I believe have been subject to overburdening criticism: *Morning Girl* (Dorris, 1992), *Encounter* (Yolen, 1992), and *Smoky Night* (Bunting, 1994).

Morning Girl, by the famous Native American writer Michael Dorris, is a lovely novella set on a Bahamian island in 1492 and focused on the relationship of a Taino boy, Star Boy, and his sister, Morning Girl. The story depicts in poetic language the family life of the Taino people and ends with Morning Girl welcoming the "white guests," the Spaniards, who has just arrived in North America. The Epilogue, a direct quote from Columbus's entry in his journal on that day, foreshadows the future domination and eventual destruction of the Taino tribe by Spanish colonists. After describing the Taino people as he saw them, Columbus wrote in the end of the entry, "They should be good and intelligent servants. . . . [A]t the time of my departure I will take six of them from here to Your Highness in order that they may learn to speak" (Dorris, 1992, p. 74). *Morning Girl* gives us a glimpse into the life of an innocent people before they are wiped out and arouses in us deep sympathy with their tragic fate. A lovely and powerful story like this, however, received a severe dose of overburdening criticism. Bigelow (1994) wrote:

A critical multiculturalism needs to invite children to draw inspiration from historical struggles against oppression. . . . Knowledge of the Taino response to Spanish colonialism could help students locate themselves as part of a tradition of caring and commitment. . . . It may be unfair to criticize Dorris for ending his book a few years earlier, but his was one of only two children's stories about these events published during the Quincentenary, and concerning resistance to Columbus et al., the book is *a partner in silence.* (p. 275, my italics)

The charge that Dorris does not portray the Taino people's resistance to Spanish colonialism is typical overburdening criticism, which demands too much from a multicultural book. If Dorris set the story before Spanish domination of Taino people, how can he possibly show their struggle? If we demand that every multicultural book include resistance to oppression, then many books can be accused of being "partners in silence." We might express regret that Dorris did not write a story portraying the Taino people as fighters in addition to writing *Morning Girl*, which shows them as victims. That would be more logical and reasonable.

Bigelow also accused Dorris of failing to portray the community life of the Taino and the social responsibilities of their children. He commented that the two children enjoyed a freedom largely cut off from the community. He went on to say that "Dorris's desire to tell a simpler brother/sister story is understandable, but he does so at the expense of suggesting how a richer community life could nurture such a relationship" (p. 274). These charges, again, are examples of overburdening criticism, of demanding too much from a book. Why should Dorris write about the community life if he chose to focus on family life? If the story is successful on a small scale, that should be sufficient.

Encounter (Yolen, 1992) is another imaginary account of the Taino people's initial encounter with Spanish colonialists. A Taino boy has had a vision of "strangers from the sky" invading the Taino people's territory and warned his tribe not to welcome them. Unfortunately, his people fail to heed his warning and treat Columbus and his followers as guests. At the end of the story the boy, now an old man, laments: "So it was we lost our lands to the strangers from the sky. We gave our souls to their gods. We took their speech into our mouths, forgetting our own" (n.p.). While acknowledging that *Encounter* is the "most exciting and useful of multicultural books produced during the Quincentenary," Bigelow (1994) criticized it for "skipping over decades of colonial theft, slavery, and brutality—and indigenous resistance, which persists to this day" (p. 273). He comments: "True, she's [Yolen] writing a children's book, which no one expects to be an encyclopedia of popular resistance. Still, Yolen could and should have included something, *anything,* to indicate that the Tainos did not passively accept their fate" (p. 272). This criticism is not fair to the book. The story actually implies a message about resistance. The Taino boy does not trust "the strangers from the sky" and indeed tells the elders to reject them. This is resistance from the very beginning of encountering Columbus. His warning to all people in the world is also about resistance, or the consequences of nonresistance. "If you do not resist them in the beginning," he seems to say, "you will suffer a fate similar to ours." The old man's monologue may sound like "self-blame," but it is definitely not passive acceptance of defeat, as Bigelow suggests. Since the story is the boy's first-person narrative, it is only natural that even in his old age he still feels strongly about his warning being lost on deaf ears.

What is more questionable about the overburdening criticism of *Encounter* is the demand that the book include some reference to popular resistance. In his criticism of *Morning Girl* and *Encounter,* Bigelow seems to require every multicultural book about interracial tension to include some reference to popular resistance; otherwise its reflection of reality is incomplete and does not meet the standards of critical multiculturalism. Historically, the Tainos fought bravely against Spanish colonialism. As Bigelow mentions in his article, they attacked Columbus's men at La Navidad in 1493, refused to plant crops for the Spaniards, and waged guerrilla warfare against them. Their resistance should be reflected in literature, but it is not necessary, or possible, to refer to it in every book about the Tainos' interaction with the Spaniards. If some reference to the resistance were interpolated into *Morning Girl* and *Encounter,* disregarding their plots, they would become more like formulaic stories.

Smoky Night also deals with the subject of interracial interaction but is set in the present time, against the background of a riot on the street. It tells how two families, one Korean American and the other Hispanic American, make friends during the riot. Before the riot, they did not get along; even their cats were not on good terms with each other. The night of the riot, ironically, brings them and their cats together. The story shows that if people reach out to each other, mutual understanding and even friendship may be achieved. *Smoky Night* was initially greeted with high acclaim—it was awarded the Caldecott medal—and then received severe criticism as well. First, the story was criticized for not including whites in the racial conflicts and for stereotyping blacks as violent rioters (Albers, 1996). This criticism is not well grounded. The text does not include any reference to the racial background of the rioters. The illustrations, especially the picture illustrating the robbery of the shoe store, show rioters of different races, although it is not easy to identify their exact race. In defense of her book, Eve Bunting (1998) writes: "There was no one group who was the bad guy—we were all guilty for that happening. There were Blacks, Whites, Mexicans, and Asians among the rioters. They were all there and I didn't single out anyone; I think we all should equally share the blame" (p. 24). What she says is true, as evidenced in the book. Other charges brought against *Smoky Night* are that: "it does not capture the complexities of the situation" and gives "no sense of *why* people living in this area rioted" (Albers, 1996, p. 276); it "oversimplifies the difficulty of living in a multicultural society . . . and denies any sort of social reason behind the riots" (Kutzer, 1996, p. 1); it preaches an incorrect message to victims of racial oppression, that "the means for solving their problems lie within them—either by hoping or by getting along with each other" (Hade, 1996, para 3). To the best of my knowledge, *Smoky Night* may be the only picture book about the Los Angeles riot. Admittedly, it does not take the reader into the center of the storm to offer some explanation of how the riot happened, but does every book about the riot have to address all the issues that the critics raise? The book definitely does not explain the complexity of the riot and the difficulty of living in a multicultural society, but to demand that explanation in a picture book may be asking too much. Can a book, especially one for children, deal with just a small aspect of the riot? Should we tell authors that if they cannot address the fundamental issues involved in the riot, they must write about something else? Of course, "getting along with each other" is not a fundamental resolution for racial tension, but it is a part of a resolution. If we try to know each other, perhaps we can avoid some racial problems or ease racial tensions (like the alienation between the Korean American and Hispanic American families), even if it cannot prevent riots from happening again. It is a significant theme, so I would argue that failure to offer a fundamental solution in the book is a limitation rather than a fault of the work. At the same time, if book after book offers only one solution again and again, then children may get the impression that this is the only solution. I think it is the teacher's responsibility to help children to see the limitations of books like *Smoky Night*.

We need more multicultural books that tackle fundamental social, and cultural issues, but we should not criticize a book, especially a picture book, for not doing so. A book that does not address fundamental issues or offer visions of drastic social changes can still be a good book, if not a great one. Many books are criticized for oversimplifying complicated social issues and providing simplistic solutions. This kind of overburdening criticism actually oversimplifies the complicated issue of literary analysis and results in simplistic, often unfair, evaluations of multicultural books. Rather than criticizing authors for not addressing fundamental issue and providing correct solutions to them, it would be more helpful to discuss how to do so in a creative, meaningful way that is understandable to children. In discussing *Smoky Night,* Hendrickson (1996) asks: "How could one write a children's picture book that could convey the complexities behind such issues as the Los Angeles riot, homelessness, and the attempted annihilation of Native Americans?" How can we "make the link between the personal and the political at a child's level?" (para. 7). We may not be pleased with many multicultural books dealing with social-cultural issues, but criticizing them for not being what they were not meant to be does not seem reasonable or convincing. Critical multiculturalism should be promoted, but overburdening criticism does not help to forward the cause. On the contrary, it could have adverse effects on the creation of multicultural literature, discouraging authors from writing about thorny social-cultural issues and making them turn to easier tasks like retelling folktales.

We hope multicultural literature about an ethnic group can reflect its complex reality and provide solutions to its social-cultural problems, but we cannot expect one book to do it all. Picture books in particular cannot encompass multiple aspects of a culture. It is reasonable, however, to expect authors to provide a more complete picture of a culture in their body of literary creations. When commenting on books about Mexican Americans, Rocha and Dowd (1993) argue for a balanced portrayal of Mexicans in children's books. In their opinion, children's books that realistically represent the Mexican American lifestyle should

portray variety in Mexican American families in terms of number of children and income (rather than depicting solely large, impoverished Mexican-American families with two parents) [and] should include Mexican-American female characters from all age groups in diversified roles, such as members of team sports or the school's Mariachi band. [Women should be presented] not only in traditional roles (cooking or keeping house) but also in nontraditional roles (such as a school P.T.A. official, police officer, mail carrier, or lawyer), since many females of Mexican descent do indeed hold such positions. (p. 62)

As they interpret it, realistic or authentic representation means accurate reflection of the "contemporary demographic and research data" of Mexican-Americans (p. 65). They do not, however, suggest that a single piece of literature about Mexican Americans should cover every aspect of the Mexican American lifestyle. Rather, they expect that books about Mexican Americans should *collectively* give a more complete picture of this ethnic group's experience. This kind of critical approach may help prevent overburdening criticism.

EMBEDDING CULTURAL CRITICISM IN CLOSE LITERARY ANALYSIS

When critiquing multicultural literature, we are urged to pay attention to "extra-literary concerns," meaning the sociocultural implications of a book (Sims Bishop, 1994; Harris, 1997). The sociocultural aspects of a book are extremely important and cannot be overemphasized. However, we may evaluate them *in addition to* the evaluation of its literary elements, as if cultural criticism were an add-on. Even the term "extra-literary concerns" may be misleading, for it suggests that cultural criticism is extra to the discussion of literary quality rather than integral to it. If cultural criticism is not imbedded in a close literary analysis of a book, it tends to look at the cultural aspects in isolation and picks up what does not meet preconceived notions of cultural correctness without examining them in the context of the whole text. It is very easy to label a book culturally insensitive or even racist by singling out culturally unacceptable aspects, without closely analyzing the whole book. In the previous sections of this chapter, we have seen how this kind of simplistic criticism ends in unconvincing and unfair evaluations of literary work, and may reinforce the misconception that cultural criticism should "take a further and still more dangerous step from literature-as-morality to literature-as propaganda" (Townsend, cited in Thomas and Woodard, 1985).

Any multicultural book, even controversial ones by outsider authors, deserves close examination before it is dismissed as culturally incorrect or even racist. *Huckleberry Finn* has been discussed and debated for a long time, and no consensus has been achieved regarding whether it is racist or antiracist. Even black critics are divided on this controversial book. In *Satire or Evasion? Black Perspectives on Huckleberry Finn* (Leonard, Tenney, and Davis, 1992), for example, sixteen black scholars express views that "exemplify the range of possible responses—from admiration to adamant opposition—and demonstrate, not surprisingly, no single position on *Huckleberry Finn* any more than there is a monolithic white one" (p. 10). Despite their differences, there is one thing in common among the scholars: they base their judgment on close analysis of the text and historical context. Perhaps no book for children or young adults, can aspire to the status of a masterpiece like *Huckleberry Finn.* Harper Lee's (1960) *To Kill a Mockingbird* may be the only exception. To be fair to all authors, whether masters or lesser ones, insiders or outsiders, all works deserve a close literary analysis like the one that has been conferred on *Huckleberry Finn.* More conversations and exchanges of opinions that are conducive to the fair judgment of a book should be encouraged.

Unlike in a social document, an author's views are usually not explicitly stated in a literary text, but rather are suggested by various implied perspectives. In the novel, "there are four main perspectives: those of the narrator, the characters, the plot, and the fictitious reader," or the intended reader (Iser, 1978, p. 5). These perspectives form a network of "schematized views," which is complex and not easy to assess. Reader response theorists hold that there is not only one reading of a book, because different readers may come up with a different configuration of these "schematized views." If we accept these premises of reader response theory, we will be more open to different opinions on controversial books and will look at all the perspectives implied in the literary elements more closely before we make a final judgment on a book.

A close analysis of the perspectives aims at yielding a unified meaning for them. This may be common knowledge in literary criticism, but in debates over multicultural books, more often than not, some perspectives are emphasized to the neglect of others, as a result of selective attention. People who are critical of a novel often underline the negative aspects while those who defend it highlight the positive ones, with both groups unwilling or unable to examine perspectives that are at odds with their own. In the politically tense and emotionally charged debates over controversial multicultural books, it is especially important to carefully weigh and consider all perspectives, explicit and implicit, to make a valid evaluation of a book.

Take the controversial novel *The Cay* (Taylor, 1969) for example, which stereotypes black people. This criticism would not be very convincing if we simply singled out the negative image of Timothy as an ugly, subservient old black man without taking into consideration other aspects of the novel. The author may object that he creates the negative image because he wants to destroy it. The following is the actual answer to this charge from the author of *The Cay:*

As a matter of story construction and nothing else, I purposely made Timothy facially ugly to enable what I thought would be an important change later on. To be blunt, had I made Timothy beautiful when Phillip awakened on that raft, I could see no valid reason for marked reaction or for the hateful fires of prejudice to be refueled. Timothy's appearance simply reinforced the position planted by Phillip's mother. (Taylor, 1975, p. 286)

In a recent attempt to defend the novel, Pinsent (1997) resorts to the literary device of the unreliable narrator. He contends that Phillip is an unreliable narrator and that the reader may misread him, thus perceiving the racist idea that black people are ugly, dirty, and less intelligent than whites without recognizing Phillip's growth in understanding Timothy's qualities. For the criticism of the stereotype to be sustained, it has to be proved that the author has not successfully destroyed the vicious stereotype in the development of the plot and that Phillip, the narrator, does not really grow in understanding Timothy. In Iser's terms, the perspective implied in the negative image of the main character should be assessed along with the perspectives implied in the plot and the narrator.

Whether the old black man, Timothy, is a subservient servant to the white boy, Phillip, or a self-sacrificing hero who brings Phillip to understand and respect him as a man of dignity depends on whether Philip substantively changes his racist attitude toward Timothy and rejects his mother's blatant racism. But that does not happen in the end. Philip may be grateful to Timothy for saving his life and may have learned some survival skills from him, but does he substantively change his racist attitude toward him? After Timothy dies, Phillip cries for a long time and then buries him. At Timothy's grave, he says: "Thank you, Timothy. Take care of him, God, he is good to me. . . . There didn't seem to be anything else to say, so I just stood by his grave for a while" (p. 115). Timothy's death can be seen as the climax in the plot line, a crucial moment in Phillip's relationship with Timothy on the island. If he had really grown to understand Timothy as a dignified, loving old man, Phillip could have said something more, showing that he has forsaken his racist notion of Timothy, or, in an interior monologue, might question his and his mother's racist attitudes toward Timothy or at least wonder why Timothy wants to protect him. The logic of the plot would dictate that the boy should be puzzled or surprised by the love and care he receives from someone his mother has taught him to disdain and hate. With no actions like these on Phillip's part, the gratitude he expresses to Timothy amounts to little more than a master's reaction toward a loyal slave who died so that he can live. If he had said that he was "a good man," it would sound much better than saying he was "good to me," which reflects a self-centered, condescending attitude.

Another crucial point in the story is the ending. In the end, the author suggests, through Phillip's actions, that his attitude toward black people has substantively changed: Phllip has spent a lot of time talking to the black people; he likes the sound of their voices and feels close to them. This "perspective of the plot" seems to imply that Phillip has finally formed a "brotherhood" with black people. However, when viewed in the context of the whole story, Phillip's actions, at the most, indicate a friendly gesture toward black people, rather than a close relationship with them. "Brotherhood" subsumes mutual understanding, respect, and love. When he goes blind after the shipwreck, Phillip has to rely on Timothy for survival. We see how Timothy cares for and protects him like a faithful servant does for his master. Phillip seems to be close to Timothy and even allows Timothy to call him by his first name, but we find no explicit or implicit evidence of substantive change in his racial attitude. He is grateful to Timothy, but gratitude alone does not constitute brotherhood. If Phillip truly loved and respected Timothy after he returned home, he would try to ask the black people for information about Timothy's past. When he tells the captain who picked him up from the cay about his experience with Timothy, he is "not sure the captain believed any of it" (p. 134). But Phillip does not insist that he told the truth, let alone showing the captain Timothy's grave on the island. Later, he also tells his parents about Timothy, but he feels that "neither of them really understood what had happened on our cay" (p. 136). Again, Phillip does not try to argue with them and expresses no anger at their apathy. It is doubtful that he has forged a close tie with black people. His parents' deep-rooted prejudice against black people is such that they show no emotion for the black man who sacrificed himself to save their son's life. The author does not take this opportunity to condemn racism by having Phillip trying to reason with his parents to make them change their attitude toward black people even just a little bit. Admittedly, Phillip has changed somewhat, but not substantively so. As Dixon (1977) points out, "At the end we're expected to believe that Phillip is a changed character but it obviously doesn't go very deep" (p. 115). Since we do not see a fundamental change of

Phillip's perspective on black people, the horrible negative image of Timothy has not been reversed.

After examining the "schematized views" implied in the literary elements of the novel, we may conclude that Timothy is a typical stereotype of black people, at both the beginning and the end of the book. The story fails to bring out his humanity and dignity beyond the stereotypical image. Even the author has to admit: "I had hoped that Timothy would emerge as a beautiful man. Obviously, for some, I failed" (Taylor, 1975, p. 287).

Pinsent (1997) argues that there are subtle shades of meaning in *The Cay* and other controversial stories. If we do not read the story closely, we may miss those meanings. Although I cannot accept his reading of *The Cay,* I concur with his proposition that we should pay close attention to the subtle, implicit meanings of a literary text. We would do better in debates over controversial books if we tried harder to uncover the "subtle shades of meaning"; our criticism would be more fair and convincing. Pinsent (1997) also makes the important point that "the child reader needs to be educated to become aware of the more subtle shades of meaning involved in a mature reading of such a text" (p. 94). I think his state-ment applies to adult readers, too.

CULTURAL CORRECTNESS AND READER RESPONSE THEORY

From the perspective of reader response theory, a story may have more than one interpretation because different readers bring different cultural backgrounds, ex-periences, knowledge, values, beliefs, personalities, and perspectives to the transac-tion with the text. This accounts for disagreements over the interpretation and evaluation of a literary work. A book on somebody's recommended list could be severely criticized by another person for being culturally incorrect. If readers' re-sponses to a book are often unpredictable and varied, then how can it be possible to apply the criteria for cultural correctness? Whose interpretation and evaluation of a book's cultural correctness count?

Although reader response theorists such as Rosenblatt and Iser emphasize the reader's role in the interpretation of literary works, they do not claim that any read-ing is adequate and acceptable. The text is not "mainly a point of departure for the critic's 'self-expression'" (Rosenblatt, 1978). Rosenblatt (1978) offers "two prime criteria of validity": "the reader's interpretation not be contradicted by any element of the text, and that nothing be projected for which there is no verbal basis" (p. 115). While we cannot predict what a reader will make of a text, we can turn to the text to judge whether his or her interpretation will meet the two criteria. In my analysis of *The Cay*, I point out that Pinsent's positive evaluation of the story con-tradicts some elements of the text. It is natural and normal to argue over whether an interpretation is substantiated by textual evidence, especially when a complicated story like *The Cay* is involved. But if our interpretation includes "responses to the total text" (Rosenblatt, 1978, p. 128) and is not limited to a personal emotional experience of it, we'd have a better chance to achieve agreement on the evaluation of a story's cultural correctness. The likelihood of agreement increases in the case of a less complicated story, because it is easier to agree on the textual evidence. For example, it would be hard to claim that the popular picture book *Tikki Tikki Tembo* (Mosel, 1968) is culturally correct. This folktale recounts how the Chinese came to give their children short names. It is supposed to be a Chinese folktale, but both the text and illustrations show that it is not. The story alleges that the ancient Chinese had long names, like the main character's: "tikki tikki tembo-no sa embochari bri ruchi-pip peri pemo." This name does not sound like Chinese, ancient or modern. As portrayed in illustrations, the buildings, the dress, and hairdo of the lady, and the clogs worn by children are in the Japanese rather than Chinese style. Once the inaccuracies are pointed out, few could argue that the book is culturally correct, even though the story is very interesting and enjoyable.

The 1942 Newbery winner *Matchlock Gun* (Edmonds, 1941) provides another example. The story stereotypes Native Americans as violent savages prowling around to attack white people and burn down their houses. When they menacingly approach the house of the Van Alstynes, we are told: "There were five of them, dark shapes on the road, coming from the brick house. They are hardly like men, the way they moved. They were trotting, stooped over, first one and then another coming up like dogs sifting up to the scent of food" (Edmonds, 1941, p. 39). Young Edward fires the huge matchlock gun and kills three Indians. He is portrayed as a hero who courageously protected his family against a bunch of terrifying savages. Unlike Wilder's *The Little House on the Prarie*, the demeaning description of American Indians seen from the white settlers' perspective in this book is not mitigated by any alternative view of American Indians. As Seale pointed out, "No reason is given for the Native attack on this decent and appealing little family, which makes it all the more horrible, all the more savage" (Slapin and Seale, 1998, p. 9). If the book were published today, it probably would not win the Newbery award. On the contrary, it is more likely that it would be castigated as an example of contributing a brazenly stereotypical view of Native Americans. Some people may still defend the book on the ground of its vivid and evocative writing, but I believe it is difficult to claim that the book is culturally correct and cite textual evidence to support the assertion.

Some literature from history, like *The Matchlock Gun,* that was not challenged, or even highly acclaimed in the past is now rejected because its text contains blatant stereotypes. One may ask, "Why did the Newbery committee ignore the plain evidence of racist depiction in this book at that time?" Obviously, the committee did not think the depiction was racist or offensive to Native Americans. In the 1940s, many educators, librarians, and critics did not find it racist. What is deemed racist now was often acceptable then. The 1942 Newbery winner gets new reviews today because criteria for judging racial bias and prejudice have changed. Even the Declaration of Independence has been reinterpreted. Before slavery was abolished, African Americans were regarded as subhuman or nonhuman. The statement that all men are created equal did not apply to them. For a long time it did not apply to Native Americans, other ethnic minorities, or women, either. Now the term "men" in the statement covers all those historically neglected groups because, as a result of civil rights and women's movements, people's notion of democracy has changed.

According to Rosenblatt (1978), in the process of evoking a literary work from the text, readers pay selective attention to different parts of the text and synthesize them into the "work-as-experienced." While "the text presents limits or controls. . .

personality and culture brought by the reader constitutes another type of limitation on the resultant synthesis" (Rosenblatt, 1978, p. 129). In the evaluation of cultural correctness, if critics bring similar cultural values and perspectives to the text, it would be more likely for them to see the same textual evidence and achieve agreement. Very often, however, this is not the case. Many problematic multicultural books are criticized only by critics of parallel cultures who can see textual evidence of cultural incorrectness in them. When writers from the mainstream culture want to write about parallel cultures, it is imperative, for them to take on the perspective of those cultures so that they can create culturally correct literature. I would contend that critics from the mainstream culture also need to take on the perspective of parallel cultures in order to identify textual evidence that is culturally incorrect.

CONCLUDING THOUGHTS

It is generally acknowledged that literature performs two functions: to entertain and to instruct. Educators and parents are particularly concerned with its function of instruction and put a premium on the moral values of children's literature, for it transmits images, ideas, beliefs, attitudes, and values that will be, consciously or unconsciously, absorbed by the impressionable young readers. Racial bias and prejudices have been instilled in children's minds by books as well as other media. Authors who create multicultural literature for children and young adults make "a move in the direction of culture maintenance or culture change" (MacCann, 1998, p. xiv). They have the social responsibility to ensure their works are culturally correct. Anyone who is concerned with the moral correctness of children's books should also be concerned with their cultural correctness. In the final analysis, what is culturally wrong is also morally wrong.

Viewed in the context of cultural wars, culturally incorrect works help to perpetuate unjust social systems, whether the author intends it or not. However, some authors deny their social responsibility. For example, Canadian author Jean Little (1990) says: "I do not believe that writers have a responsibility to society. I believe our only responsibility is to be faithful to the vision each of us is given, however fragmentary and imperfect, of the book which has claimed us as its writer" (p. 79). But I believe that most authors accept their social responsibility and are committed to promoting mutual understanding among diverse cultures. Many of the authors whose works have been criticized for racial prejudices may have good intentions but unconsciously turn out culturally incorrect works. It is likely that while these authors are trying to present a positive view, their "unexamined assumptions" and "subliminal biases" (Pinsent, 1997, p. 159) about ethnic minorities and other groups of people have surfaced in their works. If authors accept their social responsibility and are well intentioned, they should be cautious in making literary choices and more open-minded when faced with criticism. Actually, as Taxel (1995) observed, "there is a new cautiousness . . . born of a new-found respect that the parties feel when writing about the experiences of historically oppressed and powerless groups" (p. 158).

Well-intentioned outsider authors need convincing and constructive criticism from critics to help them create culturally correct works. Simplistic, doctrinal criticism may discourage respectful outsiders from writing multicultural literature. Just as outsider authors need to continuously improve the quality of their writing, so do critics need to improve the quality of their criticism. Outsider authors' important role in multicultural literature should be acknowledged. Writing from outside a culture, they may provide a perspective different from the insider authors, and their perspective may be easier for children of the mainstream culture to identify with. When they have children of the mainstream culture as their intended audience, which is often the case, they can interpret cultural differences for the intended audience and help them understand an unfamiliar culture. For example, Staples' (1989) *Shabanu: Daughter of the Wind,* an outsider account about Pakistan, would be easier for American children to understand than a book written by a Pakistani author intended for the children of Pakistan.

In the interest of multiculturalism, the standard of cultural correctness should be firmly upheld, but it should not be used as a means to exclude outsider authors. The ultimate goal for multiculturalism is to remove cultural barriers and achieve cultural rapport. A culture should not encapsulate itself, but it should open its door to well-intentioned outsiders who sincerely want to learn about and identify with it. Julius Lester (quoted in Temple et al., 1998) drives home this point when he succinctly states:

The imagination is the empathetic bridge between cultures. Instead of placing barriers around a culture and denying others permission to enter, we should be thankful that someone from outside our culture is interested, is curious, wants to learn, wants to feel a sense of belonging with us. As long as the outsider respects the culture, there is no harm. . . . One can regard his or her culture as a private reserve or as an offering. It is my hope that the people will choose the latter. (p. 96)

REFERENCES

Albers, P. (1996). Issues of representation: Caldecott gold medal winners 1984-1995. *The New Advocate 9* (4), 297-308.

Atleo, M. et al. (1999). Books to avoid: *My heart is on the ground.* 112 paragraphs. Available on-line at http://www.oyate.org.

Banfield, B. (1998). Commitment to change: The Council on Interracial Books for Children and the world of children's books. *African American Review, 32* (1), 17-22.

Bigelow, B. (1994). Good intentions are not enough: Children's literature in the aftermath of the Quincentenary. *The New Advocate, 7* (4), 265-279.

Booklist (1999). Review. *Booklist, 45* (4), 141.

Booth, W. C. (1988). *The company we keep: An ethics of fiction.* Berkeley: University of California Press.

Bunting, E. (1998). Reflections. In J. E. Brown and E. C. Stephens (Eds.), *United in diversity: Using multicultural young adult literature in the classroom* (pp. 23-26). Urbana, IL: National Council of Teachers of English Press.

Cobb, Jeanne B. (1995). *Images and stereotypes of African Americans and Hispanic Americans in contemporary children's fiction.* (ERIC Document Reproduction Service No. Ed 392 062).

Dixon, B. (1977). *Catching them young: Sex, race and class in children's literature.* London: Pluto.

Eagleton, T. (1983). *Literary theory: An introduction.* Minneapolis: University of Minnesota Press.

Gary, D. C. (1984). *A study of black characters in Caldecott and Newbery award and honor books for children.* Unpublished doctoral dissertation, Jackson State University.

Greenfield, E. (1985). Writing for children—A joy and a responsibility. In D. MacCann and G. Woodard (eds.), *The black American in books for children: Readings in racism* (pp. 19-22). Metuchen, NJ: The Scarecrow Press.

Hade, D. (1996, October 16). Child lit listserv discussion archive. 4 Paragraphs. Available on-line at http://www.dalton.org/libraries/ fairrosa/ disc/smoky_ night.html.

Harada, V. H. (1995). Issues of ethnicity, authenticity, and quality in Asian-American picture books, 1983-93. *Youth Service in Libraries, 46* (3), 135-149.

Harris, V. (1990). From Little Black Sambo to Popo and Fifina: Arna Bontemps and the creation of African American children's literature. *The Lion and the Unicorn, 14* (10), 108-127.

Harris, V. (1994). Book review. *Journal of Reading Behavior, 26* (1), 117-120.

Harris, V. (1996). Continuing dilemmas, debates, and delights in multicultural literature. *The New Advocate, 9* (2), 107-122.

Harris, V. (Ed.). (1997). *Using multiethnic literature in the K–8 classroom.* Norwood, MA: Christopher-Gordon.

Hendrickson, L. M. (1996, October 16). Child Lit Listserv discussion archive. 10 Paragraphs. Available on-line at http://www.dalton.org/libraries/ fairrosa/disc/ smoky_ night.html.

Henry, P. (1992). The struggle for tolerance: Race and censorship in *Huckleberry Finn.* In J. S. Leonard, T. A. Tenney, and T. M. Davis (Eds.), *Satire or evasion: Black perspectives on Huckleberry Finn* (pp. 25-48). Durham, NC: Duke University Press.

Hopkins, D., and Tastad, S. A. (1997). Censoring by omission: Has the United States progressed in promoting diversity through children's books? *Youth Services in Libraries, 10* (4), 399-404.

Iser, W. (1978). *The act of reading: A theory of aesthetic response.* Baltimore, MD: Johns Hopkins University Press.

Jay, G. S. (1997). Not born on the fourth of July: Cultural differences and American studies. In L. Brannon and B. M. Greene (eds.), *Rethinking American literature* (pp. 3-31). Urbana, IL: National Council of Teachers of English Press.

Kutzer, D. (Oct. 15, 1996). Child Lit Listserv discussion archive. Available on-line at http://www.dalton.org/libraries/fairrosa/disc/smoky_night._html.

Leonard, J. S., Tenney, T. A., and Davis, T. M. (Eds.). (1992). *Satire or evasion: Black perspectives on Huckleberry Finn.* Durham, NC: Duke University Press.

Little, J. (1990). A writer's social responsibility. *The New Advocate, 3* (2), 79-88.

MacCann, D. (1998). *White supremacy in children's literature: Characterizations of African Americans, 1830-1900.* New York: Garland.

McClure, A. (1995). Censorship of children's books. In S. Lehr (Ed.), *Battling dragons: Issues and controversy in children's literature* (pp. 3-30). Portsmouth, NH: Heinemann.

Mikkelsen, N. (1999). *Words and pictures: Lessons in children's literature and literacies.* Boston: McGraw Hill.

Nodelman, P. (1996). *The pleasures of children's literature* (2nd ed.). White Plains, NY: Longman.

Pang, V. O., Colvin, C., Tran, M., and Barba, R. H. (1992). Beyond chopsticks and dragons: Selecting Asian-American literature for children. *The Reading Teacher, 46* (3), 216-224.

Paterson, K. (1994). Cultural politics from a writer's point of view. *The New Advocate, 7* (2), 85-92.

Pinsent, P. (1997). *Children's literature and the politics of equality.* New York: Teachers College Press.

Ricker-Wilson, C. (1998). When the mockingbird becomes an albatross: Reading and resistance in the language arts classroom. *English Journal, 87* (2), 67-72.

Rocha, O. J., and Dowd, F. S. (1993). Are Mexican American females portrayed realistically in fiction for grades K-3? A content analysis. *Multicultural Review, 2* (4), 60-69.

Rochman, H. (1993). *Against borders: Promoting books for a multicultural world.* Chicago: ALA/Booklist Publication.

Rosenblatt, L. M. (1978). *The reader, the text, the poem: Transactional theory of the literary work.* Carbondale: Southern Illinois University Press.

Sims Bishop, R. S. (Ed.). (1994). *Kaleidoscope: A multicultural booklist for grades K-8.* Urbana, IL: National Council of Teachers of English Press.

Slapin, B. and Seale, D. (Eds.). (1998). *Through Indian eyes: The Native experience in books for children.* Philadelphia: New Society.

Stevens. C. (1999). Con-Huck Finn. 6 Paragraphs. Available on-line at http://phnet.esuhsd.org/legend/features/huck.con.html.

Sutton, R. (1992). What means we, white man? *School Library Journal, 37* (3), 155-158.

Taxel, J. (1986). The black experience in children's fiction: Controversies surrounding award-winning books. *Curriculum Inquiry, 16* (3), 245-281.

Taxel, J. (1995). Cultural politics and writing for young people. In S. Lehr (Ed.), *Battling dragons: Issues and controversy in children's literature* (pp. 155-169). Portsmouth, NH: Heinemann.

Taylor, T. (1975). A letter to the editor. *Top of the News, 31* (3), 284-288.

Temple, C., Martinez, M., Yokota, J., and Naylor, A. (1998). *Children's books in children's hands: An introduction to their literature.* Boston: Allyn and Bacon.

Thomas, J. and Woodard, G. (1985). Black perspective in books for children. In D. MacCann and G. Woodard (Eds.), *The black experience in books for children: Readings in racism* (pp. 39-51). Metuchen, NJ: Scarecrow.

Trousdale, A. M. (1990). A submission theology for black Americans: Religion and social action in prize-winning children's books about the black experience in America. *Research in the Teaching of English, 24* (2), 117-140.

Wallace, J. H. (1992). The case against *Huck Finn.* In J. S. Leonard, T. A. Tenney, and T. M. Davis (Eds.), *Satire or evasion: Black perspectives on Huckleberry Finn* (pp. 16-24). Durham, NC: Duke University Press.

Yamate, S. S. (1997). Asian Pacific American children's literature: Expanding perceptions about who Americans are. In V. Harris (Ed.), *Using multiethnic literature in the K-8 classroom* (pp. 95-128). Norwood, MA: Christopher-Gordon.

Books for Children and Young Adults

Ancona, G. (1995). *Fiesta.* New York: Lodestar.

Armstrong, W. H. (1969). *Sounder.* New York: Harper & Row.

Bruchac, J. (1998). *The heart of a chief: A novel.* New York: Dial.

Bunting, E. (1994). *Smoky night.* Ill. by D. Diaz. San Diego, CA: Harcourt Brace.

Chin-Lee, C. (1993). *Almond cookies and dragon well tea.* Ill. by Y. S. Tang. Chicago: Polychrome.

Cisneros, S. (1994). *Hair=pelitos.* New York: Knopf.

Curtis, C. P. (1999). *Bud, not buddy.* New York: Delacorte.

Dorris, M. (1992). *Morning girl.* New York: Hyperion.

Edmonds, W. D. (1941). *The matchlock gun.* Ill. by P. Lantz. New York: Dodd, Mead and Company.

Fox, P. (1973). *The slave dancer.* New York: Bantam Doubleday Dell.

Hamilton, V. (1971). *The planet of Junior Brown.* New York: Macmillan.

Hamilton, V. (1974). *M. C. Higgins, the great.* New York: Macmillan.

Hamilton, V. (1983). *Willie Bea and the Time the Martians Landed.* New York: Greenwillow.

Hurston, Z. N. (1969). *Their eyes were watching God.* New York: Negro Universities Press.

Isadora, R. (1979). *Ben's trumpet.* New York: Greenwillow.

Lee, H. (1960). *To kill a mockingbird.* Philadelphia: J. B. Lippincott.

Martinez, V. (1996). *Parrot in the oven: Mi vida: A novel.* New York: HarperCollins.

Matas, C. (1993). *Sworn enemies.* New York: Bantam.

Mochizuki, K. (1993). *Baseball saved us.* Ill. by D. Lee. New York: Lee and Low.

Morrison, T. (1972). *The bluest eye.* New York: Washington Square Press.

Mosel, A. (1968). *Tikki Tikki Tembo.* New York: Holt, Rinehart and Winston.

Myers, W. D. (1992). *Somewhere in the darkness.* New York: Scholastic.

Paterson, K. (1988). *Park's quest.* New York: Lodestar Books.

Rinaldi, A. (1999). *My heart is on the ground: The diary of Nannie Little Rose, a Sioux girl.* New York: Scholastic.

Staples, S. F. (1989). *Shabanu: Daughter of the wind.* New York: Knopf.

Taylor, M. D. (1976). *Roll of thunder, hear my cry.* New York: Dial.

Taylor, T. (1969). *The cay.* New York: Doubleday.

Villanueva, M. (1993). *Nene and the horrible math monster.* Ill. by R. Unson. Chicago: Polychrome.

Walker, A. (1982). *The color purple.* New York: Pocket Book.

Yamate, S. S. (1991). *Char siu bao boy.* Ill. by J. M. W. Jenkin. Chicago: Polychrome.

Yep, L. (1975). *Dragonwings.* New York: HarperCollins.

Yolen, J. (1992). *Encounter.* Ill. by D. Shannon. San Diego, CA: Harcourt Brace Jovanovich.

Part III

Issues Related to the Use of Multicultural

Literature in Education

7

Crossing Cultural Borders

Writers and educators agree that reading multicultural literature can help people cross cultural borders to achieve mutual understanding and intercultural harmony. As Pat Mora (1998) points out, to ease ethnic tensions, literature can be put to work as an art form that "moves readers to hear another human's voice, and thus to experience the doubts, fears, and joys of a person who may not look or sound at all like us" (p. 283). But there is no consensus on the best way to use multicultural literature for that purpose. Different approaches have been used to facilitate border crossing. These differences give rise to issues regarding the selection, evaluation, and use of multicultural books. What books best facilitate border crossing? Do books that focus on the unique experience of a culture impose isolation on it and exclude other cultures? How do we help children read multicultural books in a way that connects them to each other? Before we discuss those issues, we need to define the term cultural borders.

DEFINING CULTURAL BORDERS

Cultural borders are demarcation lines that separate one culture from another. According to Corliss (1998), there are three kinds of borders: physical borders, cultural borders, and inner borders. The term cultural borders as I use it includes all three categories, which I adapt from Corliss with some modifications. Cultural borders can be physical or geographical. When people enter into Chinatown, an Indian reservation, or a foreign country to explore the culture there, they actually cross a physical borderline. The second kind of cultural border, which I call a "difference border," is marked by cultural differences in terms of beliefs, values, experiences, history, and tradition. If we are able to understand and appreciate what is unique about another culture, we cross borders of cultural differences. The third cultural border, the inner border, exists in our minds. Our inner border can be marked by negative feelings such as fear, bias, or prejudice, which keep us from understanding and appreciating the cultures of other people.

When we overcome these factors to connect positively to another culture, we cross the inner cultural borders.

Cultural borders are frequently portrayed in multicultural literature. When we read multicultural literature, we get to know about them and experience crossing them vicariously. For example, in *Maniac Magee* (Spinelli, 1990), we see physical and inner cultural borders very clearly. The town of Two Mills is divided by a street into the East End, inhabited by blacks and the West End, inhabited by whites. The tension between the two ends is such that the physical border is almost like a battle front in a war zone. A child will get into trouble if he or she steps across the border. Because of racial prejudice, the people on one side of the street fear or even hate the people on the other side. They are separated by inner borders of prejudice as well as divided by the physical border of a street. Through the story the author suggests to the reader a way to cross those borders: to be color blind. The hero of the story Maniac Magee is color-blind, so he can cross the borders and, finally, bring the two sides together. In the eyes of some reviewers, the author's suggestion is questionable (Enciso, 1994). The questions that these reviewers raise lead us to the next issue, different approaches to border crossing.

EXAMINING ONE ASSUMPTION

An assumption underlying the call for crossing cultural borders is that knowing other cultures leads to self-growth and change. We need to cross cultural borders to broaden our vision and shape ourselves to fit into a pluralistic world. If we allow ourselves to be limited by cultural borders, Corliss (1998) warns, "the scope of who we are and who we can be individually and collectively is severely restricted" (p. xi). Rochman (1993) also stresses the need for breaking out of the limitations of one's own culture. "If you read only what mirrors your view of yourself," she states emphatically, "you get locked in. It's as if you're in a stupor or under a spell. Buried" (p. 11).

This assumption stresses the necessity for every culture to connect to other cultures. There is no denying that in an increasingly diverse world, it is important for people to reach out to other cultures and reshape their own culture by learning from them. But the assumption fails to emphasize an important point: to achieve interracial and intercultural understanding and rapport, it is crucial for people from the mainstream culture to cross the borders into parallel cultures. From the perspective of critical multiculturalism, many cultural borders, especially the inner borders, are barriers that have been erected historically by the mainstream culture to isolate and suppress the parallel cultures. If they are not broken down, no intercultural connection or rapport is possible. In the interactions between cultures, there is no even playing field for the dominated cultures. We cannot assume that intercultural connection can happen on an equal basis. Therefore, when using multicultural literature to facilitate border crossing, we should direct our efforts to helping mainstream culture children understand and respect parallel cultures. Historically, people of parallel culture background were required to "melt" into the mainstream culture. They were forced to learn in school from literature about the mainstream culture; for example, Native Americans were forced to learn the white man's culture, as portrayed in *Indian School: Teaching the White Man's Way* by Michael Cooper (1999). In fact, Native Americans know much more about the mainstream culture than people of mainstream culture know about their cultures. Therefore, crossing cultural borders, I would argue, should first be a one-way journey from the mainstream culture into parallel cultures. I am not saying that parallel cultures should not try to connect to other cultures. But the priority is for the mainstream culture to get connected to the parallel cultures, because children from parallel cultures have been, and still are, victims to alienation in an educational system dominated by the mainstream culture.

Here is an example. Patricia Ruggiano Schmidt (1995) studied cultural conflicts in a kindergarten literacy program and found that two Asian American children fell victim to prejudices during informal work and in play settings. The kindergarten teacher, of mainstream cultural background, told Schmidt that she was concerned about the two ethnic minority children, Peley and Raji, because they did not seem to enjoy the work and play, were not making friends, and did not bring anything from home for the show-and-tell. From the teacher's perspective, the two children seemed to isolate themselves from their classmates; they needed to reach out to connect with the class community. However, the fact is that Peley and Raji were alienated in this predominantly white classroom because they were different—they looked different, had different names, and behaved differently. They tried to make friends and get involved in class activities, but they were either ignored or jeered at. At the beginning of the schoolyear, Peley attempted to make friends with other children. She would ask: "Hi, will you be my friend?" Some children just ignored her, while "others looked at her quizzically" (p. 409) When the children were playing the "H word" game, Peley excitedly shouted that she had two H's in her last name "Chinh," but her playmate said, "No, you do not! I do not hear huh, huh, huh!" (p. 409). Peley was very upset, but the other children paid no attention to her and went on with their game. The children did not know Peley's last name or its spelling because it had never been used on the class roster or during attendance even though it was on her official school records. In Raji's case, cultural biases were even more obvious. Raji did not know how to tie his shoes because in India, tie shoes were uncommon and tying shoes was an unusual requirement. However, the teacher thought he lacked fine motor coordination. When the children were playing the "S letter" game, Raji talked about snakes he had seen in India, but the other children stopped him immediately, "No! Snakes!" When he created flower designs around letters—a typical schoolchildren's exercise in India—one child said mockingly: "Why do you always make flowers? You're being a girly, girly" (p. 409). Because of biases on the part of the teacher and children, the two children of parallel cultural background had very negative experiences in social interaction and in school in general. The assessment of the two children's literacy ability was also biased. Although both children could read and write stories in English, as well as or even better than, most of their classmates, they were placed in an English as Second Language class. This further isolated them from the their regular classroom. According to the author of the study, several factors account for why the two children were alienated: the teacher was not sensitive to the differences between home and school cultures; no literature from other cultures was studied in the program; and neither of the children's home cultures was considered when it came to selecting literature.

Schmidt's (1995) study reflects the reality of cultural conflicts in our schools and testifies to the need for mainstream children and their teachers to break out of ethnic encapsulation (Banks, 2001) and to cross cultural borders into parallel cultures. As Francesina Jackson points out, "Historically, 'minority' people have had to be bicultural, bidialetical, and bicognitive . . . in order to achieve in mainstream U.S. society. By the same token, few demands were made on mainstream members, including teachers, to learn about diverse cultures" (p. 59). When we talk about crossing cultural borders, it is crucial to distinguish between dominated and dominant cultures. The mainstream culture should first change and reshape itself by connecting to parallel cultures.

CRITIQUING ONE APPROACH

An approach to facilitate border crossing focuses on similarities among different cultures. The premise is that if people can appreciate their common bonds (goals, dreams, desires, needs, feelings, and challenges), it is believed that they will come to celebrate their differences (Beaty, 1997). Since we are all human beings, why should we dislike each other? If we know the similarities among human beings, the cultural borders will be easy to cross or even erase.

It is easy to find books to be used with this approach. Many multicultural books are designed to help children connect to other cultures by showing the similarities among people of different cultural backgrounds. A typical example is a recent picture book, *Whoever You Are,* by Mem Fox (1997), which highlights the bonds that tie together all human beings on earth. Despite different nationalities, appearances, languages, lifestyles, and other differences, we are all the same inside. "Joys are the same, and love is the same. Pain is the same, and blood is the same" (n.p.). Many other multicultural books carry the same message about human commonalities: despite some differences, human beings are basically the same. The following are more books with the theme of common bonds among different cultures.

Children Just Like Me (Kindersley and Kindersley, 1997) depicts children on five continents. Their foods, dress, homes, games, and beliefs are different, yet in many aspects their daily lives are very similar, and they all have curiosities, hopes, fears, and dreams. What is striking is, not their differences, but the magnificent similarities that make them very much alike.

Bein' with You This Way (Nikola-Lisa, 1994) shows a multiethnic group of children playing joyfully on an urban playground. They are different in appearance—with big or little noses, light or dark skin, curly or straight hair, blue or brown eyes, and so on—but they cheerfully celebrate their differences, which to them are "delightful, simply out-of-sightful." As they play together they also sing of their sameness: "Different—Mm-mmm, but the same, Ah-ha!" (n.p.).

People (Spier, 1980) is like a mini-encyclopedia of humankind that includes information on various aspects of humanity: size, shape, skin, color, facial features, tastes, food, clothes, work, play, holidays, etc. The book seems to emphasize how people in the world are all different, but actually has a subtext that reads: People everywhere are basically the same; they all need a home, have to work, love to play, have religious beliefs, and celebrate holidays.

To Everything There Is a Season (Dillon and Dillon, 1998) uses the biblical words of Ecclesiastes as text to show the universality of the human condition: "To everything there is a season, and a time to every purpose under the heaven: A time to be born, and a time to die; A time to plant, and a time to pluck that which is planted." (n.p.). Although the illustrations depict different cultures all around the world, from Egypt to Australia, Russia to India, Ireland to Mexico, the message of human commonality rings clear: people everywhere have a time and a purpose to everything they do in their lives.

Madlenka (Sis, 2000) portrays a girl who lives in a culturally diverse neighborhood in New York City. When she walks around to announce that she has a loose tooth, her friends, a French baker, an Indian newspaper vendor, an Italian ice-cream man, a Latin American greengrocer, an Asian shopkeeper, and others are all glad to hear the good news and help her celebrate. Again, the illustrations depict the unique culture from which each of the girl's neighbors comes, but the text delivers an unmistakable message: that love and care bind a culturally diverse group together.

Seedfolks (Fleischman, 1997) tells how a Korean girl accidentally starts a process of change in her multiethnic urban neighborhood. She plants some lima beans in a trash-filled lot, hoping to attract her dead father's spirit. The plants draw her neighbors to the lot. They decide to do some planting, too. One by one they participate in transforming it into a beautiful garden and in the process overcome cultural barriers to forge new connections among them. The once listless community thus turns vibrant.

These selections are only a small sample of the many books that illustrate to children the commonalities across cultures. We definitely need books of this type because they play an important role in helping children cross cultural borders. They demonstrate a truth that, despite various differences, we are all human beings with many commonalities and express a wish that as human beings, we should forge a close bond. They also reveal to children whose vision may have been maimed by prejudice that people who have been described as alien and inferior are basically the same as they are in many ways. As Sims Bishop (1987) points out, "Understanding our common humanity is a powerful weapon against the forces that would divide us and alienate us from one another" (p. 60). We should not underestimate the value of these books. But at the same time, we should also be ware of their limitations: they skim only superficial cultural differences; they do not delve into entrenched bias and prejudice; and they appear to offer an easy way to cross cultural borders and overcome cultural barriers. Yes, we need to present to children the bright side of a diverse world, but we should also help them see and understand the seamy side of a divided world. If children read mostly these books, they may form a false idea that, despite cultural differences, the world is always a nice place. The major problem with this approach is that it oversimplifies the difficulty of crossing cultural borders. Some of the books help the reader cross physical borders and others help with borders of superficial cultural differences, but few of them will help the reader across inner borders of deep-rooted bias and prejudice.

When discussing multicultural literature in an overview of children's literature in the last millennium, Nodelman (2000) makes a distinction between truly multicultural books and theoretically multicultural books. The books I briefly annotated here fall into the second category of his classification. Truly multicultural literature

might . . . insist occasionally on the real and deep-seated emotional and intellectual differences between people of different cultural backgrounds and demand a real tolerance hard to achieve, rather than proclaiming as most theoretically multicultural books currently do that people are basically the same. It's easy to tolerate someone like yourself, less easy to tolerate some quite truly different. (p. 9)

Nodelman's comments underscore the fact that although we are all human beings, differences between cultures are not at all trivial, but rather are profound in terms of beliefs, values, and ways of life.

Another problem with books focused on common bonds is that they rarely challenge Western mainstream ideology. On the contrary, they very often reinforce it. In analyzing books such as *People* (Spier, 1980), Nodelman (1996) comments on their potential effects on mainstream readers' attitudes. After they acknowledge and see past the superficial differences into the shared humanity, they may think the values of Western mainstream culture reflected in the books are universal truth shared by others in the world, an attitude Nodelman condemns as "dangerously chauvinistic" (p. 100).

In books like *People* and *Children Just Like Me,* people and children everywhere seem to live in peace and happiness. You do not see poverty, famine, epidemics, or the other social disasters occurring in the Third World countries, which are the consequences of past colonialization by Western imperialist powers and the present unequal global economic system. The authors of *Children Just Like Me* later came up with a sequel entitled *Children Just Like Me: Celebrations!* (1997). Again we see only the sunny side of the world. Children everywhere are having fun celebrating various holidays. In *People* and *To Everything There Is a Season,* Christianity is implied as a universally accepted religion, even in non-Christian cultures. On the dedication page of *People,* we see naked man and woman walking hand in hand through a beautiful and abundant field. They represent Adam and Eve, who live happily in the Garden of Eden. The implied message will not pass unnoticed: people everywhere in the world are descended from them. *To Everything There Is a Season* unequivocally declares that the words from Ecclesiastes are universal truth applicable to every culture in the world, despite the fact that there are so many religions in the world. In *Madlenka,* we find stereotypes of cultures represented in the illustrations. As the girl walks around the neighborhood, the pictures show her also taking a trip around the world, visiting the places her friends come from. Her school friend Cleopatra is from Africa. The image of the continent is a vast expanse of wilderness inhabited only by animals. Another friend of hers is Mrs. Kham, an old lady from Asia. We see images of the Great Wall, dragons, Peking opera masks, Taoist symbols, mermaids, and warriors, all conjuring up the old stereotypical image of Asia as an exotic, occult continent.

A recurring theme in these books is tolerance and acceptance. If we tolerate and accept differences we will form a bond with people different from us. According to Nodelman (2000), this theme has been "obsessively focused" on and "constantly reiterated and reinforced" (p. 8). White authors are prone to write on this theme. Comparing the representations of the black experience by one white and one black author/illustrator, Ray Anthony Shepard made the point that "stories of the white author/illustrators are oriented toward the liberal insistence on human similarities and sameness, whereas the Black author/illustrator celebrates the ethnic differences of Blacks" (cited in Schwartz, 1985, p. 145). What Shepard found is also true of books about other minorities. There are several possible explanations for this tendency. First, white authors shy away from the grim reality of racial prejudice and discrimination. Second, they try to avoid issues of interracial and intercultural tension that they may not be incapable of dealing with creatively. Third, they have white children as their intended readers and want to foster a tolerant attitude in them, just as they did when writing about African Americans in what Sims calls "social conscience books." There is nothing wrong with writing books about this theme itself. However, if children read mostly books of this type, they may not really know the people different from them and understand the issues of racial and cultural conflicts in reality. Together these books create a world that is more an illusion than reality.

READING MYTHS, ARCHETYPES, AND UNIVERSAL THEMES

Another proposed approach to crossing cultural borders is finding connection among different cultures in books that do not depict common human bonds like those mentioned in the previous section. The approach attempts to look beneath the cultural specificities into the universal human meaning in the collective unconscious of the human psyche. It is suggested that reading archetypal human experiences in stories from different cultures will help us connect to each other (Rochman, 1993). The assumption behind this approach is that the link of stories to archetypes in myths will form "a true multicultural bridge" (Rochman, 1993, p. 14). Archetypal experiences, such as birth, death, love, marriage, and going on a journey, and primordial images, such as the dragon, the cave, the witch, the hero, and the genie, have tremendous power to excite us at the deepest level of our psyche. Therefore, reading archetypal stories across cultures is one way to connect us to each other. How it connects us is not clearly specified. It is implied that once we enter the story, we will experience an enhanced understanding of ourselves and the world, a kind of epiphany, in discovering the universal mythical themes. Perhaps, because of the revelation, we will see how we human beings are similar to each other.

This approach is based on Carl Jung's archetypal criticism of literature and art. Jung believed that certain fundamental aspects of human experience and certain character types are archetypal. They can be found in myths and other literary and artistic forms of all cultures. The reason why mythical archetypes are found across cultures is because the human race shares a universal psyche, "the collective unconscious," which "does not develop individually, but is inherited" (Jung, cited in Robertson, 1987, p. 85). The archetypes are residues cumulated in the collective unconscious, passed down from time immemorial.

The concept of a universal collective unconscious, however, is not universally accepted. Stamiris (1986) pointed out that the existence of collective unconscious "is not confirmed by the findings of anthropology and biology. [Neither can the existence of archetypes be] scientifically verified" (p. 127). According to Stamiris, Jung's theory of archetypes is severely attacked by his critics. They contend that "One can view archetypes not as universal forms engraved in the human brain . . . but as socially necessitated and maintained common experiences, occasionally useful to literary criticism" (p. 127).

I concur with the view that the archetypes are socially mediated common experiences. They are useful to the extent that they represent some universal themes in literature and art across cultures. Readers from all cultures may find something to relate to, but whether archetypes have sufficient power to excite the readers of all cultures is open to debate. Empirical studies are needed to support the theory.

Very often Eurocentric concepts and experiences are proclaimed as universal. In the quest story of the Western world, for example, seeking to know oneself is often associated with the hero or heroine's quest. "Who am I?" is said to be an archetypal cry uttered by mythical characters on perilous journeys in ancient and contemporary stories across cultures (Rochman, 1993). But it is debatable that the cry also reverberates in all stories on the theme of going on a perilous journey to seek a grail or conquer a monster. The Chinese story of "Hua Mulan" is about an ancient girl's perilous journey to war, but she does not ask the question "Who am I?" It is only in the Disney version of the story *Mulan* that the Western theme of seeking one's true identity surfaces. In their incisive criticism of Disney's *Mulan,* Mo and Shen (2000) note that there could be various interpretations of Mulan's motive to go to war from a Chinese perspective, but "none of them would be 'true to oneself'" (p. 132). They go on to say, "An outsider's perception of another culture is often short-circuited to his/her cultural internal reality. That explains why the filmmakers interpret Mulan's going to the war in terms of 'truly being herself'" (p. 136).

Some so-called archetypes may not be universal after all. Even if we grant that all archetypes are universal, the appeal of a myth or an archetypal story from another culture does not come from the archetypes. Wendy Doniger O'Flaherty (1988), author of *Other People's Myths,* does not think so. O'Flaherty (1988) points out that Carl Gustav Jung distinguishes between "archetypes (shared by all human beings) and manifestations (appearing in each particular culture)" (p. 34). The archetypes are "inherited forms and ideas which have at first no specific content" (p. 34). It is their manifestations in individual experiences of various cultures that instill specific content in them and make them visible; an example of this is found in the archetype of perilous journey manifested in the Chinese story of Mulan. The archetypes are like "a blank check" on which people write meanings. O'Flaherty remarks:

It may be that there is a universal truth, what Jung called the archetype, that speaks to us out of a foreign myth, but it is also true that what attracts us and fascinates us is not the archetype but the particular detail of that particular, foreign version of the archetype, what Jung called the manifestation. (pp. 34-35)

While archetypes may help us find a link to "other people's myths," it is their specific manifestations in particular cultures that are really appealing and mean-ingful. People are drawn to the popular book *The Joy Luck Club* by Amy Tan (1989) less because it explores the universal mother-daughter relationship—a universal theme—than because it deals with the universal theme in the specific context of the Chinese American culture and represents its complexity brilliantly. I doubt that the book would be so fascinating if it were not about mothers and daughters who are Chinese Americans.

Archetypes, or universal themes, are undeniably a bridge to other people's stories. Being able to enter the story world and relate to the characters is a step toward connecting to the culture represented in the story, but it does not mean that the reader has really crossed cultural borders. Many readers may enjoy the story of *The Joy Luck Club* and appreciate its universal theme yet may not quite understand Chinese American culture reflected in it. According to O'Flaherty (1988), we can read a myth to learn about the unique characteristics of the cul-ture that created it, or, if we believe in universals of human experience, we can read it for universal themes that have some meaning beyond that culture. Do we want our children to find out the universal themes or do we want them to learn about the culture so that they can really understand and respect it? To help chil-dren cross cultural borders, I think we should want them to do both.

In their article, "Cross-Cultural Swapping of Mother and Grandmother Tales in a Tenth Grade Discussion of *The Joy Luck Club*," Athanases and Lew (1993) show how the classroom teacher Ann Lew (coauthor of the article) helped stu-dents, not only relate to the story, but also learn about Chinese American culture through discussion. In her class there are white students and students of varied ethnic backgrounds, including African American, Asian American, and Hispanic American. All the students recognize their mothers and grandmothers in the book and see that families are not that different from one culture to another. They also identify cross-cultural "errors" committed at the dinner table by Rich when visiting his Chinese American girlfriend's family, such as criticizing the mother's dinner, pouring soy sauce down the platter of food to spice it up, and refusing to accept a second helping. From the cultural differences in the story, the students go on to discuss cultural difference in real life in regard to table manners as they swap family food tales. In this way they understand and learn to respect cultural differences while recognizing human universals.

In the classroom, we can put together text sets about the same universal themes for children to read. They can see connections between different cultures by identifying the themes shared by the books. But that is not enough. To cross cultural borders, they should also study the cultural differences reflected in the books. For example, we can have students read and compare Gary Paulsen's (1988) *The Island* and Walter Dean Myers's (1992) *Somewhere in the Darkness* together, because they both deal with the universal theme of taking an inner journey to discover oneself. An archetypal criticism of the two books would yield some similarities between them, such as Anna O. Soter (1999) found: both stories can be classified as the Wanderer myth. The archetype "the Wanderer" is a hero who goes on "an inner quest" to "discover why he or she is here in this lifetime, and honor that discovery if and when it is made" (p. 20). In *The Island*, Wil Neuton, a white boy, fits the profile of the archetype because he finds his true self and becomes mature after meditating in the island. The black boy Jimmy, in *Somewhere in the Darkness*, is a "wanderer" like Nil in that he, too, is faced with issue of identity as he tries to choose his path and his role in life. If we stop at identifying universal themes, however, we will miss many cultural differences between them. Nil is from a white, middle-class family. The crisis in his life that forces him into seclusion on the island is very different from the problem Jimmy has. Nil's normal life is disrupted when his family has to move to a new location because of his father's promotion. Jimmy's life takes a sudden turn when his father escapes from jail to prove to Jimmy that he was mistakenly convicted of murder. Besides universal themes, there are themes of racial prejudice and discrimination in *Somewhere in the Darkness*. If we do not talk about the cultural differences between the two books, we cannot say we have helped our children bridge cultural gaps through archetypal analysis.

Carol Markstrom-Adams (1990) distinguished between universal themes and "culturally specific" themes in her analysis of the dominant themes of novels portraying Native American adolescents. Universal themes include identity, coming of age, self-consciousness, individuation, and sexual and platonic relationships, whereas culturally specific themes include prejudice and discrimination toward Native Americans with mixed-blood ancestry, and the reaffirmation of Native American cultural and spiritual systems. The culturally specific themes, rather than the universal themes, should be the focus of our attention if we intend to use other people's stories to build connections between them and us. In my opinion, the universal themes would better be seen as a springboard for accessing other cultures and relating to them. Linking books about different cultures to the myth or archetypes may be one bridge to cross-cultural connection, but it is by no means the "true multicultural bridge."

COMBATING COLOR BIAS

African American poet Joyce Carol Thomas (1993) compares color bias to a "bitter potion" for children of color. How to dispose of this "bitter potion" has been the concern of educators and parents. Many books, both fiction and nonfiction, have been published that explore and celebrate differences in skin color with a view to ridding color bias of its pernicious influence on children and help them cross the inner cultural borders. They either explain how the human race gets its skin color, like the informational book *All Colors We Are: The Story of How We Get Our Skin Color* (Kissinger, 1994), or celebrate the beauty of various skin colors, like the picture book *The Colors of Us* (Katz, 1999). In the former, the author explains how skin color is determined by the function of the skin-coloring chemical melanin, by the necessity of adapting skin color to the environment, and also by hereditary factors that affect it. In the latter, a seven-year-old girl and her mother, while on a walk through the neighborhood, see different colors in their friends' skin and find them all beautiful. Although to some extent they demystify the myth of human skin color and help children to see the beauty of different colors, books of this type have serious limitations.

Collectively, they repeat a message: under the skin of different colors we are all the same. The reader gets the impression that skin color bias is only skin deep and can be easily dispelled. But actually, the bias is deeply rooted in the history of racial domination and oppression. In a racialized society, racial distinctions such as skin color and eye color are not only descriptors of physical difference but also presumed indicators of individual worth and status. Skin color has acquired "ugly connotations that give racism the power to wound" (Cose, 1997, xxv). Color bias is an inner border that is not easy to cross. To help children cross it, we need not only books that explain how we get our skin color or why people come in different colors, but, more importantly, books that not only explain how color bias came into existence historically but also condemn it. A picture book that does that is *Sister Anne's Hands* (Lorbiecki, 1998). The story takes place in the early 1960s. Seven-year-old Ana overhears her parents talking about her new second grade teacher. "How is a woman of her color going to survive?" they wonder. Ana is curious to know what color her teacher will be. When she comes to her parochial school the first day, she is surprised to find her teacher, Sister Ann, has "skin darker than any person's" (n.p.). But very soon Ana is drawn to Sister Anne and has a great deal of fun with this kind, playful, and child-loving teacher. However, one day a paper plane sails across the classroom carrying a racist message: "Roses are red/Violets are blue/Do not let Sister Anne/get any black on you" (n.p.). Upset as she is, Sister Anne takes the opportunity to teach the children about racism. She puts up pictures of black people being lynched or shot, along with segregationist signs like "Whites Only" and "Go Back to Africa." Sister Anne gives the children a powerful lesson about racism, teaching them "some folks have their hearts open, and others are as tight as a fist. The tighter they are, the more dangerous" (n.p.). After the incident, Ana loves Sister Anne even more dearly than before. *Sister Anne's Hands* shows that the effective way to combat color bias is to expose its "true colors of hatred" (n.p.).

When people's minds are purged of color bias and the society is free of racism, all men and women will be judged by their character, not by the color of their skin. Then, as Dr. Martin Luther King, Jr., envisioned, "little black boys and black girls will be able to join hands with little white boys and white girls and walk together as brothers and sisters" (quoted in Cose, 1997, p. xviii). The ideal of a color-blind society has been pursued by Dr. King and his followers, yet it remains a dream to be realized. To realize it, we have to confront the reality of racism rather than shy away from it. However, there are people who try to be color-blind, ignoring the reality of a society divided along racial lines. George A. Woods, for example, wrote, "I try not to look at kids as white or black. . . . I do not want to break kids down into different kinds" (Lester and Woods, 1985, p. 66). Unfortunately, "denying painful and harsh realities will not make them disappear" (Nieto, 1998, p. xvi). Children are exposed to color bias in society at a very early age. "Contrary to the 'color blind' ideology," Rocha and Dowd (1993) pointed out, "children develop an awareness of cultural and physical characteristics among people at very early age, and they do so more by exposure to prevailing community attitudes about other racial groups than by immediate contact with their members" (p. 60).

People who see color-blindness, not as a vision of democracy, but as a vehicle to resolve interracial conflicts believe that if we treat everyone just as a human being, ignoring racial differences, we will be able to live in interracial harmony. This ideology is reflected in the popular book *Maniac Magee* (Spinelli, 1990), which proposes color blindness as the resolution for interracial conflict. The author should be commended for taking on a thorny social issue in his book, but his remedy for it is inadequate.

The hero in the story is a twelve-year-old white boy named Jeffrey Lionel "Maniac" Magee. What is extraordinary about him is that he is color-blind. "Maniac Magee was blind. Sort of. . . . Maniac kept trying, but he still couldn't see it, this color business" (pp. 57-58). When he runs away from his foster home to the town of Two Mills, he does not see the racial line that divides the town of Two Mills. He is able to cross between the two ends, acting like a bridge between the two sides. He miraculously makes friends with both black and white children; he explains how black people live to the white old man, Grayson, who cares for him; and he brings Mars Bar Thompson, a black boy, over to visit a white family at the East End. Through his mediation, the two sides begin to understand and help each other. Racial tension is eased, and he is able to live once again with the black family who first took him in.

Anybody who knows the inner-city neighborhoods that were torn by racial tensions in the 1990s will see that Maniac Magee's achievement of racial reconciliation is utterly unrealistic. The racial gaps cannot be bridged so easily. Even the author is aware of that. He tells us at the beginning that the story is "one part fact, two parts legend, and three parts snowball" (p. 2). "What is true, what's myth" about the hero is "hard to know" (p. 1). So let us take the story for what it is: a legendary tale with a "superboy" as its main character, which expresses a wish rather than reflect reality. "Why can't we just put aside our color bias and get to know each other as individuals?" the author seems to say wistfully. A wish should not be mistaken as a solution. The only real solution to racial problems is to destroy the value system that treats people of color as inferior, not to pretend to be color-blind.

AGAINST BORDERS

The three approaches to crossing cultural borders we have just discussed share a common stance; that is, they all attempt to blur borders instead to facing up to them. The assumption behind the three approaches is that if we focus on our common humanity, the borders between us will be easy to cross or will disappear. In cultural studies, Salvner (1998) states, we can "define ourselves by what distinguishes us (skin color, religious belief, or tribal custom) or what unites us (shared feelings, relationships, or notions of truth)" (p. xi). Apparently, the three approaches urge us to define ourselves by what unites us.

When Rochman (1993) declares that "multiculturalism means across cultures, against borders" (p. 9), she means that we should find the universals that unite us. From her perspective, focusing on what distinguishes us instead of the universals would be an exclusionary act that raises borders rather eliminates them. She remarks:

Too many lists of so-called multicultural books . . . function only as a well-meaning spotlight—shining brightly but briefly on one cultural island or another, providing overdue recognition, yes, but imposing a different kind of isolation, celebratory but still separate. The islands need a bridge to connect them, and myth offers one way to build that bridge. (p. 14)

As Rochman does not clearly specify what those multicultural books are, I can only speculate that she refers to books that deal mainly with so-called culturally specific themes. (I think this is a fairly accurate guess from the context of her remarks.) These books, in her view, isolate the parallel cultures; in other words, they create new borders around them.

A certain way of reading multicultural literature could also be exclusionary—that is what Rochman calls "a medicinal approach" which uses "stories as literal recipes for ethnic self-esteem" (p. 12). For example, Jews read about Moses to stay in touch with their tradition and Chinese women read the myth of the Woman Warrior to feel strong. Those who adopt this medicinal approach to reading "ignore the universals of story [and] fail to see the myths from many cultures as part of a living tradition" (p. 12).

While I would accept the proposition of finding universals in books across cultures (although I do not believe it should be our focus), I strongly disagree with Rochman that books celebrating parallel cultures and reading books to raise ethnic self-esteem are exclusionary and impose new isolation. Historically, parallel cultures have been marginalized, misrepresented, and even deprived of their cultural identities. Only recently were they, somewhat grudgingly, given attention and recognition for their cultural identities in art and literature. Thanks to multicultural books that shine on the "cultural islands," parallel cultures that have been submerged under the deluge of books featuring only the dominant culture are gradually being seen and acknowledged. These books give back to parallel cultures their histories and cultural identities. The importance of these books cannot be overemphasized. "Unless individuals act to retain their personal and cultural histories, as they perceive them, they can face an insignificance that presages their very distinction, as has nearly been the case with the indigenous peoples of the Americas" (Vickers, 1998, p. 2). Henry Louis Gates, Jr. also points out that each culture "lives by and *through*" the stories it "creates and preserves" (quoted in Willis, 1998, p. xii). Thanks to these multicultural books, children of parallel cultures are beginning to see themselves reflected in the books they read, know their cultural heritage, and feel a sense of pride in being who they are and also being an equal member of the society. Children of mainstream culture are also starting to understand, accept, and respect parallel cultures. In a word, such books help children connect to each other, but how ironic it is that these books are termed exclusionary and segregational (Rochman, 1993).

It is important to discover human commonalities and forge a "communal identity that may not have yet been achieved" (Gates, 1992, p. xiv). However, the first step toward that goal is to accept, tolerate, and respect cultural differences. To cross cultural borders, paradoxically, we need to recognize and face up to them first. If we do not understand and respect cultural differences, there will be no true rapport on an equal basis. Judith Thomas and Gloria Woodard (1985) wrote, "Certainly, integration and assimilation are not possible until the recognition of and respect for these differences are fully realized" (p. 15). To understand other cultures, we need to develop cross-cultural competence. By reading multicultural literature, we expect to learn about cultures different from our own and to change our perspectives on them. If we do not undergo this transformation and instead continue to perceive other cultures as alien and inferior, it will be impossible to find common ground with them.

I would conclude that the true multicultural bridge is to accept and respect cultural differences as well as seek shared human universals among us. The two aspects of the approach are not mutually exclusive, because this is not an either/or choice. Trying to ignore the differences will not help children cross the cultural borders, especially the inner borders.

REFERENCES

Athanases, S. and Lew, A. (1993). Cross-cultural swapping of mother and grandmother tales in a tenth grade discussion of *The Joy Luck Club*. *Communication Education, 42* (4), 282-287.

Banks, J. A. (2001). *Cultural diversity and education: Foundations, curriculum, and teaching* (4th ed.). Boston: Allyn and Bacon.

Beaty, J. J. (1997). *Building bridges with multicultural picture books*. Columbus, OH: Merrill.

Corliss, J. C. (1998). *Crossing borders with literature of diversity*. Norwood, MA: Christopher-Gordon.

Cose, E. (1997). *Color-blind: Seeing beyond race in a race-obsessed world*. New York: HarperCollins.

Enciso, P. (1994). Cultural identity and response to literature: Running lessons from *Maniac Magee*. *Language Arts, 71,* 524-533.

Gates, H. L., Jr. (1992). *Loose canons: Notes on the cultural wars*. New York: Oxford University Press.

Jackson, F. R. (1998). Seven strategies to support a culturally responsive pedagogy. In M. F. Opitz (Ed.), *Literacy instruction for culturally and linguistically diverse students: A collection of articles and commentaries*. Newark, DE: International Reading Association.

Lester, J., and Woods, G. (1985). Black and white: An exchange. In D. MacCann and G. Woodard (Eds.), *The black American in books for children: Readings in racism* (pp. 66-72). Metuchen, NJ: Scarecrow.

Markstrom-Adams, C. (1990). Coming of age among contemporary American Indians as portrayed in adolescent fiction. *Adolescence, 25* (127), 225-237.

Mo, W., and Shen, W. (2000). A mean wink at authenticity: Chinese images in Disney's *Mulan*. *The New Advocate, 13* (2), 129-141.

Mora, P. (1998). Confessions of a Latina author. *The New Advocate, 17* (4), 279-289.

Nieto, S. (1998). Foreword. In A. Willis (Ed.), *Teaching multicultural literature in grades 9-12: Moving beyond the canon* (pp. xv-xvii). Norwood, MA: Christopher-Gordon.

Nodelman, P. (1996). *The pleasures of children's literature* (2nd ed.). New York: Longman.

Nodelman, P. (2000). Inventing childhood: Children's literature in the last millennium. *Journal of Children's Literature, 26* (1), 8-17.

O'Flaherty, W. D. (1988). *Other people's myths: The cave of echoes*. New York: Macmillan.

Robertson, R. (1987). *C. G. Jung and the archetypes of the collective unconscious*. New York: Peter Lang.

Rocha, O. J., and Dowd, F. S. (1993). Are Mexican-American females portrayed realistically in fiction for grades K-3? A content analysis. *Multicultural Review, 2* (4), 60-69.

Rochman, H. (1993). *Against borders: Promoting books for a multicultural world*. Chicago: American Library Association.

Salvner, G. M. (1998). Foreword. In J. E. Brown and E. C. Stephens (Eds.), *Cultural sensitivity: Using multicultural young adult literature in the classroom*. Urbana, IL: National Council of Teachers of English.

Schmidt, P. R. (1995). Working and playing with others: Cultural conflict in a kindergarten literacy program. *The Reading Teacher, 48* (5), 404-412.

Schwartz, A. V. (1985). *The Cay*: Racism still rewarded. In D. MacCann and G. Woodard (Eds.), *The black American in books for children: Readings in racism* (2nd ed., pp. 144-146). Metuchen, NJ: Scarecrow.

Sims Bishop, R., (1987). Extending multicultural understanding through children's books. In B. E. Cullinan (Ed.), *Children's literature in the reading program* (pp. 60-67). Newark, DE: International Reading Association.

Soter, A. O. (1999). *Young adult literature and the new literary theories: Developing critical readers in middle school.* New York: Teachers College Press.

Stamiris, Y. (1986). *Main currents in twentieth-century literary criticism: A critical study.* Troy, NY: Whitston.

Thomas, J., and Woodard, G. (1985). Black perspective in books for children. In D. MacCann and G. Woodard (Eds.), *The black American in books for children: Readings in racism* (pp. 39-51). Metuchen, NJ: Scarecrow.

Vickers, S. B. (1998). *Native American identities: From stereotype to archetype in art and literature.* Albuquerque: University of New Mexico Press.

Willis, A. I. (Ed.). (1998). *Teaching multicultural literature in grades 9-12.* Norwood, MA: Christopher-Gordon.

Books for Children and Young Adults

Cooper, M. (1999). *Indian school: Teaching the white man's way.* New York: Clarion.

Dillon, L., and Dillon, D. (1998). *To everything there is a season.* New York: Scholastic.

Fleischman, P. (1997). *Seedfolks.* New York: HarperCollins.

Fox, M. (1997). *Whoever you are.* Ill. by L. Staub. San Diego: Harcourt Brace.

Katz, K. (1999). *The colors of us.* New York: Henry Holt.

Kindersley, B., and Kindersley, A. (1995). *Children just like me.* New York: Dorling Kindersley.

Kindersley, B., and Kindersley, A. (1997). *Children just like me: Celebrations!* New York: Dorling Kindersley.

Kissinger, K. (1994). *All the colors we are: The story of how we get our skin color.* New York: Redleaf.

Lorbiecki, M. (1998). *Sister Anne's hands.* Ill. by W. Popp New York: Dial.

Myers, W. D. (1992). *Somewhere in the darkness.* New York: Scholastic.

Nikola-Lisa, W. (1994). *Bein' with you this way.* Ill. by M. Bryant. New York: Lee and Low.

Paulsen, G. (1988). *The island.* New York: Dell.

Sis, P. (2000). *Madlenka.* New York: Farrar Straus Giroux.

Spier, P. (1980). *People.* Garden City, NY: Doubleday.

Spinelli, J. (1990). *Maniac Magee.* Boston: Little Brown.

Tan, A. (1989). *The joy luck club.* New York: Putnam's.

Thomas, J. C. (1993). *Brown honey in broomwheat tea.* Ill. by F. Cooper. New York: HarperCollins.

8

From Informing to Empowering

Incorporating multicultural literature into the curriculum is part of a democratic educational reform that addresses issues of equality and equity in schools. It aims at challenging and changing the dominant position of all white literature in the classroom. The need for multicultural literature in the curriculum is now generally acknowledged, but not totally accepted. Many schools adopt a "contribution" or "additive" approach (Banks, 1989) to integrate multicultural literature into the curriculum. Multicultural literature only appears during "multicultural weeks or months" that celebrate the contributions of parallel cultures or are added as supplementary readings to the set curriculum. There is resistance to its inclusion in the reading list of core books in elementary schools and in the canon of literature in high schools. Eurocentric "classic" literature is still the "norm" when it comes to what constitutes "cultural literacy." Studies find that the most frequently recommended books for high school and college students are still those by European or European American men (Willis, 1998). Virginia Hamilton's works may have been given the prestigious Hans Christian Anderson Award but are yet to be accepted as good as canonical works such as *Huckleberry Finn, To Kill a Mocking Bird,* and *Lord of the Flies* (Golding, 1962). Much remains to be done before high quality multicultural literature can be established as an integral part of the cannon instead of a supplement. We still need to fight for the integration of multicultural literature into the basic structure of the curriculum. Yet changing the contents of textbooks and reading lists of core books is only part of the move toward a genuinely multicultural curriculum (McMarthy, 1998). Even if multicultural literature had become an integral part of the curriculum instead of being added on as supplements, we are still faced with the questions of "What do we want it to accomplish?" and "How do we use it appropriately and effectively to achieve the goals of multicultural education?" Various approaches, strategies, and activities have been developed to use multicultural literature in the curriculum (e.g., Norton, 1990, 2000; Valedez, 1999;

Finazzo, 1996; Rasinski and Padak, 1990), but they do not share the same theoretical guidelines and seem to go in different directions. In this chapter I will discuss directions in using multicultural literature in the classroom.

INFORMING AND EMPOWERING

The ultimate goals for using multicultural literature in the curriculum are to challenge the dominant ideologies, affirm the values and experiences of historically underrepresented cultures, foster acceptance and appreciation of cultural diversity, develop sensitivity to social inequalities, and encourage transformation of the self and society. To achieve these goals, it is imperative to move from informing to empowering students when we use multicultural literature.

If used appropriately, multicultural literature can perform two functions: to inform and to empower. Through reading multicultural literature, whether nonfiction or fiction, we gain knowledge or information about the experiences, beliefs, and values of other cultures, thus enhancing our multicultural awareness and appreciation. Through reading multicultural literature we are exposed to varying perspectives on the world and challenged to look at ourselves and the world differently (Sims Bishop, 1994); we develop an ability to identify and critically analyze—and may even take action to solve—problems related to cultural or ethnic differences (Rasinski and Padak, 1990). This is how multicultural literature functions to empower us. Unless we choose to be ignorant and indifferent, good quality multicultural literature will inform or empower us or both. McGinley et al. (1997) maintain, "Stories can be a means of personal and social exploration and reflection—an imaginative vehicle for questioning, shaping, responding, and participating in the world" (p. 43). For multicultural literature to empower us, it must be used as "a means of personal and social exploration and reflection" rather than merely as a source of information.

Both functions of multicultural literature are important, and they are interrelated. Knowledge is power. The more we know about other cultures, the better equipped we are to identify and analyze cultural and ethnic issues and make decisions to act on them. Acquiring knowledge or information about other cultures is an important step toward overcoming ignorance and prejudice. It provides a basis for critical inquiry that leads to empowerment. For example, if students read informational or fictional books about the history of Chinese immigration to the United States, famous Chinese Americans, life in Chinatown, and similar topics, they will better understand Chinese American culture and perhaps rectify some misconceptions about it. With encouragement and guidance from the teacher, they can also start to examine racial and cultural issues that are reflected in the books and present in their lives. With the background knowledge gained from exploring the Chinese American culture they are in a better position to understand and analyze those issues in the real world as well as in the world of books. Although informing is important, empowering represents the more important function of multicultural literature. We should not stop at informing but must always move toward empowering.

However, many instructional activities that follow an information-driven approach do not make that move. They center on informing students about other cultures but do not tackle issues related to cultural differences. Many "multicultural weeks or months" in schools and colleges are typical examples of this type of activity. They feature the so-called four F's: food, festival, fashion, and folklore. This "holidays and celebrations" syndrome (Sims Bishop, 1994, p. xxii) is indicative of a superficial approach to using multicultural literature in education. Many multicultural books facilitate the information-driven approach (such as the cross-cultural books cited in the previous chapter), highlighting shared human conditions. They provide information on ways of life in different cultures with a view to broadening the reader's vision of cultural diversity. While they are informative and interesting, they do not deal with cultural conflicts, and many of them are somewhat superficial. They usually cannot take the students to the empowering stage. For example, a recent picture book, *On the Same Day in March: A Tour of the World's Weather* (Singer, 2000), provides interesting information on global weather and how people live in different parts of the world. It can be easily incorporated into a unit about weather, helping children understand global weather as well as the lifestyles of people in different countries. But it does not help children develop the ability to identify and analyze issues related to cultural differences.

To empower students, we need activities that adopt an issue-driven approach and use thought-provoking books that challenge children to think about issues that they may face in reality. Teachers need to create learning experiences that encourage students to empower themselves. For example, interracial relationships are an issue that all students have to deal with at some point in their lives. Adopting an issue-driven approach, a teacher may want to do a thematic unit to help students address this issue. Some of the cross-cultural books that show interactions between people of different cultural backgrounds can be used in this unit. The following are some examples. *Yo! Yes?* (Raschka, 1993) is about two boys of different ethnic backgrounds encountering each other on the street and becoming friends. Using minimal text and expressionistic illustrations, this book shows how cultural barriers can be overcome, communication achieved, and friendship formed when one party takes the initiative to approach the other. *Chicken Sunday* (Polacco, 1992) is another story about interracial friendship. The grandmother of two African American boys takes care of a Caucasian girl as if she were her own granddaughter. The boys became the girl's brothers. This story also tells how a conflict between some African American children and a Jewish hat dealer turns into friendship in the end. Another example of interracial friendship is in *Halmoni and the Picnic* (Choi, 1993). A Korean American girl's grandmother agrees to chaperone her class on a picnic. The girl is worried that her classmates may make fun of her grandma's pointed shoes and long Korean dress and may not like the Korean food her grandma prepared, but her worries turn out to be unwarranted. A friendship is formed between Halmoni and her granddaughter's class. Every child calls her Halmoni. Woodson's (2001) *The Other Side* provides a fourth example. Clove, a young African American girl, lives in a town that is segregated by a fence. Her mother tells her never to climb over to the other side because it is not safe. But one day she notices a white girl from the other side sitting on the fence. Curious about this daring girl, Clove plucks up her courage to approach her. They both brush aside the adults' injunctions and introduce themselves. A friendship is forged between them. Other children, black and white, at first stare at them in wonder, but soon join them sitting on the fence. What was originally a barrier becomes a link between the two sides. The story ends with this hopeful predication: "Someday somebody's going to come along and knock this old fence down" (n.p.). These four books begin with some sort of interracial tension but end with reconciliation or friendship. They have the potential to stimulate the reader to reflect upon the issue of interracial relationships and learn how to tackle it. To help students analyze the issue, general questions can be asked about these stories such as: What causes the tension in the story? How is it solved? How is friendship forged? What would you do if you were faced with the same problems as the characters? After discussing these questions and more specific questions related to each story, activities can be conducted to help students empathize with the characters and gain deeper insight into the issue. I will discuss moving from informing to empowering students in thematic units later in this chapter.

Some books may not directly deal with social cultural conflicts, but if we adopt an issue-driven approach to using them in the curriculum, we can still help children identify and analyze issues related to social-cultural differences. Barta and Grindler (1996) developed a five-phase procedure for exploring bias with multicultural literature, which can be used with books that are not directly concerned with social cultural issues. At phase 1, children read multicultural literature; at phase 2, children find out about cultural variation in the multicultural book they read; at phase 3, children discuss mainstream culture's biased responses to the variation; at phase 4, children learn the common human behavior represented by the cultural variation; and at phase 5, children come to understand the error of negative bias toward the variation and learn an unbiased view of them. Barta and Grindler used *Flossie and the Fox* (McKissack, 1986) as an example to show how to move children through the five phases. This folktatle tells how a black girl outwits a fox. It is not directly concerned with social-cultural conflicts. After the story is read and enjoyed, children identify the cultural variation in it, namely, Flossie's Black English Vernacular. Once the variation is defined, children discuss bias toward the dialect: it is often misperceived by mainstream culture as substandard. Then children are helped to see that, just like African Americans, all people use language in different ways to meet the needs of communication in different social contexts. Finally, unbiased information on the history and structure of Black English Vernacular is shared with children so that they further come to understand that it is wrong to be biased against a valid language. This five-phase procedure adopts an issue-driven approach that not only informs children about cultural differences but also helps them differentiate between right and wrong attitudes regarding those differences; in other words, it makes the transition from informing to empowering children.

Because empowering is the ultimate function that we want multicultural literature to perform, we must put more emphasis on it when using multicultural literature in the curriculum. Even before multicultural literature really becomes an integral part of the curriculum, we still need to move from informing to empowering. For example, the book *Halmoni and the Picnic* may be used during an Asian American Week to acquaint children with Korean culture, and it is likely that traditional Korean costumes will be displayed and Korean food tasted. But we can move from informing to empowering by asking children thought-provocative questions after they enjoy the costumes and food. Multicultural weeks or months will continue to be held in schools even after multicultural literature is woven into the existing curriculum. Such events will be more meaningful if they are not limited to providing information.

If we subscribe to a tourist view of multiculturalism (Hade, 1997), we will not move from informing to empowering. Unless students are empowered to deal with issues of social equity and justice, multicultural education will stop short of its ultimate goals. As Barta and Grindler (1996) point out, "Simply reading about cultural variations may do little to affect the degree of inequality in our society" (p. 269). Moving from informing to empowering should be a guideline for designing instructional models, for selecting multicultural books to be used with children, and for conducting multicultural activities at all levels.

STARTING TO EMPOWER CHILDREN FROM THE PRIMARY GRADES

Barta and Grindler (1996) noted that some educators and parents argue that children are too young to be exposed to issues of bias, prejudice, and discrimination. Thus, while multicultural literature is included in the instruction, those issues are seldom addressed. Children actually form misconceptions about people of parallel cultures at a very early age, due to the influences of their parents and the media. Before they come to school, they have already been exposed to cultural bias, prejudice, and discrimination; some of them have absorbed discriminatory attitudes toward people who are culturally different from them. If we do not take the step to explore bias and prejudice toward cultural differences with children, as Barta and Grindler (1996) point out, "we do little more than support" the existence of these negative forces and participate in their perpetuation (p. 270). Because children in the primary grades are at an impressionable stage of their lives, it is crucial to help them develop the right attitudes toward cultural differences and the ability to deal with social-cultural issues.

Some educators may think that even if they want to discuss issues of bias, prejudices, and discrimination, children in the primary grades may be too young to understand them. Thus, the approach they use for studying multicultural literature usually stops at presenting information. The fact is that the move to empowering can be made if the appropriate approach is used. Joyce S. Macphee (1997) provides a good example of how primary grade students can be empowered. She worked with an all European-American first-grade class of thirty-one students.

Her approach for studying multicultural literature with the children wsa a combination of Rosenblatt's (1978) transactional reader response theory and Banks' (1994) transformation approach. It encourages students to respond to characters and events in the story and challenges them to think about the social issues reflected in the books they read. The books she selected deal with interactions between European Americans and African Americans, including *Black Like Kyra, White Like Me* (Vigna, 1992), *Amazing Grace* (Hoffman, 1991), *Aunt Harriet's Underground Railroad in the Sky* (Ringgold, 1992), and *Jackie Robinson* (Sabin, 1985). The first three are realistic fiction and the last one is nonfiction. Macphee read the books during the regular read-aloud time and encourage children's personal responses to them, trying to bring their "voices into interaction with others' voices" (p. 39). Then she collects children's responses in three ways: audiotaping their spontaneous responses, asking them to draw pictures as a form of response, and meeting with the children individually and audiotaping their comments about the their pictures. When she was sharing the books with children, she asked questions and useed prompts to encourage dialogue and stimulate critical thinking about issues of racism, prejudice, and discrimination. The following is an excerpt from the transcript of some children's responses to *Black Like Kyra, White Like Me:*

Edie: Some people don't like black people. But I don't know why.
Mark: Black people used to be slaves a long time ago, and I think some people think they are still that way.
JSM [the teacher]: How do you know that, Mark?
Mark: My dad told me about that, and we talked about that in school before.
Kurt: Christy and Kyra are friends, but they met at the center for gymnastics.
JSM: So why can't everyone be friends here?
Kurt: It just happens at the Center, that's all.
JSM: Can you think of any reason why people could be friends at the Center but not in their neighborhood?
Kurt: Hmm . . . I just can't think of any. (p. 35)

In Macphee's class, children are not merely observers, but "sympathetic sharers" of the experiences of African Americans as described in the books. The books are "more than a window to look at others, becoming, instead, a vehicle for cross-cultural dialogue" (p. 33), with which children voice their opinions on the issues of social inequality and injustice. They sympathize with characters who fall victim to racism in the story and show "beginnings of social activism against unjust treatment of people" (p. 36). For example, in responding to racial segregation Jackie Robinson experienced, a child commented: "That's not fair. Everyone should be allowed to swim." Another child says strongly: "I know I would let him swim. It's a good thing that I wasn't there!" (p. 36). Macphee's approach produced positive effects of empowering the students. In a sense, it liberated the children from an ethnically encapsulated environment and prepared them to deal with situations of social injustice. Macphee's success demonstrates that with the teacher's help children in the primary grades can deal with social-cultural issues.

FROM INFORMING TO EMPOWERING IN THEMATIC UNITS

Thematic units have proved to be an effective means in organizing instruction and have been widely used in literature-based programs. Multicultural literature is gradually becoming an integral part of thematic units, as evidenced in new basal readers and classroom practices. The infusion of multicultural literature into thematic units is indicative of a more substantive transformation of the curriculum than the superficial add-ons of multicultural holidays, weeks, and months, and students now not only fulfill curricular goals in different content areas but also enhance their multicultural awareness.

There are basically two ways to make a thematic unit multicultural: either making a particular ethnic culture (e.g., American Indians) the focus of a thematic unit or incorporating multicultural literature into a thematic unit on a general cross-cultural theme (e.g., the life cycle). In both ways the study of science, social studies, language arts, and other subjects can be integrated with multicultural education. For example, in a thematic unit on the American Indians in a third grade classroom, students could read Native American legends associated with a number of tribes for language arts, study the culture, history, and contributions of American Indians for social studies, and study constellations as represented in American Indian folklore for science. Students can also discuss the conflicts between the white settlers and the Indians, examine the problems between the two cultures, identify the causes of the problems, and generate solutions as to how American Indians and white settlers could effectively coexist. Books for this thematic unit may include *When Clay Sings* (Byrd, 1972), *Desert Voices* (Byrd, 1981), *Where the Buffaloes Begin* (Baker, 1981), *Her Seven Brothers* (Goble, 1988), *The Legend of the Indian Paintbrush* (dePaola, 1991), *The Mud Pony* (Cohen, 1991), *The Turquoise Boy* (Cohlene, 1991), *Thirteen Moons on Turtle's Back* (Bruchac, 1992), *How the Stars Fell into the Sky* (Oughton, 1992), *The Lost Children* (Goble, 1993), *The Land Is My Land* (Littlechild, 1993), *Cheyenne Again* (Bunting, 1995), and *Crazy Horse's Vision* (Bruchac, 2000).

In a thematic unit on the life cycle, third-grade students are expected not only to understand different stages of life and develop an appreciation for the sacredness of life, but also to understand how life experiences differ from one culture to another. Students can study the varied life styles of ethnic cultures through multicultural literature, field trips, and community resource people. The following books may be used in this thematic unit: *Nana Upstairs, Nana Downstairs* (dePaola, 1973), *Ceremony in the Circle of Life* (White Deer of Autumn, 1991), *On the Day You were Born* (Fraiser, 1991), *The Keeping Quilt* (Polacco, 1988), *Family Pictures* (Garza, 1990), *A Boy Becomes a Man at Wounded Knee* (Wood, 1992), *Pablo's Tree* (Mora, 1994), *Patchwork Quilt* (Flournoy, 1996), *The Secret of the Stones* (San Souci, 2000), *Halmoni's Day* (Bercaw, 2000), and *Quinnie Blue* (Johnson, 2000).

These two examples of multicultural thematic units are taken from Ms. Mary Guenther's third grade classroom. Mary teaches at a school in a midwestern city.

She has been experimenting with multicultural thematic units in her literature-based classroom for several years. Throughout the school year, multicultural literature is incorporated into the curriculum through thematic units. Mary's class is comprised of students of various cultural heritages including European, African, Asian, Native, and Hispanic American. Mary believes that a major goal of a multicultural curriculum is to help students acquire the knowledge, attitude, and abilities they will need to be full participants in a culturally diverse society. Therefore, it is important to teach students to know, to reflect and to act on issues of cultural difference. Mary does not stop at the level of presenting information about other cultures, but encourages her students to view events, concepts, issues, and problems from the perspective of diverse racial and ethnic groups. In the following I will describe in some detail how Mary moves from informing to empowering in a thematic unit called "Celebrating American Immigration."

Throughout the unit, one curricular goal was to inform the students about immigration. The students read books about immigration and also did a heritage project to research their families' history of immigration at the end of the unit. The students had more than fifty books about immigration at different difficult levels to choose from, including fiction and nonfiction. These books provided ample information on experiences of immigrating to a new country. Here are a few examples: *Angel Child, Dragon Child* (Surat, 1989), *Watch the Stars Come Out* (Levinson, 1985), *Making a New Home in America* (Rosenburg, 1986), *I Speak English for My Mom* (Stanek, 1989), *Goodbye, Vietnam* (Whelan, 1992), *Grandfather's Journey* (Say, 1993), *My Name Is Maria Isabel* (Ada, 1995), *A Day's Work* (Bunting, 1994), and *I Was Dreaming to Come to America* (Lawlor, 1995).

After reading the books students came to know the reasons why people wanted to immigrate to the United States, problems the immigrants encountered, and the cultural values they brought with them. By reading *I Speak English for My Mom* and *A Day's Work*, for example, the students learned about economic problems some Mexican American families face because of their parents' or grandparents' lack of proficiency in English and the tremendous responsibility of the young children to translate for their parents or grandparents. Students wrote in their journals about the various ways each family dealt with the language barrier to obtain better jobs. A girl wrote:

In *I Speak English For My Mom*, Lupe's mom had to learn English in order to get a better job. Lupe knew to speak English because she had to learn it to go to school. Lupe had to talk for her mom because she didn't speak English. But Lupe's mom knew she couldn't live by Lupe talking for her. So she went to English school.

They also learned about the strong work value of these immigrant families. A boy wrote:

In the book *A Day's Work* the boss was willing to hire Grandfather again even though he didn't know English. It was because Grandfather showed that he knew to tell the truth and to work hard and to do his best. Grandfather would not accept pay until the job was done correctly.

The unit, however, did not stop at informing the students about various aspects of immigration, but moved them through the empowering phase. First, the students were asked to identify with the characters and take on their perspectives. After reading *Goodbye Vietnam*, for example, the students were asked to put themselves in the position of the Vietnamese family encountering the problems and dangers on the journey and share how they might feel if they were traveling with this family. Many stated their fears about crowded conditions, food shortage, and imprisonment. Others were concerned about leaving their friends and valued possessions behind. The following are excerpts from their journals:

It would be scary and I would be hungry! I would miss my pets. I wouldn't want to leave my toys behind. And I would be tired from the journey.

I would feel nauseated and I would have claustrophobia on the boat. I would feel bad, and I would want to be in America right away.

I would feel happy because we are getting away from the problems in Vietnam. I would feel sad about the food shortage on the journey and concerned about grandma getting caught by the police.

By relating to the characters in the story, students can sympathize with their situation, understand their feelings, and look at immigration from a new perspective.

The students were also challenged to reflect on issues of discrimination experienced by immigrants upon their arrival in the new country. They were asked, not only to think about why it was wrong to discriminate, but also how they would react to the injustice. They read two books about discriminatory attitudes toward new immigrants: *Angel Child, Dragon Child,* which is about a Vietnamese immigrant girl, Ut, who is teased about her language, clothing, and food by classmates. and *My Name Is Maria Isabel,* which tells how Maria, a Puerto Rican immigrant, encounters learning problems in school because the teacher has changed her name to Mary. After reading *Angel Child, Dragon Child,* students shared their thoughts on how they would react to Ut, if they were her classmates:

I would ask her to tell me about her country to make her feel important.

I would explain to Ut that the students don't mean to laugh at her. They do it because they don't know Ut's country.

I would try to make her feel at home. And try to be her friend. I would teach her some English if she didn't know a lot.

I would teach her how to eat with our utensils . . . and get her used to our clothes. I would play with her at recess. I would sit with her at lunch. I would help her understand what the teacher was saying. I would stand up for her if someone was teasing her. I would learn how to speak Vietnamese so I could speak to her, and last but not least, I would be her friend.

After reading *My Name Is Maria Isabel*, students recognized the importance of Maria's name to her family. They shared their feelings if their names had been changed and talked about how they would react. One child wrote in his journal:

I would feel bad and embarrassed. I would talk to the teacher about my feelings. And if that didn't work I would correct her when she called me by a different name.

After discussing the issues of discrimination against immigrants, students were asked to explain how they would use what they had learned to make this world a better place? The following are examples of the students' responses:

I would use this information to make the world a better place by giving people from another culture a chance, by encouraging them, and by respecting them.

It was a big thing for me to learn about all the kids that come to this country. I think that if I was some person, that was the president or somebody, I would make a change.

The students did not just talk about issues in the book world; they actually took up immigration issues in the local community. Immigration was a hot topic in the community because of the growing Hispanic immigration population. Throughout the unit there were articles in two local newspapers focused on immigrants from Mexico who had been hired by a local meat-packing company. Many issues about immigration being highlighted in the papers were also those addressed in the immigration unit. After analyzing the issues, the students wanted to learn more about the Mexican culture and contributions made by Hispanics and decided to take actions that will enable the school to present a more accurate and positive view of the Hispanic culture.

If an information-driven approach is used to implement a thematic unit on immigration, the students will learn about many aspects of immigration, such as what countries the immigrants come from, why they want to immigrate to a new country, what the cultural differences are between their home country and the new country, and what immigration procedures they go through to obtain their legal status of residence. The unit will end after providing this information to the students. But in Mary's thematic unit, as we have seen, students are not just receiving information; they are also learning to be reflective social critics and participants in social change (Banks, 1989, 1994).

CRITIQUE OF ONE APPROACH TO THE STUDY OF MULTICUL-TURAL LITERATURE

Norton (2000) proposed "a five-phase approach for the study of multicultural literature that proceeds from ancient to contemporary literature" (p. 4). It is designed for the study of African/African American, Asian/Asian American, Native American, Latino, and other ethnic literature in the reading curriculum. Students are supposed to study traditional literature of a particular culture at phase one; traditional literature from a specific area at phase two; historical nonfiction at phase three; historical fiction at phase four; and contemporary literature at phase five. Following this sequence of study, students explore the literature of the culture systematically. Throughout the course, students are encouraged to search for themes, symbols, values, and beliefs that run through the ancient and contemporary literature of that culture. As a result of the in-depth studies, students are expected to develop a solid knowledge base of the literature and gain insights into the culture depicted in it.

This approach is basically an information-driven approach. The goals for each phase indicate that the approach focuses on acquiring knowledge about the literature and culture of an ethic group rather than analyzing issues related to cultural differences and conflicts depicted in the literature. Take phase three "historical nonfiction" and phase four "historical fiction" for example. The three goals for phase three are: (a) "Analyze nonfiction for the values, believes, and themes identified in traditional literature"; (b) "Compare adult autobiographies and children's biographies (if possible)"; and (c) "Compare information in historical document with autobiographies and biographies" (Norton, 2000, p. 5). The goals for phrase four are: (a) "Evaluate historical fiction according to the authenticity of the conflicts, characterizations, settings, themes, language, and traditional beliefs and values"; (b) "Search for the role of traditional literature in historical fiction"; and (c) "Compare historical fiction with autobiographies, biographies, and historical information" (Norton, 2000, p. 5).

If these goals are accomplished, there is no doubt that students will gain a clear understanding of the philosophy, values, and beliefs of an ethnic culture as well as develop an ability to evaluate the authenticity of literature about it. The importance of this understanding should not be underestimated. However, what is missing from the picture is goals that aim at challenging and changing students' perspectives and developing their ability to identify, analyze, and act on social cultural issues. If students are to be empowered, those goals need to be added—goals that highlight the link between the study of literature about the history of an ethnic group and the social historical struggles it waged against injustices, and also goals that emphasize students' personal responses to social injustice as portrayed in the literature. Specific goals could possibly include: "Understand how historical fiction and nonfiction reflect discrimination and domination of the minority ethnic groups and their struggle against it," "Compare different perspectives on a historical figure or event to understand how the dominant culture has the power over the interpretation of history," and "compare what you already know about a historical event and what you learn from the books you read." The goals for phase five, contemporary literature, also lack a close link between conflicts in the book world and social issues in the real world. The main goal for phase five is "encourage students to search for continuity among traditional literature, nonfiction, historical fiction, and contemporary writings and to consider the themes, values and conflicts that emerge in contemporary writings" (Norton, 2000, p. 8). It needs to be expanded to include objectives that would encourage students to reflect and act on social issues in contemporary world, for example, "Identify issues in your life that are similar to those represented in the book" and "Compare perspectives on, and solutions to, those issues."

The goals we set affect our selection of reading materials and instructional activities for the study of multicultural literature. Since the goals focus on acquiring knowledge, most instructional activities suggested for the five phases also indicate an orientation more toward informing than empowering. They are more text oriented than reader oriented. For example, for phases three and four in the study of Asian literature, the following two activities are suggested: "Integrating Literature and Geography" (Norton, 2000, p. 220) and "Identifying Traditional Values and Historical Happenings" (Norton, 2000, p. 222). In the first activity, students are asked to read about the Silk Route, which linked ancient China to Europe, and identify five fundamental themes in geography: "location," "place," "relationships with place," "movement," and "regions" (Norton, 2000, p. 221). In the second activity, students are asked to read books set in earlier historical periods "to search for continuing cultural threads and to authenticate historical happenings" (Norton, 2000, p. 222). For example, students could read Erik Christian Hauggard's (1991) *The Boy and the Samurai,* which is set in feudal Japan, and find out how the author includes "cultural traditions and beliefs" in the text and "create vivid settings and believable conflicts" (Norton, 200, p. 222). For phase five, the suggested activity is "Compare Biographies of One Biographical Character" (Norton, 2000, p. 223). Three biographies of Gandhi are selected for the activity. Its purpose is to "evaluate and compare the accuracy of characterization" (Norton, 2000, p. 223) and to analyze other literary elements in the biographies. These suggested activities are useful in helping students understand and appreciate the values, beliefs, and traditions of parallel cultures but have limitations in helping them develop the ability to identify, analyze, and make decisions on issues arising from cultural differences. If goals for empowering students are to be included, alternative books and activities must be added. For example, in phase five, when students read biographies of Gandhi, in addition to examining the literary elements, they may be asked to do further research on Gandhi's philosophy, its influence on Martin Luther King, Jr., and how it can be applied to the resolution of conflicts in our time.

Norton's five-phase approach provides a very useful framework for in-depth study of multicultural literature in the curriculum. It is of great value in helping students gain a comprehensive understanding of the values, beliefs, and traditions as well as the literary forms of parallel cultures. However, if a component of empowerment is worked into the framework, the approach will be more effective in accomplishing the goals for multicultural education.

READING MULTICULTURALLY AS A MEANS OF EMPOWERING

When multicultural literature is incorporated into the curriculum, we want children to read it for social justice and change in addition to enhancing their awareness and appreciation of cultural differences. We want them to develop the ability to identify, analyze, and act on issues associated with cultural differences. When they read literature in general we also want them to read it critically for the same purpose. To accomplish the goals, they need to read it from a multicultural perspective, or to use Hade's (1997) term, read it multiculturally. In the following discussion, I'll expand on this topic, which I touched on in Chapter 1.

To read multiculturally is to adopt a critical approach that seeks to interpret the signs of race, gender, class and other cultural differences in literature, and critique the author's ideological stances implied in those signs. When Hade (1997) discussed the Disney movie, *The Lion King,* with his daughters, he applied cultural criticism to the movie and surfaced meanings that his daughters and other audience overlooked. He was reading the signs of gender and criticizing expressions of sexism in the movie. According to him the movie is sexist for portraying the lionesses as subservient to male lions. Even though they are physically strong enough to defeat Skar, the cruel leader of the pride, they quietly accept his rule.

To further illustrate how to read multiculturally, I will analyze the presentation and interplay of race, class, and gender issues in two recently published books: *Voices in the Park* (Browne, 1998) and the 1999 Newbery winner *Holes* (Sachar, 1998). Since these two books are not classified as multicultural literature by most definitions of the term, readers may not notice those issues. When teachers use them with children in class, they may not call students' attention to the social cultural issues in the books and thus may miss an opportunity to help them identify and analyze them.

Voices in the Park is a picture book of animal fantasy. A rich female gorilla takes her son and their pedigree Labrador for a walk in a park. They meet with a poor male gorilla with his daughter and their dog. The two children become friends immediately and have a great time together, sliding down slides and swinging on climbing bars. The two dogs also "race around like old friends" (n.p.). But the rich lady is not happy that her son and dog mingle with a "rough looking" girl and her "scruffy mongrel" (n.p.). She cuts short her walk and takes her son and dog home. The message about class distinction is quite apparent in the story, but it can be lost on readers who do not read it multiculturally. The mother is prejudiced against the poor. The moment they enter the park, she is concerned that they will run into "frightful types" (n.p.) of people. From her perspective, the girl and her father are among them. This is evident from the epithets she uses to describe the girl and her dog. But her son and her dog do not share her prejudice and therefore are able to cross class boundary to befriend a poor person. This is a story that condemns class prejudice. It is also a story that undoes gender stereotype: the girl is portrayed as more outgoing and daring than the boy. At first the boy seems to be timid and withdrawn. It is the girl who plays the leading role in the story. When the boy is led away by his mother, he looks sad but does not protest. The contrast between the boy's and the girl's characters reflects back on the issue of class distinction. An implied message is that the rich woman's way of bringing up her children is too restrictive. The story is told respectively from the perspectives of the mother, son, father, and daughter. There are four voices speaking in the park. The multiple points of view add to the difficulty of reading the multicultural message in the story. It can be easily read as a story about play and friendship only, and used to teach the literary element of point of view. But in addition to that we should also read the signs of class and gender in the story; in other words, we should read it multiculturally.

Holes is realistic fiction bordering on fantasy. The protagonist, Stanley Yel-nats, a white boy from a poor family, is wrongly convicted of stealing a pair of sneakers donated by a famous baseball player for charity and is sent to a juvenile detention center. He believes his bad luck is caused by a curse on the family incurred by his "no-good-dirty-rotten-pig-stealing-great-great-grandfather." The detention center, which is called the Green Lake Camp, is actually situated in an area of desert. Every inmate must dig a hole five feet deep and five feet in diameter every day, supposedly to build character. In fact, they are digging holes because the Warden, a witch-like woman, is searching for buried treasures. At the center Stanley makes friends with a black boy nicknamed Zero. Stanley teaches him how to read, and in return, Zero helps him dig. When Zero runs away from the center, Stanley is deeply concerned that he will die in the desert. He leaves to look for him, hoping to bring him back. He finds Zero under an overturned boat, still alive, and both escape to a mountain on the edge of the desert. They survive the scorching heat in the desert, living on jars of onion juice that have been left in the sand for a century. They come back to the camp and dig up treasures that belonged to Stanley's great-grandfather. In the end, Stanley is cleared and the corrupt Warden is punished. In a story within the story, which takes place one hundred years ago, the reader learns that a black man called Sam concocted onion juice to treat various ailments. Sam was killed by a white racist because he was in love with a white school teacher named Katherine. Disillusioned with the society, Katherine became an outlaw. It was she who robbed Stanley's great-grandfather and buried his treasure in the desert. The white man who killed Sam and caused the death of Katherine turns out to be the wicked Warden's great-grandfather.

This is a well-crafted story that deals with several universal themes: friendship, survival, fatalism, and retribution. Yet, if we read it multiculturally, we will uncover other layers of meaning associated with class, race, and gender. With respect to class issues, the story condemns an unjust legal system that victimizes the poor. Stanley's parents cannot afford a lawyer, so even though he tells the truth in court, he is still convicted of a crime he did not commit. His trial is delayed several months to fit the schedule of the rich and famous athlete, who is a witness. If Stanley had also been a rich and famous person, that might not have happened. Zero was living on the street when he was arrested. The boy has no parents and nobody cares about him. When the Warden plots to destroy his records after he runs away, she asks one of the counselors at the center: "Is there anyone who might ask questions? Some social worker who took an interest in him?" The guard replied: "He had nobody. He was nobody" (p. 144). The system is totally indifferent to Zero's well-being and neglects his education but does not hesitate to punish him the moment he has a brush with the law.

With respect to racial issues, the story strongly condemns the institutionalized racism that had Sam murdered in cold blood. "It is against the law for a Negro to kiss a white woman," the sheriff said to Katherine (p. 113). The punishment for the crime was hanging. When Katherine told him that he would have to hang her too because she kissed Sam back, he replied that it was not against the law for a white woman to kiss a black man. Katherine tried to reason with him, "We're all equal under the eye of God." The corrupted officer brazenly offered her a deal: "One sweet kiss, and I won't hang your boyfriend. I'll just run him out of town" (p. 114). Katherine ran out and tried to escape with Sam in a boat, but Sam was shot and killed. This tragedy happened one hundred ten years ago. The story unequivocally condemns racism in the past. However, its message about today's racial relations is a positive one. The detention center seems to be free of racial problems. The counselors do not discriminate against black inmates. There is no racial strife among the inmates, either. In Stanley's group, three inmates are black, three are white, and one is Hispanic. "Stanley was thankful that there were no racial problems . . . On the lake they were all the same reddish brown color— the color of dirt" (p. 84). These boys are not unaware of racism in the past, though. They mock Stanley when Zero helps dig his hole: "Same old story . . . The white boy sits around while the black boy does all the work. Ain't that right?" Racism appears to be but a joking matter. The past racial tension is replaced by racial harmony. How realistic is this description? I think the author expresses a good wish rather than portrays a realistic picture of racial relations today.

With respect to gender issues, the story presents a strong female character in Katherine, who is in advance of her time but still believable. She defies racist attitude and legislation to love a black onion picker. She tries to save him when his life is in danger. When Sam is murdered, she would rather die with him than being rescued. After Sam's death, she kills the sheriff and becomes a rebel against an unjust society. Another female character, the Warden, is a villain who rules the center ruthlessly. She paints her fingers with rattlesnake venom and scratches anybody who disobeys her. She fits the stereotype of wicked witch of fairy tales. By contrast, Katherine is not cast in the traditional gender role of a beautiful but weak fairy tale princess. She is beautiful and strong. Instead of depending on a "prince" for protection, she takes her fate into her own hand.

Besides racism, classism, and sexism, the story also criticizes discrimination against obese people. Stanley is overweight, and the kids at his school often tease him about his size. "Even his teachers sometimes made cruel comments without realizing it." When his math teacher teaches ratios, she uses the ratio of

Stanley's weight and that of the lightest child in the class as an example, "unaware of how much embarrassment she caused both of them" (p. 7).

Reading a book multiculturally elucidates the issues of race, class, gender, and other cultural differences in it, which might have been overlooked in a "purely" aesthetic study. It enhances students' multicultural awareness and their ability to identify and analyze issues of cultural differences. Reading multiculturally does not mean censoring problematic books; rather, it means interpreting the signs of race, class, gender, and other cultural differences (Hade, 1997). It is, in essence, a kind of cultural criticism that examines "literary works in their historical and cultural context rather than as disembodied texts" (Purves, 1993, p. 358). Its aim is to teach literature, not just as an intellectual discipline, but also for social critique and social change. If we are to empower students, reading multiculturally should be made an integral part of literature programs.

OPPORTUNITIES FOR TEACHERS TO INFORM AND EMPOWER THEMSELVES

Teaching multicultural literature is new and challenging to many teachers. As Soter (1999) points out, "teachers interested in using literature of other cultures (whether ethnic or global) [are concerned that] they do not know enough about the cultures represented in those books" (p. 86). Thus, to introduce multicultural literature into their classroom, teachers need to study it first. Before teaching a piece of multicultural literature, Willis and Palmer (1998) suggest that teachers do some research into it:

They should compile a biographical sketch of the author, a historical review of the setting, a historical review of the period in which the author wrote, and a listing of cultural footnotes to enhance an understanding of the novel. [The research would give teachers and their students] a better understanding of the culture under study. (p. 228)

No expert knows every culture in the world. For all teachers and teacher educators teaching multicultural literature is a continuing process of researching and learning about other cultures.

Acquiring knowledge of other cultures, however, is only the first step. In learning to teach multicultural literature, teachers should also move from informing to empowering themselves. To help students explore, and perhaps transform, their cultural perspectives, teachers should first engage in examining their own. They need to go "through the same journey of introspection of self and exploration of other voices that they are expected to lead their students through" (Wilkinson and Kido, 1997, p. 256). They should be willing and able to "unlearn biases, prejudices, and stereotypes [and develop] a cultural consciousness that responds to difference in a sensitive and thoughtful manner" (Willis and Palmer, 1998, p. 216).

Wilkinson and Kido (1997) offer a good example of how teachers examine and transform their cultural beliefs and attitudes in a teacher education program. One of the approaches they used was combining reader response and transformation, similar to the one Macphee used in her first grade classroom. The new and practicing teachers in the program read multicultural texts that appealed to them as adults, recorded their reflections in double-entry response journals, and engaged in dynamic dialogues to share their responses. Their responses demonstrated that they were affected and transformed by good quality multicultural literature, as evidenced in the following examples:

Before I read this essay and other parts of his autobiography, I used to think Malcolm X was a black man who hated white people, never stopping to realize why he hated us so much. I assumed that his hatred stemmed from our history of slavery, how blacks were so poorly treated during that era. However, I now realize that he had other good reasons to hate white people, especially white supremacists who brutally murdered his father. This is not to say that I condone his hatred, but I understand how he [came] to hate.

After reading [Ortiz-] Cofer's (1990) *Silent Dancing: A Partial Remembering of a Puerto Rican Childhood,* I have some understanding now what it is to experience "cultural schizophrenia," as Cofer describes her double identity and bi-cultural life. She shattered my stereotypical views of Puerto-Rican/Latino women. I will always remember: "It is custom, however, not chromosomes that leads us to choose scarlet over pink." (pp. 254-258)

With new visions and voices they acquired from the program, the teachers were "better able to meet with the challenges of dealing with issues of diversity in the classroom" and some were able to bring about "notable transformations" among their students (p. 259).

Jordan and Purves (1993) point out that "few teachers possessed the necessary training or support needed to teach multicultural literary texts as cultural artifacts" (p. 18) and implement multicultural education. If multicultural literature is to play its role of informing and empowering students, both preservice and in-service teachers should be given an opportunity to inform and empower themselves in college courses or workshops that employ approaches like those developed by Wilkinson and Kido (1997) and by Willis and Palmer (1998). Studies have shown that if teachers are not informed and empowered, multicultural literature "runs the risk of being trivialized and misused" (Fang, et al., 1999, p. 259). Instead of promoting understanding of the "self" and "other," it may reinforce misconceptions, stereotypes, and prejudices.

NOTE

The section "From Informing to Empowering in Thematic Units" in this chapter is based in part on a paper I coauthored with Mary Guenther, which was presented at the NCTE Convention in Detroit in 1997. I want to thank Mary for graciously allowing me to use part of the paper here.

REFERENCES

Banks, J. A. (1989). Multicultural education: Characteristics and goals. In J. A. Banks and C. A. M. Banks (Eds.), *Multicultural education: Issues and perspectives* (pp. 2-27). Boston: Allyn and Bacon.

Banks, J. A. (1994). Transforming the mainstream curriculum. *Educational Leadership, 51* (8), 4-8.

Barta, J., and Grindler, M. C. (1996). Exploring bias using multicultural literature for children. *The Reading Teacher, 50* (3), 269-270.

Fang, Z., Fu, D., and Lamme, L. L. (1999). Rethinking the role of multicultural literature in literacy instruction: Problems, paradox, and possibilities. *The New Advocate, 12* (3), 259-276.

Finazzo, D. A. (1996). *All for the children: Multicultural essentials of literature.* Albany, NY: Delmar.

Hade, D. D. (1997). Reading multiculturally. In V. Harris (Ed.), *Using multiethnic literature in the K–8 classroom* (pp. 233-256). Norwood, MA: Christopher-Gordon.

Jordan, S., and Purves, A. C. (1993). *Issues in the responses of students to culturally diverse texts: A preliminary study* (Report Series 7.3). Albany, NY: National Research Center on Literature Teaching and Learning.

Macphee, J. S. (1997). "That's not fair!" A white teacher reports on white first graders' responses to multicultural literature. *Language Arts, 74* (1), 33-40.

McCarthy, C. R. (1998). Multicultural education, minority identities, textbooks, and the challenge of curriculum reform. In A. Willis (Ed.), *Teaching and using multicultural literature in grades 9-12: Moving beyond the canon* (pp. 1-16). Norwood, MA: Christopher-Gordon.

McGinley, W., Kamberelis G., Mahoney, T., Madigan, D., Rybicki, V., and Oliver, J. (1997). Re-visiting reading and teaching literature through the lens of narrative theory. In T. Rogers and A. O. Soter (Eds.), *Reading across cultures: Teaching literature in a diverse society* (pp. 42-68). New York: Teachers College Press.

Norton, D. E. (1990). Teaching multicultural literature in the reading curriculum. *The Reading Teacher, 44* (10), 28-40.

Norton, D. E. (2000). *Multicultural children's literature: Through the eyes of many children.* Columbus, OH: Merrill.

Purves, A. (1993). Toward a reevaluation of reader response and school literature. *Language Arts, 70,* 348-361.

Rasinski, T., and Padak, N. D. (1990). Multicultural learning through children's literature. *Language Arts, 69,* 576-580.

Rosenblatt, L. M. (1978). *The reader, the text, the poem.* Carbondale: Southern Illinois University Press.

Sims Bishop, R. (1994). Introduction. In R. Sims Bishop (Ed.), *Kaleidoscope: A multicultural booklist for grades K-8.* Urbana, IL: National Council of Teachers of English Press.

Soter, A. O. (1999). *Young adult literature and the new literary theories: Developing critical readers in middle school.* New York: Teachers College Press.

Valedez, A. (1999). *Learning in living color: Using literature to incorporate multicultural education into the primary curriculum.* Boston: Allyn and Bacon.

Wilkinson, P. A., and Kido, E. (1997). Literature and cultural Awareness: Voices from the journey, *Language Arts, 74,* 255-265.

Willis, A. (Ed.). (1998). *Teaching multicultural literature in grades 9-12: Moving beyond the canon* (pp. 215-250). Norwood, MA: Christopher-Gordon.

Willis, A., and Palmer, M. D. (1998). Negotiating the classroom: Learning and teaching multicultural literature. In A. Willis (Ed.), *Teaching multicultural literature in grades 9-12: Moving beyond the canon* (pp. 215-250). Norwood, MA: Christopher-Gordon.

Books for Children and Young Adults

Ada, A. F. (1995). *My name is Maria Isabel.* Ill. by K. D. Thompson. New York: Simon and Schuster.
Baker, O. (1981). *Where the buffaloes begin.* Ill. S. Gammell. New York: F. Warne.
Bercaw, E. C. (2000). *Halmoni's day.* Ill. R. Hunt. New York: Dial Books for Young Readers.
Browne, A. (1998). *Voices in the park.* New York: DK Publishing.
Bruchac, J. (1992). *Thirteen moons on turtle's back.* Ill. by T. Locker. New York: Philomel.
Bruchac, J. (2000). *Crazy Horse's vision.* Ill. by S. D. Nelson.
Bunting, E. (1994). *A day's work.* Ill. by R. Himler. New York: Clarion.
Bunting, E. (1995). *Cheyenne again.* Ill. by Toddy. New York: Clarion.
Byrd, B. (1972). *When clay sings.* Ill. T. Bahti. New York: Scribner.
Byrd, B. (1981). *The desert voices.* Ill. P. Parnall. New York: Scribner.
Cohen, C. L. (1991). *Mud pony.* Ill. S. Begay. New York: Scholastic.
Choi, S. N. (1993). *Halmoni and the picnic.* Boston: Houghton Mifflin.
Cohlene, T. (1991). *The turquoise boy: A Navajo legend.* Ill. C. Reasoner. Mahwah, NJ: Troll Communications.
dePaola, T. (1973). *Nana upstairs, Nana downstairs.* New York: Putnam.
dePaola, T. (1991). *The legend of the Indian paintbrush.* New York: Putnam.
Flournoy, V. (1996). *Patchwork quilt.* Ill. by J. Pinkney. New York: Scholastic.
Fraiser, D. (1991). *On the day you were born.* San Diego, CA: Harcourt Brace Jovanovich.
Garza, C. L. (1990). *Family pictures.* San Francisco, CA: Children's Book Press.
Goble, P. (1988). *Her seven brothers.* New York: Bradbury.
Goble, P. (1993). *The lost children: The boys who are neglected.* New York: Bradbury.
Golding, W. (1962). *Lord of the flies.* New York: Coward, McCann and Geoghegan.
Hauggard, E. C. (1991). *The boy and the samurai.* Boston: Houghton Mifflin.
Hoffman, M. (1991). *Amazing Grace.* Ill. by C. Binch. New York: Dial.
Johnson, D. (2000). *Quinnie Blue.* Ill. J. Ransome. New York: Henry Holt.
Lankford, M. D. (1992). *Hopscotch around the world.* Ill. by K. Milone. New York: Morrow Junior Books.
Lawlor, V. (Ed.). (1995). *I was dreaming to come to America.* New York: Viking.
Levinson, R. (1985). *Watch the stars come out.* New York: Dutton.
Littlechild, G. (1993). *This land is my land.* Emeryville, CA: Children's Books.
McKissack, P. (1986). *Flossie and the fox.* Ill. by R. Isdora. New York: Dial.
Mora, P. (1994). *Pablo's tree.* Ill. by C. Lang. New York: Macmillan.
Oughton, J. (1992). *How the stars fell into the sky: A Navajo legend.* Ill. by L. Desimini. Boston: Houghton Mifflin.
Polacco, P. (1988). *The keeping quilt.* New York: Simon & Schuster.
Polacco, P. (1992). *Chicken Sunday.* New York: Morrow.
Raschka, C. (1993). *Yo! Yes?* New York: Orchard.
Ringgold, F. (1992). *Aunt Harriet's underground railroad in the sky.* New York: Crown.
Rosenberg, M. B. (1986). *Making a new home in America.* New York: Lothrop, Lee and Shepard.

Sabin, R. (1985). *Jackie Robinson.* New York: Troll.

Sachar, L. (1998). *Holes.* New York: Farrar, Straus and Giroux.

San Souci, R. D. (2000). *The secret of the stones.* Ill. by J. Ransome. New York: Phyllis Fogelman.

Say, A. (1993). *Grandfather's journey.* Boston: Houghton Mifflin.

Singer, M. (2000). *On the same day in March: A tour of the world's weather.* Ill. by F. Lessac. New York: HarperCollins.

Stanek, M. (1989). *I speak English for mom.* Ill. by J. Friedman. Morton Grove, IL: Albert Whitman.

Surat, M. (1989). *Angel child, dragon child.* Ill. by V. D. Mai. New York: Little Brown.

Vigna, J. (1992). *Black like Kyra, white like me.* Ill. by N. B. Westcott. Morton Grove, IL: Albert Whitman.

Whelan, G. (1992). *Goodbye, Vietnam.* New York: Random House.

White Deer of Autumn. (1991). *Ceremony in the circle of life.* Ill. by D. San Souci. Hillsboro, OR: Beyond Words Publishing.

Wood, T. (1992). *A boy becomes a man at Wounded Knee.* New York: Walker.

Woodson, J. (2001). *The other side.* Ill. by E. B. Lewis. New York: Putnam's Sons.

9

Investigating Reader Responses to Multicultural Literature

Reader response theory, especially Rosenblatt's (1978) transactional theory, has been driving literary instruction for over half a century. This theory emphasizes readers' lived-through experience of a literary text and values their personal input into its interpretation. Instructional methods based on reader response theory encourage students to immerse themselves in literature, engage in the story world, express their personal feelings and thoughts, and share their responses through group discussion to achieve a fuller and richer interpretation of the text. A reader response approach is appropriate for teaching multicultural literature in terms of engaging readers in stories about unfamiliar cultures and making them reflect on their own and others' values, beliefs, and perspectives. It should be noted, however, that "much of reader-response theory ignores the issues of race, class, and sex, and give no hint of the conflicts, sufferings, and passions that attend these realities" (Schweickart, 1986, p. 21). Therefore, transactional theory should, and can be, combined with theories of cultural criticism such as post-colonial, critical multicultural, Marxist, and feminist criticism, for reader response theory can accommodate cultural criticism (Cai, 2000). Despite its limitations (Rogers and Soter, 1997), reader response theory still has an important role to play in enhancing cross-cultural understanding and appreciation. In the previous chapter, we have seen how it is combined with Banks's (1994) transformation approach in some studies to empower students and teachers.

To implement a reader response approach in teaching multicultural literature, teachers need to know what happens when readers read multicultural literature. It is more complicated than it appears. I propose a multidimensional model for the study of reader response to multicultural literature. For researchers, this model may provide guidance for reviewing previous studies and conducting further investigation. For teachers, it will provide insights into the various ways in which students may respond to multicultural literature and factors that may affect their response. In this chapter, I first explain the conceptualization of the model and then use it to schematize studies that have been conducted.

A MULTIDIMENSIONAL MODEL

In a report on research and the pedagogical application of reader response to children's literature, Michael Benton (1993) found that five themes have emerged in the research. One of them is found in "culturally oriented" studies concerning with "children's concepts and social attitudes." These studies are divided into three groups:

Multicultural and feminist studies, which explore how far literature can be helpful in teaching about issues of race and gender; whole culture studies, which consider children's response to literature in the context of the broad range of their interests; and cross-cultural studies, which compare the responses of young readers from different countries to the same texts to identify similarities and cultural differences. (p. 22)

Benton illustrated the thrust of each group of studies with examples. An example for the first group is a study by Beverley Naidoo (1992) that shows how exploring multicultural literature using reader response methods may help readers clarify and change their values and attitudes. A study by Beach and Freedman is given as an example for the second group. Their study examines adolescents' responses to magazine ads and short stories as an act that reflects their teenage culture. One of the examples for the third group is Bunbury and Tabbert's study that compares Australian and German children's responses to an Australian bush-ranger story (Benton, 1993). Of the three groups, the second one does not fall within the purview of what I term the study of reader response to multicultural literature, because it subscribes to a broader definition of culture and focuses on teenage culture. Reader response to multicultural literature is also a broader field for exploration than is covered in the studies of the first and third groups. Many studies go beyond the scope mapped out by of Benton's classification.

To better understand the complex act of responding to multicultural literature requires the proposed multidimensional model, which encompasses important areas of research and incorporates various reader response theories that guide the research. This model draws upon schema theory (Adams and Collins, 1977), structuralist theory (Culler, 1975), transactional theory (Rosenblatt, 1978), phenomenological theory (Iser, 1974, 1978), the theory of intersubjective reading (Bleich, 1986), the theory of interpretive community (Fish, 1980), and cultural theory of response (Beach, 1993). These theories provide different lenses for examining three dimensions of reader response to multicultural literature: cognitive-developmental, affective-attitudinal, and social-communal (Fig. 9.1). These three dimensions are integral to the main inquiry into the relationship between culture and response to literature. As reader response is an organic process, the three areas of investigation are interrelated. "Instead of thinking of reading as a linear process," Rosenblatt (1985) notes, "we have to think rather of a complex network or circuit of inter-relationships, with reciprocal interplay" (pp. 100-101). However, the three dimensions are studied separately for the purpose of analysis and explication. Their interconnections make overlap among them un-avoidable. As a matter of fact, many studies focus on one dimension but also touch upon others. For example, Taylor's (1997) study, "Multicultural Literature Preferences of Low-Ability African American and Hispanic American Fifth-Graders," focuses on students' preferences in multicultural literature, a theme in the "affective-attitudinal" area, but in the analysis of findings, the author also discusses the influences of students' background knowledge and cultural envi-ronment on their responses, which fall into the categories of "cognitive-developmental" and "social-communal," respectively.

Figure 9.1
A Multidimensional Model

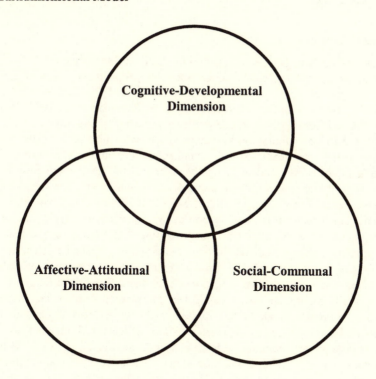

COGNITIVE-DEVELOPMENTAL DIMENSION

Research in the cognitive-developmental dimension of reader response looks into reader's cognitive ability to comprehend and interpret a literary text, the strategies they use to process the text, patterns of responding behavior, and the development of cognitive ability through responding to literature. Schema theory, transactional theory, and structuralist theory all stress the importance of the background knowledge (knowledge of the world and knowledge of literature), prior experience, perspectives, and values that readers bring to bear upon the text. These factors affect their comprehension and interpretation of it. What readers bring to the transaction with at text may be culturally specific. Knowledge of the world, for example, may refer to knowledge of a specific culture, and knowledge of literature may refer to that of the literary forms, conventions, and features of that particular culture. Such culturally specific knowledge, experience, perspective, and values constitute a person's cultural identity. Studies in the cognitive-developmental area deal with the relationship between readers' cultural identity and their comprehension and interpretation of the text. Many focus on how culturally specific background knowledge or schemata affect the process and outcome of readers' transaction with the text.

Comprehension

Many studies have been conducted on the basis of schema theory. They try to demonstrate the difference between an culturally informed and uninformed readers in comprehension of the text (e.g., Anderson et al., 1977; Kintsch and Green, 1978; Steffensen, Joag-Dev, & Anderson, 1979; Reynolds et al., 1982; Nelson, 1987; Flores Duenas, 1997). These studies either compare the responses of readers from different cultural backgrounds to the same text or compare the responses of the same reader to texts about different cultures. The results of the research indicate that readers comprehend better and recall more information from culturally familiar texts than culturally unfamiliar texts. The following are three examples. The study by Steffensen et al. (1977) compared Indian (natives of India) and American readers' responses to a letter about a typical American wedding and one about a typical Indian wedding. The finding reveals that subjects read the culturally familiar passage more rapidly, recalled a larger amount of information from the text, and "produced more culturally appropriate elaboration of the native passage" (p. 10). Conversely, the subjects took longer to read the culturally unfamiliar text, recalled less information from it, and misinterpreted it. Reynolds et al. (1982) studied randomly selected black and white eighth graders' responses to the same text. The subjects read a letter that "dealt with an instance of 'sounding,' a form of verbal ritual insult found in the black community" (p. 353). The results showed that "black students tended to interpret the passage as being about verbal play, whereas white students tended to interpret it as about physical aggression" (p. 353). Flores Duenas (1997) investigated four Mexican American fifth grade bilingual students' responses to stories by Mexican American and non-Mexican American authors. One of the findings was that the subjects understood the themes and events of stories by Mexican American authors much better than stories by non-Mexican American authors. They also wrote better retellings of the Mexican American stories. All three studies found a correlation between readers' cultural schemata and comprehension of text, either informational or literary.

Other studies are more process oriented than product oriented, focusing on strategies that readers use or response patterns that emerge as readers process a text. They show differences in the use of reading strategies for processing culturally familiar and unfamiliar text (Lee, 1985; Malik, 1990; Pritchard, 1990; Cai, 1992). Lee (1985) compared the responses of sixty Korean and forty-one American college students' responses to two stories, one from each culture and found, among others, significant differences in categories of response strategies (Purves and Rippere, 1968) between the two groups. "Korean students made more engagement responses, more interpretative responses, and more miscellaneous responses to the stories than American students, while American students made far more evaluative responses to the stories" (p. 115). Lee believed that these differences in response patterns reflected cultural values: "emotionalism, indirectness, and collectivism are emphasized . . . in the Korean culture while rationalism, directness, and individualism are emphasized in the American culture" (120). Pritchard's (1990) study developed a taxonomy of twenty-two processing strategies in five categories and compared the use of these strategies by thirty eleventh graders from the United States and thirty eleventh graders from the Pacific Island nation of Palau as they read culturally familiar and unfamiliar text. The subjects were found to use some categories of strategies more often to process the culturally unfamiliar text than familiar text. They "rely more heavily on strategies for developing awareness, accepting ambiguity, or establishing intrasentential ties" (p. 288). They may use these strategies more frequently with unfamiliar text because "they encounter difficulty in relating stimulus sentences to other portions of the text or to their own background knowledge" (p. 288). Pritchard concluded that cultural schemata affect readers' processing strategies as well as comprehension of text.

Interpretation

Readers' cultural schemata (including culturally specific literary schemata) also affect their interpretation of literary elements and aesthetic features in text. Noda (1980) studied the responses of a Japanese reader and an American reader to six modern Japanese stories and found significant differences between the two readers' responses to both the cultural and aesthetic features of the stories. The American reader had difficulty interpreting the Japanese cultural symbols; they either did not recognize or made negative comments on the uniquely Japanese aesthetic features, such as "the sense of beauty in death, mortality, and the fragility of life" (p. 361), which the Japanese reader understood and savored. When interpreting the literary elements such as setting and plot, the American reader generally tended to discuss them as aspects of the form or structure, whereas the Japanese reader tended to interpret them "as meaningful vehicles for conveying human emotions and mood" (p. 357). Bunbury and Tabbert's (1989) study com-

pared Australian and German children's responses to the ironic portrayal of an
Australian national hero in the novel *Midnite*. They found that children of both
countries are capable of ironic identification. The difference between them lies
in the fact that the Australian children's responses were culturally specific, recognizing the hero as "a variation of the traditional image of the bushranger" (p.
31), whereas the German children's responses were more general, identifying
him as a variation from their notion of a hero or a robber. In a study that compared American and Chinese readers' responses to an American short story, a
Chinese folktale, and a Chinese poem (Cai, 1992), I found significant difference
between Chinese American readers' response to the literary element of style.
Because the Chinese subjects had acquired the literary schema and developed
the literary competence (Culler, 1975) to understand the traditional Chinese poetry, they performed better in interpreting and appreciating the style of the poem
than the American subjects. I also found that the subjects interpreted the themes
and characterization of the literary works in ways consistent with their respective
cultural schemata.

Complex Relationship

Although many studies have proved that readers' cultural background influences their comprehension of a text, the correlation between the two should not
be understood in a rigid manner (Sinha, 1995). Recent studies have shown that
readers' cultural background cannot guarantee that they are familiar with a text
that reflects his or her culture and therefore understand the text better than other
readers. Grice and Vaughn (1992) studied nine black and four white third grade
students' responses to twenty-four culturally conscious books and found that
students could not fully understand and appreciate these books because they
were unfamiliar with African and African American culture and history. Only a
"slightly greater percentage of black than white youngsters responded favorably
to the 24 books." "Consequently," they concluded, "just being black or living in
the inner city was not necessarily a prerequisite for benefiting from what was
read" (p. 161). Students need to receive "thoughtful lessons on African and
Afro-American culture" preceding exposure to culturally conscious books. We
cannot assume that membership in an ethnic group automatically assures full,
accurate knowledge of that ethnic group.

Based on many of the studies cited previously, we may assume that that readers' prior cultural knowledge helps them comprehend a text. But sometimes the
opposite is true. Some research has revealed that students' prior cultural experiences may be an impediment rather than an aid to their comprehension of text.
Wilson and Thomas (1995) found that some African American students misin-
terpret an essay entitled "Black Family Life" "because it doesn't immediately
confirm their own experiences" (p. 61). They rejected the essay for stereotyping
African American family experiences, despite the fact that the description of
African American families is "put forward . . . as the foil for a straw man argu-

ment" (p. 54). The authors point out that prior knowledge should not be constructed as monolithic. Rather, it is shaped by "an intricate web of cultural myths, emotional experiences, and prior assumptions" (p. 63). As such, it may complicate the comprehension of text. More research is needed to prove that this also holds true of readers from other ethnic backgrounds.

We may also assume that members of the same ethnic group may have the same background knowledge about their culture and neglect possible difference in their response to literature. "Cultural knowledge is in part personal construct" (Leung, 1995, p. 29). Members of the same ethnic group acquire knowledge of their culture from various sources—from family, school, community, literature, television shows, movies, and so on. Their cultural knowledge varies in depth and scope. Lueng studied four girls' (three Chinese American and one Caucasian) responses to Jean Fritz's fictional autobiography, *Homesick, My Own Story* (1992), and found not only differences between the Chinese American girls and the Caucasian girl but also differences among the Chinese American girls. One Chinese American girl had limited knowledge of Chinese history and culture. She found it difficult to read *Homesick,* which was set in China in the 1920s, a period marked by political chaos and civil war. But the book did not pose big problems for the other two Chinese American girls because they were more knowledgeable about Chinese history and culture. This study shows that different developmental levels of cultural knowledge among readers of the same ethnic group affect their response to literature.

How to develop students' cross-cultural competence is a major concern in multicultural education. However, studies that focus on the developmental aspect of reader response to multicultural literature are surprisingly rare. Further research could be done in this area, for example, comparing readers who have been given instruction in multicultural literature and readers who have not. One might explore research questions similar to those raised by Sims (1983) with regard to response to African American literature: "Does exposure over time make a difference, i.e. when children have been exposed to Black literature as an integral part of their reading experience, do they respond differently from those with limited and experimental exposure?" (p. 27). Besides time of exposure, comparison can be made between the effects of different reading materials, curricula, instructional methods, and so on. The central question is: do these factors help to develop students, both mainstream and ethnic minority students, into informed readers of multicultural literature?

AFFECTIVE-ATTITUDINAL DIMENSION

The affective component of one's schemata plays an important part in reader response to multicultural literature: In reading, as Iser (1974) notes, the reader actively exercises his or her faculties, "generally the emotional and cognitive" (p. xiii). The affective, or emotional, aspects of reader response include the readers' preferences for various books, like or dislike of characters, identification with characters, and involvement in the story. In terms of transactional theory, these responses lean to the aesthetic end of the response continuum whereas the cognitive aspect of response leans to the efferent end (Rosenblatt, 1978). The affective aspect of response is associated with a reader's attitude toward the text, which influences his or her responses. According to the cultural theory of response (Beach, 1993), readers are socialized by various institutions to adopt certain "reading formations," that is, "acquired ideological stances that constitute certain subject positions or desired ways of responding" (p. 129). Readers' "reading formations" or "subject positions," which reflect their cultural beliefs and attitudes, partly determine their acceptance, resistance, or rejection of a text. Research in this area also addresses the effects of reading multicultural literature on changing or modifying readers' attitudes about themselves and people of other racial or ethnic backgrounds.

Preference, Like/Dislike, and Identification

Readers' preference for books in the stories has been the focus or an aspect of many studies. Sims (1983) did a landmark case study of an almost eleven-year-old black girl's responses to fiction about African Americans. Her findings revealed that the black child prefered books related to her personal experiences and characters with whom she could identify. Nevel (1999) did a thirteen-week case study of 10 tenth grade students to examine how students of mixed ethnic backgrounds respond to multicultural poetry. The students read poems from four major minority cultures and participated in reader response activities. The results showed that 75 % of the students of color expressed a preference for literature from their own cultures, and fully 100% connected most to literature from their own cultures. The white students had a lower percentage of connection to literature about people of color.

In a study of fourteen African American and ten Hispanic American fifth-graders' preferences for multicultural books, Taylor (1997) narrowed down the investigation to preferences for different types of multicultural literature, including culturally conscious books, melting books, folktales, and others. The subjects read twenty-four picture books—mainly melting pot and culturally conscious books—and chose their favorites. The results were mixed. The top three favorite books for all students were a melting pot story, a culturally conscious book, and a folktale. The top three books preferred by African American students were culturally conscious books. However, three culturally conscious books were also among the least favorites. This was also the case with the Hispanic American students; they ranked some culturally conscious books high and others low on their scale of preference. This study revealed that lack of understanding about, and appreciation of, African American history and culture prevented them from fully understanding and appreciating some culturally conscious books about African Americans.

Towell et al. (1997) studied the responses of 110 primary-aged children to eight books that portrayed male and female children of different racial or ethnic backgrounds and found no evidence to indicate a relationship between children's cultural identity and their preference of books or identification with characters in the story. "The majority of the children liked the books without reference to ethnicity as one of the reasons except for a few children in grades two and three" (p. 11). They concluded that a good story may transcend ethnicity in the minds of young children, at least in the primary grades.

Towell et al.'s (1997) and Taylor's (1997) studies found no direct relationship between readers' ethnicity and preferences for books, while Sims' (1983) and Nevel's (1999) studies revealed that readers' ethnicity affects readers' preferences. The mixed results of the studies indicate that, like the relationship between readers' ethnic identity and the comprehension of multicultural literature, the relationship between readers' cultural identity and their preferences for multicultural literature or identification with characters in the story is complex. Further research is needed to help us understand it. A factor to consider in future studies is the readers' developmental stage of ethnic identity formation. The subjects in Sims' (1983) study and Nevel's (1999) study are older than those in Towell et al.'s (1997) study and Taylor's (1997) study. They may have been more aware of their ethnicity and more able to express their understanding of it.

In some studies of readers' preferences for stories, characters, and other literary aspects, researchers examine specifically the relationship between their cultural values and their responses. Ho's (1990) study of Singaporean adolescents' responses to U.S. young adult literature focused on the conflict between the readers' cultural values and the characters' values in the fiction. The discrepancy between the two sets of values influenced the readers' preferences and appreciation of the characters. The readers found the portrayal of some parent figures unreasonable because by Singaporean standards, they behaved cruelly to their children; they considered the unconformable behaviors of some teenage characters irresponsible or inconsiderate; and they admired some characters' defiance of their parents because sometimes they felt their own parents imposed too many restrictions on them. "Their responses are unique," the author concluded, "because Singapore society and culture are unique" (p. 257). Hopper-Weil (1989) compared Puerto Rican and American reader responses to culturally familiar and unfamiliar short stories and found that the Americans tended to view the individual positively, emphasizing the needs of self, while the Puerto Ricans, as consistent with their positive view of family, tended to value the love and union of family over individual needs and desires. Readers' judgmental responses to stories and characters can be explained in terms of what Beach (1995) calls the "cultural model." Beach maintains that readers may experience "tension between their own cultural models and the portrayal of cultures in literature that differ from their own culture" (p. 88). For example, when reading *Shabanu* by Suzanne Staples (1989), some readers may feel a tension between their own and a fundamentalist Islamic cultural model regarding family roles and gender equity. Students with a "feminist" cultural model may be highly critical of Shabanu's mistreatment by her father. . . . The high-level goals of an Islamic cultural model [are] based on the belief in the need for the father to maintain authority over the family. . . . Students with an evangelical Christian cultural model, in which the father is perceived to be "head of the household," may be less critical of the family's patriarchal attitudes. (p. 88)

The interaction between readers' cultural models and the portrayal of culture in multicultural literature is an area worth more research.

Identification with characters in stories is another important subject for study. Some of the aforementioned studies had touched upon this subject, but do not focus on it. The following are three more studies that in part deal with identification. In a case study, Smith (1995) investigated African American students' response to literature and found that they selected books that most closely reflected their own "cultural frame of reference" (p. 574). In responding to these self-selected books, they showed a close personal connection with the characters who shared their experiences and language patterns. Their responses to the experiences of African American characters were strongly personal and emotional.

Peggy Rice (1999) conducted a study of white mid- to high middle-class fifth graders' responses to Gary Soto's short stories and found, among other things, that "with limited or no understanding of Hispanic culture, the students had difficulty relating to the experiences of the protagonists in the stories, even though these experiences were 'universal'" (p. 8). She noted that an implication of this finding is that "it is important not to assume that children will identify with the universal experiences portrayed by characters in culturally conscious stories" (p. 8).

A study conducted by Liaw (1995) investigated eleven six- to ten-year-old Chinese children's response to three picture books that contained Chinese characters. One interesting finding in terms of identification with character is that the majority of the subjects could not relate to the Chinese girl in the picture book *I Hate English* (Levine, 1989) because they never hated English and learning English was easy for them. One child even crossed out the title and changed it to *I Like English*. This finding shows that personal experiences can be an important factor when it comes to identification with characters in multicultural literature. It also suggests that some multicultural books may not capture the reality of a particular culture.

Involvement

Research in the readers' involvement in multicultural literature is relatively limited. The two studies done by Altieri (1993, 1996) stand out conspicuously in this area. Both studies attempted to determine if there was a relationship between students' ethnicity and level of aesthetic involvement. The 1993 study used 60 third-grade students of varied ethnic backgrounds as subjects. The 1996 study replicated the study with some modifications, using a larger number of subjects in higher grades (122 fifth and 118 seventh grade students). In both studies, the subjects listened to multicultural stories read to them by the researcher and were told, "Write anything you want about the story" (Altieri, 1996, p. 239). The written responses were analyzed using an instrument that measured six levels of aesthetic involvement. The results of data analysis indicated that the students' ethnicity did not influence their involvement in the story. "Subjects, regardless of ethnicity or culture portrayed in text consistently demonstrated aesthetic involvement in the stories" (Altieri, 1996, p. 242). Grade was also not found a significant factor in determining level of involvement. The only significant relationship between students' ethnicity and culture portrayed in the story existed for one out of five responses focuses, the "story world" focus, which demonstrated "the reader placing himself/herself into the character's shoes" (Altieri, 1996, p. 243). African Americans were least likely to focus on the story world when reading white stories, and white students were the least likely to focus on the story world when responding to African American stories.

Reader involvement is a very important part of aesthetic experience of a text. As Altieri (1996) points out, "research shows that by becoming personally involved in a story students obtain a higher level of understanding than those who respond efferently" (p. 238). Further research in this area is very much needed. Based on her finding, Altieri (1996) claims that "students are able to become involved in texts which are not of their culture and thus have a rich literary experience" (p. 245). If future research can provide support for this claim, teachers will be more assured about using multicultural literature in the curriculum.

Resistance

In contrast to involvement to multicultural literature is resistance to it. Researchers have documented students' resistance to the study of multicultural materials in various ways and for various reasons. Ruzich (1999) reported that conservative, working-class white students in two colleges where she has taught resisted the study of multicultural literature for several reasons. They believed that "these works are irrelevant to their future employment skills and goals, or that these works aren't the kind of 'classic works' that can help them to become well-rounded, educated people" (p. 299). They also viewed the readings and discussions of these works as "threats and responded with belligerent silence" (Ruzich, 1999, p. 299). In their study of issues in student responses to multicultural literature, Jordan and Purves (1993) found that students "tend to resist points of view that they are unfamiliar with, ideas that they haven't heard from friends and family" (p. 10). They also rejected a text because the experience it described were alien to them or because they did not understand it due to a lack of background knowledge about the culture in the text.

Beach's (1997) study of students' resistance to engagement with multicultural literature showed how the "subject positions" of some white students in a suburban high schools led them to various forms of resistance in responding to multicultural literature: they resented challenges to white supremacy, denied racial differences, accepted stereotyped instead of authentic portrayals of racial difference, and exhibited reluctance to adopt alternative cultural perspectives and change the status quo.

Not only white readers resist multicultural texts; readers of parallel culture backgrounds may also become "resisting readers." When their subject positions are at odds with those of the author (e.g., subject positions that reflect ignorance, bias, prejudice, or racism), parallel culture readers will "read against" the text. In a study conducted in 1992, I compared American readers and Chinese readers' responses to an excerpt from *Footprints of the Dragon* by Oakes (1949)(for a summary and critique of the book, see Chapter 3). The results indicated that Chinese readers were more sensitive to racial bias in the text than American readers and also felt more strongly about it than American readers. They responded very negatively to the story and the stereotyped main character, Hi Wo, who is portrayed as workaholic and subservient (Cai, 1992).

Parallel culture readers may resist engagement with a multicultural text in a very different way. Their resistance arises, not from the conflict between their subject positions and those of the implied author, but from fear and anger at the racial injustice in the story world and its connection to the real world. Möller and Allen (2000) terms this kind of resistance "engaged resisting" (p. 172) in their study of 4 fifth grade girls' responses to Mildred Taylor's (1987) *The Friendship*. Their engaged resisting took a variety of forms: they resisted not only the text, but also the implied outcomes of the story and the discussion of disturbing connections to reality. "In its most intense forms, resisting took the form of detachment—attempts to dissociate from the character or to disengage from the book and the related discussion" (p. 174).

As the aforementioned studies indicate, resistance to multicultural literature may stem from various causes and take different forms. It is a complex phenomenon and a sensitive issue, which reflects conflicts of ideological and political positions. We need more research to probe into its complex nature. Future studies may further investigate parallel culture readers' resistance, which has not been studied as much as the resistance of mainstream readers.

Racial Attitude

Rosenblatt (1995) believed that books might help change attitudes toward different races. Many studies have been conducted to determine whether reading multicultural literature would affect readers' racial attitudes. Some studies focused on how it affects the self-concept of minority students. Woodward (1970) studied the effect of teaching all black literature on ninth grade black students' reading ability and self-concept. A class, the treatment group, was taught a collection of black literature, while another class, the control group, was taught material from the state-adopted text, both for one semester. The results of the study showed that studying black literature enhanced the self-esteem of the black students. Guzman-Trevino (1996) studied Mexican American students' responses to Mexican American literature in a book-club setting and found that it validated the students as well as motivated them to read. Other studies investigate whether reading multicultural literature brings about attitudinal changes concerning race and ethnicity in white readers. Spears-Bunton's (1990) study of how students in an eleventh grade English class reacted to the introduction of African American literature into their curriculum showed that students' attitudes toward such texts were drawn on ethnic and racial lines. While African American students embraced literature that reflected their experiences, European American students resisted it. The cultural tension in the classroom came to a head when a European American boy declared publicly "I hate Black literature" (p. 570). As the class progressed, however, "subtle changes" occurred. The reading of Virginia Hamilton's (1968) *House of Dies Drear* marked a turning point in their attitudinal change. McKenna (1996) investigated the effects of "ethnobibliotherapy" on ethnic identity development of a group of mostly white in-service teachers. Ethnobibliotherapy is a combination of reader response and "bibliotherapeutic instructional strategies which fostered identification, catharsis, and insight using works by authors representing races or ethnic cultures other than one's own" (p. 14). The researcher found that through the treatment, the participants developed increased awareness of their ethnicity and changed their racial attitudes. Benson (1995) also reported positive results of responding to multicultural literature. She investigated how primarily Caucasian pre-service teachers made meaning of ethnicity within the context of a multicultural education course. Engaging in reading and responding to multicultural literature and interacting with peer participants not only helped the participants understand their ethnicity but also initiated change in their attitudes and beliefs about ethnicity. They progressed through three stages of development, from "denying differences" to " accepting differences" and then to "valuing differences" (pp. 76-78).

The findings of these studies provide support for the claim that exposure to multicultural literature affects readers' attitudes about race and ethnicity. Research conducted by Litcher and Johnson (1969) and by Bazelak (1974) also found positive effects of reading multicultural literature on changing students' attitudes toward race and ethnicity. Some other studies, however, showed no significant effects or inconclusive results (Brewbaker, 1972; Lancaster, 1971; Walker, 1972; Gwinn, 1998; McCabe, 1998). In her study, Lancaster (1971) tested the hypothesis that reading books with black characters might affect the racial preferences of white children. Fifty-six good-quality books with black characters were read by 125 fifth grade white students during classtime on a voluntary basis. A comparison was made between pre- and posttest scores on the Race/Activity Decision Criteria Picture Test scale (Horowitz, cited in Lancaster, 1971). The results were mixed. For one group of students, the more books they read, the less often they used race as a decision-making criterion. For another group, the greater number of books read was significantly correlated with higher prejudice scores. Walker (1971) did a study to determine the effects of hearing stories that portrayed blacks in a positive manner on the racial attitudes of black and white kindergarten children. Thirty-five books were read to two experimental groups each day for six weeks, while the stories read to the control groups were animal stories or informational books. The results indicated that hearing stories that portrayed blacks in a positive manner was insufficient to change the negative attitudes of black and white kindergarten children toward blacks.

It is interesting and revealing to compare two dissertation studies that investigated the effects of reading Mark Twain's *Huckleberry Finn* on readers' racial attitudes. Frankel's (1972) study had two groups of ninth grade boys, including both white and black, as its subjects. The experimental group (twenty whites and seven blacks) read the novel individually in five daily installments and also participated in classroom activities organized around the book. The control group (sixteen whites and nine blacks) read the book at home as "outside reading," with no classroom teaching or discussion. The results showed positive effects on attitudes of white students toward blacks and the self-concept of black students in the experimental group. Jones (1985) also investigated the effects of reading *Huckleberry Finn* on ninth grade students but with a larger sample (n=300). He found no consistent positive results across measurements in two treatment groups. Although students in the book and discussion treatment group expressed more positive racial attitudes to "interactions with Blacks," students in the book only treatment group did not. The results also "indicated a tendency to perceive Black characters in stereotypic terms" (p. 86) across both treatment groups.

Purves and Beach (1972) wrote:

The effects of literature upon readers are . . . many, and they are usually uncertain. One cannot predict that a certain poem or story will be approached by or affect all readers in the same way. Too much of the effect. is related to the reader and the circumstances of reading. (p. 177)

This statement provides some explanation for the mixed results of the research in the effects of reading multicultural literature on racial attitudes. In the studies I have just surveyed, there is a lot of variation in the reader (from kindergarten children to college students) and the circumstances of reading (from reading alone to reading with reflection and discussion). Although readers' responses to literature may be unpredictable and varied, we never question the functions of literature: to entertain and instruct. Neither do we overlook its effects on readers, especially those of an impressionable age. Just as with literature in general, multicultural literature will inevitably affect the reader. The key is treatment in studies, which includes types of multicultural books to read for the treatment, forms of treatment, and length of treatment. More studies, especially longitudinal ones, are needed to decide how multicultural literature can be an effective tool to increase respect for racial difference.

SOCIAL-COMMUNAL DIMENSION

Reading is not only a cognitive and affective activity but also an intersubjective, social process, not only a personal act, but also a communal event (Fish, 1980; Bloome, 1985; Bleich, 1986). It involves the interaction among readers in a group or communal setting. As David Bloome (1985) defines it, reading as a social process is "an activity by which people orient themselves to each other, communicate ideas and emotions, control others, control themselves, acquire status or social position, acquire access to social rewards and privilege, and engage in various types of social interaction" (p. 165). Along with the text and the reader, the social context of a reading event conditions the construction of meaning. The participants in a reading event negotiate the meaning of text through interaction. Perhaps nowhere is intersubjective interaction more intense than in group discussions of multicultural literature. Multicultural literature brings social, cultural, and political issues into the classroom and provides a forum where students encounter the vicarious experiences of diverse cultures and are offered alternative perspectives on the world" (Green, 1993). Diverse perspectives and "subject positions" bring sociocultural richness to the classroom. On the other hand, they also bring sociocultural tension. The classroom becomes a site for "struggles of interpretation" (Eagleton, 1983, p. 132). If consensus is achieved, it does not mean dialogue with no conflict or contradiction; rather, it retains its original Latin meaning of sensing together (McKenna, 1996). There are many studies that investigate the collaborative meaning making of literary texts in general. For example, Eeds and Wells (1989) studied what happened when literature study groups of fifth and sixth grade students discussed literary texts and found some patterns of responding behaviors: constructing a simple agreed-upon meaning of the text; sharing personal responses; participating in hypothesizing, interpreting, and verifying; and critiquing the text as literature. But what happen when a group of readers talk about multicultural texts? What is unique about the discussion of multicultural literature as compared with literature in general? Research in the social-communal dimension of reader response to multicultural literature should focus on relationship between readers' cultural identity and their collective meaning-making process. It may investigate the function of interpretive community, negotiation of social cultural meanings of text, intercultural interaction among readers, and the influence of historical and social context on the readers' responses. Let us look at some studies that dealt with the social-communal dimension of reader response to multicultural literature.

Interpretive Community

The term *interpretive community* (Fish, 1980) is used loosely by researchers and educators to mean a social community of readers who negotiate the meaning of literary texts. The community could be a class, a book club, a literature circle, or any other literature study group (e.g., Eeds and Wells, 1989; Möller and Allen,

2000). The original meaning of *interpretive community* means a community of readers who share the same interpretive strategies. For example, an interpretive community may subscribe to the values of feminism and use the strategies of feminist criticism to approach a literary text. The concept of interpretive community was advanced by Fish (1980) to explain the stability and variation of interpretation. If a group of people agrees on an interpretation of a text, it is because they belong to the same interpretive community. If they do not, then they belong to different interpretive communities. Whereas the concept of interpretive community stresses similarity among its members, the concept of reading as social process is oriented to the interactions and negotiations of the participants. When the term *interpretive community* is used to refer to a literature study group, it actually means a social community in which the members construct meaning of texts through interaction and "learn to share certain common assumptions and strategies" (Beach, 1993, p. 119). Rogers (1997) conducted a year-long ethnographic study of community, texts, and cultural conversation in an urban high school English class. This study did not explicitly address reader response to multicultural literature; rather, it was concerned with opening up curricular spaces for social and cultural inquiry in an English classroom. However, Rogers touched on the social-communal dimension of response to multicultural literature in some ways. In the study, Rogers (1997) described how the English teacher tried to construct an interpretive community in which students felt free to voice their opinions, even if this involved some risk taking, and to listen to, and respect each other's responses. In this community, both author and reader were seen as culturally situated, and their cultural situatedness was considered an important factor that determined how they constructed meaning. Students were encouraged to bring their personal, social, and cultural experiences to the texts and respond in ways that reflected their subject positions. Their stories were considered "texts" and valued as much as the authors' texts. They were also encouraged to "set their beliefs against those articulated in the texts" (p. 105). To create this interpretive community, the teacher moved away from the role of interpretive authority to that of a community member like the students and became a mediator in collectively constructing the meaning of texts.

Möller and Allen's (2000) researched the social-communal dimension as one of the major inquiries in their study. They analyzed the interpretive community of 4 fifth grade girls of diverse ethnic backgrounds, as created in a five-day transaction with Mildred Taylor's (1980) *The Friendship,* a story about black children encountering racism in rural Mississippi in the 1930s. In their report, they proposed a new concept, the "response development zone" (p. 148) in an interpretive community. "Within this zone, the reader actively constructs meaning, drawing on prior knowledge and experiences as well as on textual and contextual information, in a setting where support is provided by knowledgeable peers and a teacher who mediates learning and encourages shared knowledge and social interaction" (p. 148). When responding to multicultural literature within this zone, teachers and students participate in "explicit dialogue on personal, societal and political issues and guide each other towards deeper or alternative interpretations of text, self, and the world, creating a new kind of individual, but socially connected knowledge" (pp. 156-157). The four girls' collective transaction with multicultural texts in the response development zone was described as a four-act drama: "Act 1: understanding characters and specific actions," "Act 2: Shift to the big-picture—Historical and textual racism," "Act 3: Shift to the Present—Fear and the search for safety," "Act 4: Actors in real and possible worlds." Möller and Allen found that the girls were not only spectators of the story world but became actors in it, through transacting with multicultural literature in the interpretive community. The teacher, although remaining offstage, challenged and supported their inquiry into historical and present-day reality.

Negotiation of Meaning

Readers socially negotiate the meaning of texts in an interpretive community through responding to the texts and also to each other's responses. Some studies that investigated the discussion of multicultural literature described how readers shared their reactions to text to gain an understanding of it. For example, Lehr's (1995) study of how fourth graders read, wrote, and talked about the theme of freedom in novels set in foreign countries showed that the students used their background knowledge as "familiar markers" (p. 135) to guide their understanding of the perspectives of the characters and different concepts of oppression and freedom. Other studies focused on the participants' interactions as they negotiate the meaning of the text. Enciso's (1994) study, for instance, described ways in which two groups of predominantly white fifth and sixth graders "negotiated the meaning of difference" in the text and "among themselves" (p. 17) as they discussed *Maniac Magee* (Spinelli, 1990). It not only showed how students used their "cultural resources" as "familiar framework" (p. 24) for constructing their interpretation of the text but also how they differed from one another on the racial issues represented in it. When talking about skin color, for example, white students sided with Maniac Magee in dismissing it as irrelevant while an African American student "asserted race as a significant dimension of the story" (p. 21).

McKenna's (1996) study also described interaction among readers in literature study groups. Preservice teachers compared and contrasted different perspectives on characters and character relations while collaboratively constructing meaning of multicultural texts. Drawing on each other's varied perspectives, they were able to question the implicit values and assumptions they brought to bear on the text and open up to alternative interpretations.

Unlike these two studies, a study conducted by Bean et al. (1999) investigated the effect of interpretive stance on group discussion of multicultural literature. Twenty preservice teachers discussed the ethnic identity development of the main character in Gary Soto's (1991) *Taking Sides,* working in literature circles. Three of the five groups were told to adopt a literary analysis stance, while the other two used a personal association stance. The results suggested that the participants' stance affects the negotiation of meaning: the literary analysis stance limited the preservice teachers' ability to gain cross-cultural insights, while the personal associations stance enabled them to identify with characters in the novel and better understand the culture depicted in it.

Intercultural Tension

In discussion, readers position themselves in relation to one another as well as in relation to the text (Enciso, 1994). The subject positions that readers of various ethnic backgrounds bring to the text are likely to conflict, not only with the author, but also with each other, resulting in intercultural tension among the readers. Diaz-Gemmati (1995) did a naturalistic study of the literature discussion in her racially mixed eighth grade class and found that exploring themes of racism and prejudice sometimes resulted in an explosion of heated debates, arguments, and conflicts among members of literature circles. When students discussed *To Kill a Mocking Bird* (Lee, 1992), a major disagreement erupted between a black girl and a white girl over the use of the pejorative term "Nigger" in the novel. "Soon the entire group was talking at one another rather than talking to each other" (p. 7). During the discussion of *Roll of Thunder, Hear My Cry* (Taylor, 1976), heated debates again broke out, this time over the issue of white privileges, as the students connected the history reflected in the novel with the present-day reality in their lives. The battle line was drawn between the minority students, who were bused in, and the white students who lived in the neighborhood. Reconciliation occurred, if momentarily, when the students were asked to share their personal experiences of prejudice and discrimination. The discussion ended with "new insights" into the novels and "raw feelings" among the students as well. A conclusion drawn from the study was that "hard talk can take place within the safety of classroom walls" (p. 23). It permitted the students to "air some of their previously hidden feelings and helped them begin to separate their opinions from those of their parents" (p. 14).

Relatively few studies have investigated the social-communal dimension of reader response to multicultural literature as compared with research in the other two dimensions. The dynamic and dramatic interaction among readers deserves more attention by researchers. Two themes that have been touched upon but not expanded on also need further exploration: the teacher's role and intertextuality. The particular social-cultural position that the teacher takes exerts great influence on the students. A teacher who takes a conformist or assimilationist position may enforce interpretation based on the values of the dominant culture. But if the teacher adopts a more open or truly multiculturalist position, the result may be acceptance of various interpretations based on different systems of cultural values. Some studies (e.g., Lehr, 1995; Rogers, 1997) looked at how the teacher functioned as a facilitator and mediator but did not examine in depth how their subject positions affected the discussion. Intertextual discourse that connected various texts (books, movies, songs, and personal stories) was also reported as an important component of group discussion in several studies (Lehr, 1995; Rogers, 1997; Enciso, 1994), but it was not the focus of investigation. Future research could examine how such discourse enters the conversation and affects construction of meaning. An area that has rarely been explored in the studies of reader response to multicultural literature cited here is the large social context beyond the interpretive community in the classroom. How the social, cultural, and political milieu of a school, a community, or a historical period affects readers' responses to multicultural literature could be a profitable research question for future study.

CONCLUDING THOUGHTS

If we expect multicultural literature to "have a liberating and fortifying effect in the ongoing life of the reader" (Rosenblatt, 1995, p. 277), it is not enough to know multicultural literature itself; it is imperative also to know how children will respond to it. The model I propose for the study of reader response to multicultural literature is intended to conceptualize the complex and multidimensional nature of reader response to multicultural literature and to map out multiple channels for research in this field. My survey of the studies indicates what research has been accomplished in the cognitive-developmental, affective-attitudinal, and social-communal areas, and it also points to what research remains to be done (not only in areas where research is relatively limited but also in areas where there are inconclusive or contradictory findings). Jordan and Purves (1993) raised an issue regarding the relationship between liking and comprehension. Do students need to like a text in order to comprehend it, or do they need to comprehend it first to like it? Further research may provide answers to these and other similar questions that have been left unanswered.

Research in reader response to multicultural literature has great implications for the instruction of multicultural literature. Teachers can learn from the results of the studies that children's response to multicultural literature is a complex phenomenon. They can become aware of the many factors that affect children's responses and various ways in which children of different ethnic backgrounds may respond. Perhaps they will realize that children do not necessarily respond in ways that teachers tend to project and therefore will be motivated to find out more about their students. This is important: "Knowing more about students and their transactions with literature can only enhance the effectiveness of teaching" (Purves and Beach, 1972, p. 182): Teachers who understand how students respond in the cognitive-developmental, affective-attitudinal, and social-communal areas will certainly do a better job when selecting books and structuring instruction to fit the needs of their students.

We have discussed and debated various issues regarding multicultural literature. Ultimately, they boil down to one fundamental question: "How does multicultural literature produce the desired effects of inculcating the ideals of social justice and equality in our children?" For authors, critics, publishers, teachers, and school administrators, nothing is more important than the end result of education. Research in all three areas of reader response to multicultural literature may provide clues to what kind of multicultural literature we need and how to use it as an instructional instrument to achieve the goal of multicultural education.

REFERENCES

Adams, M. J., and Collins, A. (1977). *A schema-theoretic view of reading.* Center for the Study of Reading Technical Report No. 32. Urbana: University of Illinois.

Altieri, J. L. (1993). African-American stories and literary responses: Does a child's ethnicity affect the focus of a response? *Reading Horizon, 33* (3), 236-244.

Altieri, J. L. (1996). Children's written responses to multicultural texts: A look at aesthetic involvement and the focuses of aesthetically complex responses. *Reading Research and Instruction, 35* (3), 237-248.

Anderson, R. C. (1977). *Schema-directed processes in language comprehension.* Center for the Study of Reading Technical Report No. 50. Urbana: University of Illinois.

Banks, J. A. (1994). Transforming the mainstream curriculum. *Educational Leadership, 51* (8), 4-8.

Bazelak, L. P. (1974). *A content analysis of tenth-grade students' responses to black literature, including the effect of reading this literature on attitudes toward races.* Unpublished doctoral dissertation, Syracuse University.

Beach, R. (1993). *A teacher's introduction to reader-response theories.* Urbana, IL: National Council of Teachers of English.

Beach, R. (1995). Constructing cultural models through responding to literature. *English Journal, 84* (6), 87-94.

Beach, R. (1997). Students' resistance to engagement with multicultural literature. In T. Rogers and A. O. Soter (Eds.), *Reading across cultures: Teaching literature in a diverse society* (pp. 69-94). New York: Teachers College Press.

Bean, T. W., Valerio, P. C., and Mallette, M. H. (1999). Preservice teachers' discussion of a multicultural young adult novel. *Reading Research and Instruction, 38* (3), 197-210.

Benson, M. L. (1995). *Understanding ethnicity: Preservice teachers' construction of the meanings of ethnicity.* Unpublished doctoral dissertation, Florida State University.

Benton, M. (1993). *Reader response criticism in children's literature.* Occasional paper No. 15. (ERIC Document Reproduction Service No. ED 390 045).

Bleich, D. (1986). Intersubjective reading. *New Literary Study,* 17, 401-421.

Bloome, D. (1985). Reading as a social process. *Advances in Reading/Language Research,* 2, 165-195.

Brewbaker, J. M. (1972). *The relationship between the race of characters in a literary selection and the literary response of Negro and white adolescent reader.* Unpublished doctoral dissertation, University of Virginia.

Bunbury, R., and Tabbert, R. (1989). A bicultural study of identification: Reader response to the ironic treatment of a national hero. *Children's Literature in Education, 20* (1), 25-35.

Cai, M. (1992). *Towards a multidimensional model for the study of reader response to multicultural literature.* Unpublished doctoral dissertation, Ohio State University.

Cai, M. (2000). Reflections on transactional theory as a theoretical guide for literacy and literature education. *The New Advocate, 14* (1), 19-32.

Culler, J. (1975). *Structuralist poetics: Structuralism, linguistics and the study of literature.* Ithaca, NY: Cornell University Press.

Diaz-Gemmati, D. M. (1995). *And justice for all.* Occasional Paper No. 41. Berkeley, CA: National Center for the Study of Writing and Literacy.

Eagleton, T. (1983). *Literary theory: An introduction.* Minneapolis: University of Minnesota Press.

Eeds, M., and Wells, D. (1989). Grand conversations: An exploration of meaning construction in literature study groups. *Research in the Teaching of English, 23* (1), 24-29.

Enciso, P. (1994). Cultural identity and response to literature: Running lessons from *Maniac Magee. Language Arts, 71,* 524-533.

Fish, S. (1980). *Is there a text in this class?* Cambridge, MA: Harvard University Press.

Flores Duenas, L. (1997). *Second language reading: Mexican American student voices on reading Mexican American literature.* Unpublished doctoral dissertation, University of Texas at Austin.

Frankel, H. L. (1972). *The effects of reading* The Adventures of Huckleberry Finn *on the racial attitudes of selected ninth grade boys.* Unpublished doctoral dissertation, Temple University, Philadelphia.

Green, M. (1993). The passions of pluralism: Multiculturalism and the expanding community. *Educational Research, 22* (1), 13-18.

Grice, M. O., and Vaughn, C. (1992). Third graders respond to literature for and about Afro-Americans. *Urban Review, 24* (2), 149-164.

Guzman-Trevino, S. (1996). *Constructing lives, constructing stories: Responses of Mexican-American students to Mexican-American literature.* Unpublished doctoral dissertation, University of Texas at Austin.

Gwinn, C. B. (1998). *The effect of multicultural literature on the attitudes of second grade students.* Unpublished doctoral dissertation, University of Minnesota.

Ho, L. (1990). Singapore readers' response to U.S. young adult fiction: Cross-cultural differences. *Journal of Reading, 33,* 4, 252-258.

Hopper-Weil, S. (1989). *Literature and culture: An analysis of the effects of cultural background on Puerto Rican and American reader response to selected short stories.* Unpublished doctoral dissertation, New York University.

Iser, W. (1974). *The implied reader: Patterns in communication in prose fiction from Bunyan to Beckett.* Baltimore, MD: John Hopkins University Press.

Iser, W. (1978). *The act of reading: A theory of aesthetic response.* Baltimore, MD: Johns Hopkins University Press.

Jones, W. T. (1985). The effects of reading *Adventures of Huckleberry Finn* on the racial attitudes of white ninth-grade students. Unpublished doctoral dissertation, The Pennsylvania State University.

Jordan, S., and Purves, A. C. (1993). *Issues in the responses of students to culturally diverse texts: A preliminary study* (Report Series No. 7.3). Albany, NY: National Research Center on Literature Teaching and Learning.

Kintsch, W., and Green, E. (1978). The role of culture specific schemata in the comprehension and recall of stories. *Discourse Processes, 1,* 1-3.

Lancaster, J. W. (1971). *An investigation of the effect of books with black characters on the racial preferences of white children.* Unpublished doctoral dissertation, Boston University.

Lee, S. (1985). *Comparative responses to literature by Korean and American college students.* Unpublished doctoral dissertation, University of Pittsburgh.

Lehr, S. (1995). Fourth graders read, write, and talk about freedom. In S. Lehr (Ed.), *Battling dragons: Issues and controversy in children's literature* (pp. 114-140). Portsmouth, NH: Heinemann.

Leung, C. B. (1995). *Bicultural perspectives and reader response: Four young readers respond to Jean Fritz's* Homesick. Unpublished manuscript.

Liaw, M. (1995). Looking into the mirror: Chinese children's responses to Chinese children's books. *Reading Horizon, 35* (3), 185-197.

Litcher, J. H., and Johnson, D. W. (1969). Changes in attitudes toward Negroes of white elementary school students after use of multiethnic readers. *Journal of Educational Psychology, 60* (2), 148-152.

Malik, A. A. (1990). A psycholinguistic analysis of the reading behavior of EFL-proficient readers using culturally familiar and culturally nonfamiliar expository texts. *American Educational Research Journal, 27* (1), 205-223.

McCabe, C. T. (1998). *Multicultural children's literature: Its effect on the cultural attitude of fifth-grade students.* Unpublished doctoral dissertation, Virginia Commonwealth University.

McKenna, H. R. (1996). *Ethnobibliotherapy: Ethnic identity development through multicultural literature.* Unpublished doctoral dissertation, University of Washington.

Möller, K. J., and Allen, J. (2000). Connecting, resisting and searching for safer places: Students respond to Mildred Taylor's *The Friendship. Journal of Literacy Research, 32* (2), 145-186.

Naidoo, B. (1992). *Through whose eyes? Exploring racism: Reader, text, and context.* London: Trentham Books.

Nelson, G. L. (1987). Culture's role in reading comprehension: A schema theoretical approach. *Journal of Reading, 30,* 424-429.

Nevel, D. A. (1999). *Students' transactions with multicultural poetry in the high school classroom: A case study.* Unpublished doctoral dissertation, Georgia State University.

Noda, L. A. (1980). *Literature and culture: Japanese and American reader responses to modern Japanese short stories.* Unpublished doctoral dissertation, New York University.

Pritchard, R. (1990). The effects of cultural schemata on reading processing strategies. *Reading Research Quarterly, 25* (4), 273-295.

Purves, A. C. and Beach, R. (1972). *Literature and the reader: Research in response to literature, reading interests, and the teaching of literature.* Urbana, IL: National Council of Teachers of English.

Purves, A. C. and Rippere, V. (1968). *Elements of writing about a literary work: A study in response to literature* (NCTE Research Report No. 9). Urbana, IL: National Council of Teachers of English.

Reynolds, R. E., Anderson R. C., Steffensen, M. S., and Taylor, M. (1982). Cultural schemata and reading comprehension. *Reading Research Quarterly, 17* (3), 353-366.

Rice, P. (November, 1999). *It "ain't" always so: Students' interpretations of multicultural stories with universal themes.* Paper presented at the Convention of the National Council of Teachers of English, Denver, CO.

Rogers, T., (1997). No imagined peaceful place: A story of community, texts, and cultural conversations in one urban high school English classroom. In T. Rogers and A. O. Soter (Eds.), *Reading across cultures: Teaching literature in a diverse society* (pp. 95-115). New York: Teachers College Press.

Rogers, T., and Soter, A. O. (Eds.). (1997). *Reading across cultures: Teaching literature in a diverse society*. New York: Teachers College Press.

Rosenblatt, L. M. (1978). *The reader, the text, the poem: Transactional theory of the literary work*. Carbondale: Southern Illinois University Press.

Rosenblatt, L. M. (1985). Viewpoints: Transaction vs. interaction—a terminological rescue operation. *Research in Teaching English, 19*, 96-107.

Rosenblatt, L. M. (1995). *Literature as exploration* (5th ed.). New York: The Modern Language Association of America.

Ruzich, C. M. (1999). White students' resistance to multicultural literature: Breaking the sullen silence. *Teaching English in the Two Year College, 26* (3), 299-304.

Schweickart, P. P. (1986). Reading ourselves: Toward a feminist theory of reading. In E. B. Flynn and P. P. Schweickart (Eds.), *Gender and reading* (pp. 31-62). Baltimore, MD: Johns Hopkins University Press.

Sims, R. (1983). Strong black girls: A ten year old responds to fiction about Afro-Americans. *Journal of Research and Development in Education, 16* (3), 21-28.

Sinha, S. (1995). *The role of culture in children's response to literature*. Unpublished doctoral dissertation, University of Illinois, Urbana-Champaign.

Smith, E. (1995). Anchored in our literature: Students responding to African American literature. *Language Arts, 72*, 571-574.

Spears-Bunton, L. A. (1990). Welcome to my house: African American and European American students' responses to Virginia Hamilton's *House of Dies Drear. Journal of Negro Education, 59*, 566-576.

Steffensen, S. M., Joag-Dev, C., and Anderson, R. C. (1979). A cross-cultural perspective on reading comprehension. *Reading Research Quarterly, 15* (1), 10-29.

Taylor, G. S. (1997). Multicultural literature preferences of low-ability African American and Hispanic American fifth-graders. *Reading Improvement, 34* (1), 37-48.

Towell, J. H., Schulz, A., and Demetrulias, D. M. (1997). Does ethnicity really matter in literature for young children? (ERIC Document Reproduction Service No. ED 412 571).

Walker, P. (1972). *The effects of hearing selected children's stories that portray blacks in a favorable manner on the racial attitudes of groups of Black and White kindergarten children*. Unpublished dissertation, University of Kentucky.

Wilson, M., and Thomas, S. (1995). Holy smoke! I missed something here: Cultural experience and the construction of meaning. *English Education, 27* (2), 53-65.

Woodward, M. A. (1970). *The effects of teaching black literature to ninth grade class in a Negro high school in Picayu, Mississippi*. Unpublished doctoral dissertation, University of Tennessee.

Books for Children and Young Adults

Fritz, J. (1982). *Homesick, my own story*. New York: Putnam.
Hamilton, V. (1968). *The house of Dies Drear*. New York: Macmillan.
Lee, H. (1992). *To kill a mockingbird*. Boston: G. K. Hall.
Levine, A. (1989). *I hate English*. New York: Scholastic.
Oakes, V. (1949). *Footprints of the dragon*. Philadelphia, PA: John C Winston.

Soto, G. (1991). *Taking sides.* San Diego: Harcourt Brace Jovanovich.
Spinelli, J. (1990). *Maniac Magee.* Boston: Little Brown.
Staples, S. F. (1989). *Shabanu: Daughter of the wind.* New York: Knopf.
Taylor, M. D. (1976). *Roll of thunder, hear my cry.* New York: Dial.
Taylor, M. D. (1987). *The friendship.* New York: Dial.

Appendix

Websites Related to Multicultural Literature

GENERAL LITERATURE FOR CHILDREN AND YOUNG ADULTS

Carol Hurst's Children's Literature Site (http://www.carolhurst.com/index)

At this website, there are two sections under "Subject" that are related to multicultural literature: "Multicultural, Diversity, and Tolerance" and "Native Americans." They offer titles of multicultural literature about Native Americans and links to other multicultural sites. Reviews of multicultural books and biographical information on authors of parallel cultures can be found in two other categories, "Books" and "Authors."

Cynthia Leitich Smith Children's Literature Resources (http://www.Cynthia leitichsmith.com/index1)

In addition to offering information and resources about children's literature, this site has a "Multiculturalism" section that gives visitors access to many Web pages that are concerned with issues of culture and gender in literature for children and young adults. In the "Topic Bibliographies" section, briefly annotated bibliographies of books about Asian Americans, Native Americans, and interracial families are provided.

Fairrosa Cyber Library of Children's Literature (http://www.dalton.org/libraries /fairrosa)

This site contains booklists of literature for children and young adults literature as well as links to book review sources. Multicultural titles can be found in the lists. In a discussion section, there are threads from archived discussion of children's literature on the Child listserv. Some of the postings cover controversial multicultural books.

Key E. Vandergrift's Special Interest Page (http://scils.rutgers.edu /%7Ekvander/ index.html)

This comprehensive site of children's literature has sections that discuss gender and cultural issues in picture books, including lists of recommended picture books that present positive images of the parallel cultural groups and a rather extensive bibliography of background readings in gender and culture.

Multicultural and International Children's Literature Links (http://www.home. earthlink.net/~elbond/multicultural.htm)

This comprehensive site offers a global perspective. It contains multiple links to multicultural resources in the United States and also in other countries.

CENTERS, ORGANIZATIONS, AND CONFERENCES

Barahona Center (http://www.csusm.edu/csb/)

Barahona Cener for the Study of Books in Spanish for Children and Young Adults is located at California State University, San Marcos. Its stated mission is to inform educators about books centered on Latino people and books in Spanish. Its homepage contains recommended books in Spanish and English, references books by I. Schon, and links to many other multicultural resources.

Center for Multilingual Multicultural Research (http://www-rcf.usc.edu/~cmmr/)

The website of this center at the University of Southern. California offers abundant information on multilingual multicultural education. Among its many sections there are the center's projects and programs, on-line resources on African American, Asian American, Latino/Hispanic American, and Native American cultures, language policy and rights, and language, literacy, and learning. Visitors can access numerous related sites.

Cooperative Children's Book Center (CCBC) (http://www.soemadison.wisc.edu/ ccbc/)

Cooperative Children's Book Center is a research library at the School of Education at the University of Wisconsin-Madison. Its site contains many multicultural resources, including a list of 50 multicultural books every child should know, its publications of multicultural literature bibliographies, and statistics on books by and about people of color published in the United States. In the library's listserv forum on children's and young adult literature, multicultural titles are often among the chosen topics for discussion.

Cultural Mosaics (http://www.coe.ohio-state.edu/edtl/llc/cm.html)

This site is part of the Ohio State Martha L. King Literacy Center homepage. It features monthly selections of multicultural books on a theme from the issue of *Cultural Mosaics* published by the center. It also contains a directory of on-line multicultural resources: multicultural Links from A-Z.

Oyate (http://www.oyate.org)

Oyate (the Dakota word for "people") is a Native American organization whose stated mission is to see that Native American lives and histories are portrayed honestly. The Website has a catalog of recommended books, teaching materials, and other products. The section "Books to Avoid" presents an insider's perspective on books that misrepresent Native American culture.

United States Board on Books for Young People (USBBY) (http://www.usbby.org/)

USBBY is a branch of the International Board on Books for Young People (IBBY). Its goal is to "build bridges to international understanding through children's and young adult books." The Website contains information about the organization, its conferences, its "Bridge to Understanding Award," and the IBBY publication *Bookbird,* a quarterly journal on international children's literature. Visitors can also find links to many international sites.

Virginia Hamilton Conference (http://dept.kent.edu/virginiahamitonconf/index.html)

This conference focuses exclusively on multicultural literature for children and young adults. It has several features at its site: information on the conference, authors and illustrators, articles based on previous conferences, archives, Virginia Hamilton Awards, and biographical information on Virginia Hamilton.

BIBLIOGRAPHIES, BOOK REVIEWS, AND TEACHING IDEAS

Celebrate Cultural Diversity Through Children's Literature (http://www.multiculturalchildrenslit.com)

This site is developed and maintained by Robert F. Smith. It offers annotated bibliographies of children's literature about parallel cultures. Each bibliography is divided by genre. It also has links to many sites related to each culture covered in the site.

Children's Literature: Beyond Basals (http://www.beyondbasals.com)

This site offers "Book Guides" for incorporating literature into the curriculum. They provide lessons plans and extension activities for each title listed, including multicultural titles are included in the guides.

Critical Bibliography of North American Indians, for K-12 (http://nmnhwww.si.edu/anthro/outreach/Indbibl/bibliogr.html)

This site is hosted by the Anthropology Outreach Office at the Smithsonian Institution. The bibliography focuses on materials for primary and secondary school students, although it also lists publications of interest to the general public. It is preceded by a long introduction and divided into 11 sections organized by cultural areas and tribes. Each section is further divided into subsections by genre. Numerous books about North American Indians are included in the bibliography.

Culture Connections in Classrooms (http://www.cedu.niu.edu/~carger/culture)

This site was created by Chris Liska Carger of Northern Illinois University for the purpose of encouraging educators to integrate multicultural children's literature into the curricula. It features book reviews, author studies, lesson plans, and thematic unit plans.

Making Multicultural Connections through Trade Books (http://www.mcps.k12.md.us/curriculum/socialstd/MBD/Books_Begin.html)

At this site multicultural trade books that have a specific instructional connection to content areas are chosen and briefly annotated for teachers to use in their classroom. The books are indexed by both title and theme. For some books, a specific lesson plan is also provided to illustrate how they can be used as a multicultural link to extend students' learning experience in a content area.

Multicultural Book Review Homepage (http://www.isomedia.com/homes/jmele/homepage.html)

In addition to annotated bibliographies of books about parallel cultures in the United States and books in English from other countries, this site has a special feature, "Review of the Month." Visitors are encouraged to write and submit their own book reviews to the site.

Multicultural Lesson Plans (http://www.coe.ohio-state.edu/dyford/lessons_plans.htm)

Created by Donna Y. Ford of Ohio State University, this site offers sample lesson plans that are multicultural, literature based, and interdisciplinary. It also provides numerous multicultural readings and resources.

Multicultural Literature in the Classroom (http://www.educ.sfu.ca/gentech/pbl/titlepage.html)

This site was created for teachers by teachers. It has many links to educational resources and classroom activities to promote an active multicultural classroom. It contains textual resources, curriculum resources, a research base, and other categories.

Multicultural Resources for Children (http://falcon.jmu.edu/~ramseyil/multipub.htm)

This is the Internet School Library Media Center (ISLMC) multicultural page. It contains general resources about multicultural literature and a wealth of bibliographies of books about parallel cultures for children and young adults. There is also a bibliography of books with gay and lesbian themes for K-12.

Native American Books (http://www.kstrom.net/isk/books/bookmenu.html)

This is a rich resource site for exploring books about Native American experience and reviews from a Native American perspective. It has an index of all Native American books, grouped by both author and tribe, and an index of books for young readers grouped by grade level. The reviews are divided into subject categories. Each recommended book is marked with a thumbs-up icon, and each unrecommended one with a thumbs-down. A special section called "Big Baddies" reviews books that misrepresent Native American culture.

Pacific Children's Literature (http://www.uog.edu/coe/paclit/)

This site specializes in children's literature about Pacific Islanders. It includes book reviews, teaching ideas, and information on authors, illustrators, and storytellers. It also features original works created by students of the University of Guam and members of the Guam communities.

South Asian Children's Books and Software (http://www.umiacs.umd.edu /users/ sawweb/sawnet/ kidsbooks.html)

This site is a starting place for locating South Asian children's books. Briefly annotated bibliographies are offered. There is also information on where to obtain South Asia-oriented computer software for children.

MULTICULTURAL PUBLISHERS AND DISTRIBUTORS

African World Press (http://store.yahoo.com/africanworld/index.html)

The homepage of this press offers comprehensive information on African American history, politics, political economy, literature, linguistics, religion, organizations, and other topics. In the section "Children and Young Readers," visitors can find titles of children's literature that the press has published.

Asian Kids (http://www.afk.com/index.tmpl)

Besides an on-line catalogue of books and other products related to Asia, this site presents useful resources and information for teachers and parents, including parents' corner, teachers' corner, author's corner, country facts, ethnic calendar, Lunar New Year, Moon festival, etc.

Children's Book Press (http://www.cbookpress.org)

This site contains an on-line catalog of multicultural books published by the press and a section that provides teaching and learning resources, including workshops developed by authors and artists, links to sites developed by teachers, and samples of students' works.

Curstone Press (http://www.curstone.org)

This publisher of multicultural books has the following features at its Website: books and authors, outreach programs, events, teaching resources, forum, e-mail and links. The links to many other on-line multicultural resources make the site a gateway to information on multicultural publications, movies, radio, television broadcasts, and organizations.

Just Us Books (http://www.justusbooks.com)

This press publishes books for young people about the black experience. Its Website has several categories: its catalog of publications and other products, an author/illustrator corner, tips for writers, and a parent/teacher center. It also provides connections, information, and materials of African American concerns for the purpose of enhancing teaching and learning.

Lee & Low (http://www.leeandlow.com)

In addition to on-line catalog of Lee & Low books, there are teaching guides, a column with an editor's advice on writing and publishing multicultural books for young people, interviews with authors and illustrators and a calendar of their appearances, and a contest to win a multicultural book.

MPEC Listing of Multicultural Publishers and Distributors (http://www.mpec.org /publishe.html)

The Multicultural Publishing and Education Catalog (MPEC) is a national network for independent publishers, authors, educators, and librarians fostering authentic multicultural books and materials. Its home page provides information on multicultural publishers and distributors of books and magazines.

North American Native Authors On-line Catalogue (http://www.native authors.com)

This site offers many titles authored or coauthored by American Indian poets, writers, historians, storytellers, and performers. It also has a section on featured authors.

Pinata books/Arte Publico (http://www.arte.uh.edu/Pinata_Books/pinata_books. html)

These presses specialize in publishing children books about Hispanic Americans. In addition to on-line catalogs, the site also has the following sections: "Recovering the U.S. Hispanic literary heritage," "The Americas Review," "News and Events," and links to other sites.

Polychrome Publishing Corporation (http://home.earthlink.net/~polypub/)

At this site visitors can find children's books that tell "Asian American stories from the Asian American community" published by the corporation.

Shen's (http://www.shens.com/)

Shen's distributes and publishes multicultural books. Its catalog includes many titles about Asian cultures. The section "In Search of Cinderella" list many tales similar to the Cinderella story from various cultures in the world. There are also booklists for thematic units.

Small Presses Owned and Operated by People of Color (http://www.soemadison. wisc.edu/ccbc/pclist.htm)

This site is part of Cooperative Children's Book Center's homepage. It provides a directory of small presses of children's literature that are owned and operated by people of color. There is also a list of other small presses committed to publishing multicultural literature.

AUTHOR'S NOTE

These websites were selected for informational purposes only, and are not necessarily endorsed by the author. The Internet is an ever-changing world, so some sites may change or disappear.

Selected Bibliography

Albers, P. (1996). Issues of representation: Caldecott gold medal winners 1984-1995. *The New Advocate 9* (4), 297-308.

Altieri, J. L. (1993). African-American stories and literary responses: Does a child's ethnicity affect the focus of a response? *Reading Horizon, 33* (3), 236-244.

Altieri, J. L. (1996). Children's written responses to multicultural texts: A look at aesthetic involvement and the focuses of aesthetically complex responses. *Reading Research and Instruction, 35* (3), 237-248.

Athanases, S., and Lew, A. (1993). Cross-cultural swapping of mother and grandmother tales in a tenth grade discussion of *The Joy Luck Club. Communication Education, 42* (4), 282-287.

Austin, M. C., and Jenkins, E. (1973). *Promoting world understanding through literature, K-8.* Littleton, CO: Libraries Unlimited.

Banfield, B. (1998). Commitment to change: The Council on Interracial Books for Children and the world of children's books. *African American Review, 32* (1), 17-22.

Banks, C. A. M., and Banks, J. A. (1995). Equity pedagogy: An essential component of multicultural education. *Theory into practice, 34* (2), 152-158.

Banks, J. A. (1979). Shaping the future of multicultural education. *Journal of Negro Education, 68,* 237-252.

Banks, J. A. (1994). Transforming the mainstream curriculum. *Educational Leadership, 51* (8), 4-8.

Banks, J. A. (2001). *Cultural diversity and education: Foundations, curriculum, and teaching.* Boston: Allyn and Bacon.

Banks, J. A., and Banks, C. A. M. (1997). (Eds.). *Multicultural education: Issues and perspectives.* Boston: Allyn and Bacon.

Barrera, R. B. (1992). The cultural gap in literature-based literacy education. *Education and Urban Society, 24* (2), 227-243.

Barrera, R. B., Thompson, V. D., and Dressman, M. (Eds.). (1997). *Kaleidoscope: A multicultural booklist for grades K-8.* Urbana, IL: National Council of Teachers of English.

Barta, J., and Grindler, M. C. (1996). Exploring bias using multicultural literature for children. *The Reading Teacher, 50* (3), 269-270.

Bar-Tal, D., Graumann, C. F., Kruglanski, A. W., and Strobe, W. (Eds.). (1989). *Stereotyping and prejudice: Changing concepts* (pp. 3-34). New York: Springer-Verlag.

Bazelak, L. P. (1974). *A content analysis of tenth-grade students' responses to black literature, including the effect of reading this literature on attitudes toward races.* Unpublished doctoral dissertation, Syracuse University.

Beach, R. (1993). *A teacher's introduction to reader-response theories.* Urbana, IL: National Council of Teachers of English.

Beach, R. (1995). Constructing cultural models through responding to literature. *English Journal, 84* (6), 87-94.

Bean, T. W., Valerio, P. C., and Mallette, M. H. (1999). Preservice teachers' discussion of a multicultural young adult novel. *Reading Research and Instruction, 38* (3), 197-210.

Beaty, J. J. (1997). *Building bridges with multicultural picture books.* Columbus, OH: Merrill.

Benson, M. L. (1995). *Understanding ethnicity: Preservice teachers' construction of the meanings of ethnicity.* Unpublished doctoral dissertation, Florida State University.

Benton, M. (1993). *Reader response criticism in children's literature.* (Occasional papers No. 15) (ERIC Document Reproduction Service No. ED 390 045).

Bigelow, B. (1994). Good intentions are not enough: Children's literature in the aftermath of the Quincentenary. *The New Advocate, 7* (4), 265-279.

Bird, E. (Ed.). (1996). *Dressing in feathers: The construction of the Indian in American popular culture.* Boulder, CO: Westview.

Bleich, D. (1978). *Subjective criticism.* Baltimore, MD: Johns Hopkins University Press.

Bleich, D. (1986). Intersubjective reading. *New Literary Study, 17,* 401-421.

Bloome, D. (1985). Reading as a social process. *Advances in Reading/Language Research, 2,* 165-195.

Booth, W. C. (1961). *The rhetoric of fiction.* Chicago: University of Chicago Press.

Booth, W. C. (1988). *The company we keep: An ethics of fiction.* Berkeley: University of California Press.

Brewbaker, J. M. (1972). *The relationship between the race of characters in a literary selection and the literary response of Negro and white adolescent readers.* Unpublished doctoral dissertation, University of Virginia.

Broderick, D. (1973). *Image of the Black in children's fiction.* New York: Bowker.

Brown, J. E., and Stephens, E. C. (Eds.). (1998). *Cultural sensitivity: Using multicultural young adult literature in the classroom.* Urbana, IL: National Council of Teachers of English.

Bullard, S. (1991). Sorting through the multicultural rhetoric. *Educational Leadership, 49* (4), 32-36.

Bunbury, R., and Tabbert, R. (1989). A bicultural study of identification: Reader response to the ironic treatment of a national hero. *Children's Literature in Education, 20* (1), 25-35.

Cai, M. (1992a). A balanced view of acculturation: Comments on Laurence Yep's three novels. *Children's Literature in Education, 23* (2), 107-108.

Cai, M. (1992b). *Towards a multidimensional model for the study of reader response to multicultural literature.* Unpublished doctoral dissertation, Ohio State University.

Cai, M. (1992c). Values and valuables in historical fiction for children. *The New Advocate, 5* (4), 279-291.

Cai, M. (2000). Reflections on transactional theory as a theoretical guide for literacy and literature education. *The New Advocate, 14* (1), 19-32.

Cai, M. and Sims Bishop, R. (1994). Multicultural literature for children: Towards a clarification of the concept. In A. H. Dyson & C. Genishi (Eds.), *The need for story: Cultural diversity in classroom and community* (pp. 57-71). Urbana, IL: National Council of Teachers of English.

Cassuto, L. (1997). *The inhuman race: The racial grotesque in American literature and culture.* New York: Columbia University Press.

Clemetson, L. (1998). Caught in the cross-fire: A young star teacher finds herself in a losing racial battle with parents. *Newsweek, 132,* 38-39.

Corliss, J. C. (1998). *Crossing borders with literature of diversity.* Norwood, MA: Christopher-Gordon.

Cortes, C. E. (1994). Multiculturation: An educational model for a culturally and linguistically diverse society. In K. Spangenberg-Urbschat & R. Pritchard (Eds.), *Kids come in all languages: Reading instruction for ESL students* (pp. 22-35). Newark, DE: International Reading Association.

Cose, E. (1997). *Color-blind: Seeing beyond race in a race-obsessed world.* New York: HarperCollins.

Coyle, L. R. (1991). The creative use of stereotypes in the short stories of Norma Fox Mazer. *The Alan Review, 18* (1), 7-8.

Culler, J. (1975). *Structuralist poetics: Structuralism, linguistics and the study of literature.* Ithaca, NY: Cornell University Press.

Dasenbrock. R. W. (1987). Intelligibility and meaningfulness in multicultural literature. *PMLA, 102* (1), 10-19.

Dasenbrock, R. W. (1999). Why read multicultural literature: An Arnoldian perspective. *College English, 61* (6), 691-701.

Dixon, B. (1977). *Catching them young: Sex, race and class in children's literature.* London: Pluto.

Dorris, M. (1994). *Paper trail: Essays.* New York: HarperCollins.

Durbin, K. (1988, June 21). A new, if not improved, stereotype. *New York Times,* 24.

Dyer, R. (1993). *The matter of images: Essays on representations.* London: Routledge.

Dyson, A. H., and Genishi, C. (Eds.). (1994). *The need for story: Cultural diversity in classroom and community.* Urbana, IL: National Council of Teachers of English.

Eagleton, T. (1983). *Literary theory: An introduction.* Minneapolis: University of Minnesota Press.

Eagleton, T. (2000). *The idea of culture.* Malden, MA: Blackwell.

Eeds, M., and Wells, D. (1989). Grand conversations: An exploration of meaning construction in literature study groups. *Research in the Teaching of English, 23* (1), 24-29.

Elmeel, S. L. (1993). Toward a real multiculturalism. *School Library Journal, 39* (11), 50.

Enciso, P. (1994). Cultural identity and response to literature: Running lessons from *Maniac Magee. Language Arts, 71,* 524-533.

Estrada, K, and McLaren, P. (1993). A dialogue on multiculturalism and democratic culture. *Educational Research, 22* (3), 27-33.

Fang, Z., Fu, D., & Lamme, L. L. (1999). Rethinking the role of multicultural literature in literacy instruction: Problems, paradox, and possibilities. *The New Advocate, 12* (3), 259-276.

Finazzo, D. A. (1996). *All for the children: Multicultural essentials of literature.* Albany, NY: Delmar.

Fish, S. (1980). *Is there a text in this class?* Cambridge, MA: Harvard University Press.

Fishman, A. R. (1995). Finding ways in: Redefining multicultural literature. *English Journal, 84* (6), 73-79.

Fleishman, A. (1971). *The English historical novel.* Baltimore, MD: The John Hopkins University Press.

Flores Duenas, L. (1997). *Second language reading: Mexican American student voices on reading Mexican American literature.* Unpublished doctoral dissertation, University of Texas at Austin.

Frankel, E. R. (1996). Bias and stereotypes in the portrayal of Palestinian-Arabs in American juvenile trade fiction, 1957-1985: An analysis of a selected bibliography. *Multicultural Review, 3* (30), 48-52.

Frankel, H. L. (1972). *The effects of reading* The Adventures of Huckleberry Finn *on the racial attitudes of selected ninth grade boys.* Unpublished doctoral dissertation, Temple University, Philadelphia PA.

Galda, L., and Cullinan, B. E. (2002). *Literature and the child* (5th ed.). Belmont, CA : Wadsworth/Thomson Learning.

Gates, H. L., Jr. (1991, November 24). "Authenticity," or the lesson of Little Tree, *New York Times*, pp. 1, 26-30.

Gates, H. L., Jr. (1992). *Loose canons: Notes on the cultural wars.* New York: Oxford University Press.

Goebel, B. (1995). Expanding the literary canon and reading the rhetoric of "race." *English Journal, 85* (4), 42-48.

Grice, M. O., and Vaughn, C. (1992). Third graders respond to literature for and about Afro-Americans. *Urban Review, 24* (2), 149-164.

Guzman-Trevino, S. (1996). *Constructing lives, constructing stories: Responses of Mexican-American students to Mexican-American literature.* Unpublished doctoral dissertation, University of Texas at Austin.

Gwinn, C. B. (1998). *The effect of multicultural literature on the attitudes of second grade students.* Unpublished doctoral dissertation, University of Minnesota.

Hade, D. D. (1997). Reading multiculturally. In V. Harris (Ed.), *Using multiethnic literature in the K-8 classroom* (pp. 233-256). Norwood, MA: Christopher-Gordon.

Harada, V. H. (1995). Issues of ethnicity, authenticity, and quality in Asian-American picture books, 1983-93. *Youth Service in Libraries, 46* (3), 135-149.

Harris, V. (1990). From Little Black Sambo to Popo and Fifina: Arna Bontemps and the creation of African American children's literature. *The Lion and the Unicorn, 14* (10), 108-127.

Harris, V. (Ed.). (1992). *Teaching multicultural literature: In grades K-8.* Norwood, MA: Christopher-Gordon.

Harris, V. (1994a). Book review. *Journal of Reading Behavior, 26* (1), 117-120.

Harris, V. (1994b) No invitation required to share multicultural literature. *Journal of Children's Literature, 20* (1), 9-13.

Harris, V. (1994c). Review of Against Borders: *Promoting books for a multicultural world. Journal of Reading Behavior, 26* (1), 117-120.

Harris, V. (1996). Continuing dilemmas, debates, and delights in multicultural literature. *The New Advocate, 9* (2), 107-122.

Harris, V. (Ed.). (1997). *Using multiethnic literature in the K-8 classroom.* Norwood, MA: Christopher-Gordon.

Hearn, B. (1993, August). Respect the source: Reducing cultural chaos in picture books, part two. *School Library Journal,* pp. 33-37.

Hirsch, E. D., Jr. (1967). *Validity in interpretation.* New Haven, CT: Yale University Press.

Hirschfelder, A. B., Molin, P. F., and Wakim, Y. (1999). (Eds.), *American Indian stereotypes in the world of children: A reader and bibliography* (2nd ed.). Lanham, MD: Scarecrow.

Hirschfelder, A. B., and Singer, B. R. (Eds.). (1992). *Rising voices: Writings of young Native Americans.* New York: Charles Scribner's Sons.

Ho, L. (1990). Singapore readers' response to U.S. young adult fiction: Cross-cultural differences. *Journal of Reading, 33,* (4), 252-258.

Holland, N. N. (1968). *The dynamics of literary response.* New York: Oxford University Press.

Holland, N. N. (1980). Unity identity text self. In J. Tompkins (Ed.), *Reader-response criticism: From formalism to post-structuralism* (pp. 118-134). Baltimore, MD: The Johns Hopkins University Press.

Hopkins, D., and Tastad, S. A. (1997). Censoring by omission: Has the United States progressed in promoting diversity through children's books? *Youth Services in Libraries, 10* (4), 399-404.

Hopper-Weil, S. (1989). *Literature and culture: An analysis of the effects of cultural background on Puerto Rican and American reader response to selected short stories.* Unpublished doctoral dissertation, New York University.

Horning, K. T., Kruse, G. M., and Schliesman, M. (1997). *CCBC Choices 1996.* Madison: University of Wisconsin Press.

Huck, C. S., Hepler, S., Hickman, J., and Kiefer, B. Z. (2001). *Children's literature in the elementary school* (7th ed.). Boston: McGraw Hill.

Iser, W. (1974). *The implied reader: Patterns in communication in prose fiction from Bunyan to Beckett.* Baltimore, MD: John Hopkins University Press.

Iser, W. (1978). *The act of reading: A theory of aesthetic response.* Baltimore, MD: Johns Hopkins University Press.

Jay, G. S. (1997). Not born on the fourth of July: Cultural differences and American studies. In L. Brannon and B. M. Greene (Eds.), *Rethinking American literature* (pp. 3-31). Urbana, IL: National Council of Teachers of English.

Jones, W. T. (1985). The effects of reading *The Adventures of Huckleberry Finn* on the racial attitudes of white ninth-grade students. Unpublished doctoral dissertation, Pennsylvania State University.

Jordan, S., and Purves, A. C. (1993). *Issues in the responses of students to culturally diverse texts: A preliminary study* (Report Series No. 7.3). Albany, NY: National Research Center on Literature Teaching and Learning.

Kearney, R. (1988). *The wake of imagination: Toward a postmodern culture.* Minneapolis : University of Minnesota Press.

Kincheloe, J. L., and Steinberg, S. R. (1997). *Changing multiculturalism.* Buckingham, England: Open University Press.

Kintsch, W., and Green, E. (1978). The role of culture specific schemata in the comprehension and recall of stories. *Discourse Processes,* 1, 1-3.

Kruse, G. M., and Horning, K. T., (1990). Looking into the mirror: Considerations behind the reflections. In M. V. Lindgren (Ed.), *The multicolored mirror: Cultural substance in literature for children and young adults.* Fort Atkinson, WI: Highsmith.

Kruse, G. M., Horning, K. T. and Schliesman, M. (1997). *Multicultural literature for children and young adults.* Madison, WN: Cooperative Children's Book Center.

Lancaster, J. W. (1971). *An investigation of the effect of books with black characters on the racial preferences of white children.* Unpublished doctoral dissertation, Boston University.

Langer, S. K. (1957). *Philosophy in a new key: A study in the symbolism of reason, rite, and art.* Cambridge, MA: Harvard University Press.

Larrick, N. (1965, September 11). The all-white world of children's books. *Saturday Review, 48,* 63-65.

Leask, N. (1988). *The politics of imagination in Coleridge's critical thought.* New York: St. Martin's Press.

Lee, M. (1995). Building bridges or barriers? *The Horn Book Magazine, 71* (2), 233-236.

Lee, S. (1985). *Comparative responses to literature by Korean and American college students.* Unpublished doctoral dissertation, University of Pittsburgh.

Lee, S. J. (1996). *Unravelling the "model minority" stereotype: Listening to Asian American youth.* New York: Teachers College Press.

Lehr, S. (Ed.). (1995). *Battling dragons: Issues and controversy in children's literature* (pp. 3-30). Portsmouth, NH: Heinemann.

Leonard, J. S., Tenney, T. A., and Davis, T. M. (Eds.). (1992). *Satire or evasion: Black perspectives on* Huckleberry Finn. Durham, NC: Duke University Press.

Lester, N. A. (1999). Roots that go beyond big hair and a bad hair day: *Nappy Hair* pieces. *Children's Literature in Education, 30* (3), 171-183.

Lester, P. M. (Ed.). (1996). *Images that injure: Pictorial stereotypes in the media.* Westport, CT: Praeger.

Leu, S. (2001). Reimagining a pluralistic society through children's fiction about Asian Pacific American immigrants, 1990-1999. *The New Advocate, 14* (2), 127-142.

Levy, M. (1995). Reflections on multiculturalism and the tower of psychoBable. *The ALAN Review, 22* (3), 11-15.

Liaw, M. (1995). Looking into the mirror: Chinese children's responses to Chinese children's books. *Reading Horizon, 35* (3), 185-197.

Lindgren, M. (Ed.). (1991). *The multicolored mirror: Cultural substance in literature for children and young adults.* Fort Atkinson, WI: Highsmith.

Litcher, J. H., and Johnson, D. W. (1969). Changes in attitudes toward Negroes of white elementary school students after use of multiethnic readers. *Journal of Educational Psychology, 60* (2), 148-152.

Little, J. (1990). A writer's social responsibility. *The New Advocate, 3* (2), 79-88.

MacCann, D. (1998). *White supremacy in children's literature: Characterizations of African Americans, 1830-1900.* New York: Garland.

MacCann, D., and Woodard, G. (Eds.). (1985). *The black American in books for children: Readings in racism* (2nd ed.). Metuchen, NJ: Scarecrow.

Macphee, J. S. (1997). "That's not fair!" A white teacher reports on white first graders' responses to multicultural literature. *Language Arts, 74* (1), 33-40.

Malik, A. A. (1990). A psycholinguistic analysis of the reading behavior of EFL-proficient readers using culturally familiar and culturally nonfamiliar expository texts. *American Educational Research Journal, 27* (1), 205-223.

Markstrom-Adams, C. (1990). Coming of age among contemporary American Indians as portrayed in adolescent fiction. *Adolescence, 25* (127), 225-237.

May, J. P. (1995). *Children's literature & critical theory.* New York: Oxford University Press.

McCabe, C. T. (1998). *Multicultural children's literature: Its effect on the cultural attitude of fifth-grade students.* Unpublished doctoral dissertation, Virginia Commonwealth University.

McKenna, H. R. (1996). *Ethnobibliotherapy: Ethnic identity development through multicultural literature.* Unpublished doctoral dissertation, University of Washington.

Meltzer, M. (1987). A common humanity. In B. Harrison and G Maguire (Eds.), *Innocence and experience* (pp. 490-497). New York: Lothrop.

Mikkelsen, N. (1998). Insiders, outsiders, and the question of authenticity: Who shall write for African American children? *African American Review, 32* (1), 33-49.

Mikkelsen, N. (1999). *Words and pictures: Lessons in children's literature and literacies.* Boston: McGraw Hill.

Miller, S., and McCaskil, B. (Eds.). (1993). *Multicultural literature and literacies: Making space for difference*. Albany: State University of New York Press.

Miller-Lachmann, L. (Ed.) (1992). *Our family, our friends, our world: An annotated guide to significant multicultural books for children and teenagers*. New Providence, NJ: Bowker.

Mo, W., and Shen, W. (2000). A mean wink at authenticity: Chinese images in Disney's *Mulan*. *The New Advocate, 13* (2), 129-141.

Möller, K. J., and Allen, J. (2000). Connecting, resisting and searching for safer places: Students respond to Mildred Taylor's *The Friendship*. *Journal of Literacy Research, 32* (2), 145-186.

Moore, O. (1985). Picture books: The un-text. In D. MacCann and G. Woodard (Eds.), *The black American in books for children: Readings in racism* (pp. 183-191). Metuchen, NJ: the Scarecrow Press.

Mora, P. (1998). Confessions of a Latina author. *The New Advocate, 17* (4), 279-289.

Morrison, T. (1992). *Playing in the dark*. Cambridge, MA: Harvard University Press.

Murphy, B. (1993). Letter to the editor. *The Horn Book Magazine, 69* (4), 389.

Naidoo, B. (1992). *Through whose eyes? Exploring racism: Reader, text, and context*. London: Trentham Books.

Nelson, G. L. (1987). Culture's role in reading comprehension: A schema theoretical approach. *Journal of Reading, 30,* 424-429.

Nevel, D. A. (1999). *Students' transactions with multicultural poetry in the high school classroom: A case study*. Unpublished doctoral dissertation, Georgia State University.

Noda, L. A. (1980). *Literature and culture: Japanese and American reader responses to modern Japanese short stories*. Unpublished doctoral dissertation, New York University.

Nodelman, P. (1988). Cultural arrogance and realism in Judy Blume's *Superfudge*. *Children's Literature in Education, 19* (4), 230-241.

Nodelman, P. (1996). *The pleasures of children's literature* (2nd ed.). White Plains, NY: Longman.

Nodelman, P. (2000). Inventing childhood: Children's literature in the last millennium. *Journal of Children's Literature, 26* (1), 8-17.

Noll, E. (1995). Accuracy and authenticity in American Indian children's literature: The social responsibility of authors and illustrators. *The New Advocate, 8* (1), 29-43.

Norton, D. E. (1990). Teaching multicultural literature in the reading curriculum. *The Reading Teacher, 44* (10), 28-40.

Norton, D. E. (1999). *Through the eyes of a child: An introduction to children's literature* (5th ed.). Columbus, Ohio: Merrill.

Norton, D. E. (2000). *Multicultural children's literature: Through the eyes of many children*. Columbus, OH: Merrill.

Nye, N. S. (1999). Singing the long song: Arab culture in books for young readers. *The New Advocate, 12* (2), 119-126.

O'Flaherty, W. D. (1988). *Other people's myths: The cave of echoes*. New York: Macmillan.

Pang, V. O., Colvin, C., Tran, M., and Barba, R. H. (1992). Beyond chopsticks and dragons: Selecting Asian-American literature for children. *The Reading Teacher, 46* (3), 216-224.

Paterson, K. (1991). Living in a peaceful world. *Horn Book Magazine, 69* (1), 32-38.

Paterson, K. (1994). Cultural politics from a writer's point of view. *The New Advocate, 7* (2), 85-91.

Pinsent, P. (1997). *Children's literature and the politics of equality*. New York: Teachers College Press.

Pitts, L. Jr. (1998, December 5). Politics of hair speaks volumes about black pride. *The Miami Herald*, 1g-2g.

Pratt, L., and Beaty, J. J. (1999). *Transcultural children's literature*. Columbus, OH: Merrill.

Pritchard R. (1990). The effects of cultural schemata on reading processing strategies. *Reading Research Quarterly, 25* (4), 273-295.

Purves, A. (1993). Toward a reevaluation of reader response and school literature. *Language Arts, 70*, 348-361.

Purves, A. C., and Beach, R. (1972). *Literature and the reader: Research in response to literature, reading interests, and the teaching of literature*. Urbana, IL: National Council of Teachers of English.

Purves, A. C., and Rippere, V. (1968). *Elements of writing about a literary work: A study in response to literature*. NCTE Research Report No. 9. Urbana IL: National Council of Teachers of English.

Rabinowitz, P. J. (1987). *Before reading: Narrative conventions and the politics of interpretation*. Ithaca, NY: Cornell University Press.

Rabinowitz, P. J., and Smith, M. W. (1988). *Authorizing readers*. New York: Teachers College Press.

Rasinski, T., and Padak, N. D. (1990). Multicultural learning through children's literature. *Language Arts, 69*, 576-580.

Reimer, K. M. (1992). Multiethnic literature: Holding fast to dreams. *Language Arts, 69*, 14-21.

Reynolds, R. E., Anderson R. C., Steffensen, M. S., and Taylor, M. (1982). Cultural schemata and reading comprehension. *Reading Research Quarterly, 17* (3), 353-366.

Ricker-Wilson, C. (1998). When the mockingbird becomes an albatross: Reading and resistance in the language arts classroom. *English Journal, 87* (2), 67-72.

Robertson, R. (1987). *C. G. Jung and the archetypes of the collective unconscious*. New York: Peter Lang.

Rocha, O. J., and Dowd, F. S. (1993). Are Mexican American females portrayed realistically in fiction for grades K-3?: A content analysis. *Multicultural Review, 2* (4), 60-69.

Rochman, H. (1993). *Against borders: Promoting books for a multicultural world*. Chicago, IL: ALA Books / Booklist Publications.

Rogers, T., and Soter, A. O. (Eds.). (1997). *Reading across cultures: Teaching literature in a diverse society*. New York: Teachers College Press.

Rosenblatt, L. M. (1978). *The reader, the text, the poem: Transactional theory of the literary work*. Carbondale: Southern Illinois University Press.

Rosenblatt, L. M. (1985). Viewpoints: Transaction vs. interaction—a terminological rescue operation. *Research in Teaching English, 19*, 96-107.

Rosenblatt, L. M. (1995). *Literature as exploration* (5th ed.). New York: The Modern Language Association.

Ruzich, C. M. (1999). White students' resistance to multicultural literature: Breaking the sullen silence. *Teaching English in the Two Year College, 26* (3), 299-304.

Said, E. W. (1978). *Orientalism*. New York: Pantheon Books.

Schmidt, P. R. (1995). Working and playing with others: Cultural conflict in a kindergarten literacy program. *The Reading Teacher, 48* (5), 404-412.

Scholes, R. (1985). *Textual power: Literary theory and the teaching of English*. New Haven, CT: Yale University Press.

Schon, I. (1993). Good and bad books about Hispanic people and culture for young readers. *Multicultural Review, 2* (1), 28-31.

Schwartz, A. V. (1977). The five Chinese brothers: Time to retire. *Interracial Books for Children Bulletin, 8* (3), 3-7.

Schweickart, P. P. (1986). Reading ourselves: Toward a feminist theory of reading. In E. B. Flynn and P. P. Schweickart (Eds.), *Gender and reading* (pp. 31-62). Baltimore, MD: Johns Hopkins University Press.

Shannon, P. (1994). I am the canon: Finding ourselves in multiculturalism. *Journal of Children's Literature, 20* (1), 1-5.

Silvey, A. (1993). Varied carols. *The Horn Book Magazine, 69* (2), 132-133.

Sims, R. (1982). *Shadow and substance: Afro-American experience in contemporary children's fiction.* Urbana, IL: National Council of Teachers of English.

Sims, R. (1983). Strong black girls: A ten year old responds to fiction about Afro-Americans. *Journal of Research Development in Education, 16* (3), 21-28.

Sims, R. (1984). A question of perspective. *The Advocate 3*, 145-156.

Sims Bishop, R. (1987). Extending multicultural understanding through children's books. In B. E. Cullinan (Ed.), *Children's literature in the reading program* (pp. 60-67). Newark, DE: International Reading Association.

Sims Bishop, R. (1994). A reply to Shannon the canon. *Journal of Children's Literature, 20* (1), 6-8.

Sims Bishop, R. (1994). (Ed.). *Kaleidoscope: A multicultural booklist for grades K-8.* Urbana, IL: National Council of Teachers of English.

Sims Bishop, R. (1996). Letter to the editor. *The New Advocate, 9* (2), vii-viii.

Sinha, S. (1995). *The role of culture in children's response to literature.* Unpublished doctoral dissertation, University of Illinois, Urbana-Champaign.

Sipe, L. (1997). In their own words: Authors's view on issues in historical fiction. *The New Advocate, 10* (3), 243-258.

Slapin, B., and Seale, D. (1998). *Through Indian eyes: The Native experience in books for children.* Los Angeles: American Indian Studies Center, University of California.

Smith, E. (1995). Anchored in our literature: Students responding to African American literature. *Language Arts, 72*, 571-574.

Smith, K. P. (1993). The multicultural ethic and connections to literature for children and young adults. *Library Trends, 41* (30), 340-353.

Soter, A. O. (1999). *Young adult literature and the new literary theories: Developing critical readers in middle school.* New York: Teachers College Press.

Spears-Bunton, L. A. (1990). Welcome to my house: African American and European American students' responses to Virginia Hamilton's *House of Dies Drear. Journal of Negro Education, 59*, 566-576.

Stamiris, Y. (1986). *Main currents in twentieth-century literary criticism: A critical study.* Troy, NY: Whitson.

Steffensen, S. M., Joag-Dev, C., and Anderson, R. C. (1979). A cross-cultural perspective on reading comprehension. *Reading Research Quarterly, 15* (1), 10-29.

Stolz, M. (1993). Letter to the editor. *The Horn Book Magazine, 69*, (5), 516.

Stotsky, S. (1994). Academic guidelines for selecting multiethnic and multicultural literature. *English Journal, 84*, (2), 27-34.

Sutton, R. (1992). What means we, white man? *School Library Journal, 37* (3), 155-158.

Taxel, J. (1981). The American Revolution in children's books: Issues of racism and classism. *Interracial Books for Children Bulletin, 12* (7, 8), 3-9.

Taxel, J. (1986). The black experience in children's fiction: Controversies surrounding award-winning books. *Curriculum Inquiry, 16*, 245-281.

Taxel, J. (1992). The politics of children's literature: Reflections on multiculturalism and Christopher Columbus. In V. Harris (Ed.), *Teaching multicultural literature in grades K-8* (pp. 1-36). Norwood, MA: Christopher-Gordon.

Taxel, J. (1995). Cultural politics and writing for young people. In S. Lehr (Ed.), *Battling dragons: Issues and controversy in children's literature* (pp. 155-169). Portsmouth, NH: Heinemann.

Taxel, J. (1997). Multicultural literature and the politics of reaction. *Teachers College Record, 98* (3), 415-448.

Taylor, G. S. (1997). Multicultural literature preferences of low-ability African American and Hispanic American fifth-graders. *Reading Improvement, 34* (1), 37-48.

Temple, C., Martinez, M., Jokota, J., and Naylor, A. (2001). *Children's books in children's hands: An introduction to children's literature* (2nd ed.). Boston: Allyn and Bacon.

Tomlinson, C. M. (Ed.). (1998). *Children's books from other countries.* Lanham, MD: Scarecrow.

Tomlinson, C. M. (1999). Children's books from and about other countries. *Journal of Children's Literature, 25* (1), 8-17.

Tompkins, J. (Ed.) (1980). *Reader-response criticism: From formalism to post-structuralism.* Baltimore, MD: Johns Hopkins University Press.

Trousdale, A. M. (1990). A submission theology for black Americans: Religion and social action in prize-winning children's books about the black experience in America. *Research in the Teaching of English, 24* (2), 117-140.

Valedez, A. (1999). *Learning in living color: Using literature to incorporate multicultural education into the primary curriculum.* Boston: Allyn and Bacon.

Vickers, S. B. (1998). *Native American identities: From stereotype to archetype in art and literature.* Albuquerque: University of New Mexico Press.

Walker, P. (1972). *The effects of hearing selected children's stories that portray blacks in a favorable manner on the racial attitudes of groups of black and white kindergarten children.* Unpublished doctoral dissertation, University of Kentucky.

West, C. (1993). *Race matters.* Boston: Beacon Press.

Wilkinson, P. A., and Kido, E. (1997). Literature and cultural awareness: Voices from the journey, *Language Arts, 74,* 255-265.

Willis, A. T. (Ed.). (1998). *Teaching multicultural literature in grades 9-12: Moving beyond the canon.* Norwood, MA: Christopher-Gordon.

Wilson, M., and Thomas, S. (1995). Holy smoke! I missed something here: Cultural experience and the construction of meaning. *English Education, 27* (2), 53-65.

Woodson, J. (1998, January/February). Who can tell my story. *The Horn Book Magazine,* pp. 34-38.

Woodward, M. A. (1970). *The effects of teaching black literature to ninth grade class in a Negro high school in Picayu, Mississippi.* Unpublished doctoral dissertation, University of Tennessee.

Yep, L. (1987). A Chinese sense of reality. In B. Harrison and G. Maguire (Eds.), *Innocence and experience* (pp. 485-489). New York: Lothrop.

Yokota, J. (1993). Issues in selecting multicultural children's literature. *Language Arts, 70,* 156-167.

Yokota, J. (Ed.). (2000). *Kaleidoscope: A multicultural booklist for grades K-8* (3rd ed.). Urbana, IL: National Council of Teachers of English.

Index

About the Author

MINGSHUI CAI is Associate Professor of Literacy Education at the University of Northern Iowa. He is a member of the editorial board of *The Journal of Children's Literature* and has also served on the editorial board of *Language Arts*. His articles have appeared in *The New Advocate, Bookbird, Children's Literature in Education*, and other journals.

DATE DUE

DEC '17 '0

#47-0108 Peel Off Pressure Sensitive